MODERN WOODEN
YACHT CONSTRUCTION

MODERN
WOODEN YACHT CONSTRUCTION

Cold-Molding • Joinery • Fitting Out

By JOHN GUZZWELL

INTERNATIONAL MARINE PUBLISHING COMPANY

CAMDEN, MAINE

All photos by Maureen Guzzwell except where otherwise indicated.

Copyright © 1979
by International Marine Publishing
Library of Congress Catalog Card Number 78-64787
International Standard Book Number 0-87742-106-4
Typeset by A&B Typesetters, Inc., Concord, New Hampshire
Printed and bound by The Alpine Press, South Braintree, Massachusetts

Second printing, 1981

Published by International Marine Publishing Company
21 Elm Street, Camden, Maine 04843

For my sons James and John, fellow boatbuilders

CONTENTS

PART II Finishing the Hull

Acknowledgments

The author gratefully acknowledges the assistance and cooperation of the following in the preparation of this book:

William Garden, Jay Benford, Frank Fredette, Betty Simmerer, Laurent Giles & Partners, John Spencer, the American Institute of Timber Construction, Forest Products Limited, New Zealand, Department of Primary Industries, Australia, Timber Research & Development, Bucks, England, U.S. Forest Products Laboratory, Mr. James Elder of David W. Evans Inc., John Mallitte, New Zealand, James W. Layton, Sydney, Australia, Ron Libkuman, Hawaii, and above all my wife, Maureen, who typed the manuscript and coordinated all the material.

Part I

Building the Hull

1

General Discussion

The use of wood as a material for building vessels dates far back in time. Although Noah may possibly be the earliest recorded boatbuilder, man undoubtedly began fashioning wooden vessels of some sort shortly after he came in contact with large bodies of water. Throughout this long history, techniques have remained basically unchanged for periods lasting thousands of years. Examples of early craft found in burial tombs or at archaeological excavation sites show methods of construction that are still in use today in various parts of the world.

The remains of early Viking longships show a form of construction where each plank edge is lapped over and fastened to its neighbor plank. Transverse framing, either sawn or bent to shape, often with the use of hot water or steam, formed the desired shapes of the skeleton framework to which the planking was secured. This type of construction is now known as clencher or lapstrake construction, and is commonly used today for building small craft. The use of reliable metal fastenings, such as copper rivets and bronze nails and screws, has replaced more primitive fastening methods, which ranged from sewing the edges of planking together to fastening them with hardwood pegs. However, the basic principles remain the same as when the Norsemen ventured out on the oceans in their longships.

Another method that has survived from the past is the one known as carvel construction. The great ships of the Spanish, Portuguese, Dutch, and English navies during the Middle Ages were built with this technique. Although similar to lapstrake construction in some ways, carvel construction differs in that the plank is fastened directly to the frame so that the edges are butted up against one another. The tapered seam created by the planks' juncture is made watertight by caulking it with natural fibers such as cotton or oakum. Traditional carvel construction continues to be used in vessels ranging from navy minesweepers, commercial fishing vessels, and tugs, to small pleasure yachts, both power and sail.

Why, then, should there be a need for another book on wooden boatbuilding when the subject has already been covered extensively over the years? I have several answers to this question, the main one being that because of the many new materials that have been developed during recent years, the modern wooden boatbuilder now has available to him a new set of techniques that allows him to do things with wood that were never before possible. This new engineering with wood exploits its many superb qualities yet also avoids its pitfalls, and the end result is a superior wooden structure that is durable, leakproof, and extremely strong for its weight. The techniques described in this book should enable the keen amateur or young professional builder to follow each of the steps required to build a modern wooden yacht and to take advantage of the superior qualities offered by many of these new materials, which were not available when most of the standard texts on boatbuilding were published.

Another important reason for adopting modern construction techniques is the fact that it is no longer possible to obtain the same quality lumber that was customarily used in the past. Less than 100 years ago in the Pacific Northwest, vessels measuring over 100 feet overall were being built with full-length planking. Today it is frequently difficult to obtain planking much longer than 18 to 20 feet. As a professional builder, I realize the difficulty of obtaining the quality materials of yesteryear, yet there are still plenty of good alternative lumbers. These, combined with the products from the chemical and plastics industries, allow the construction of wooden vessels that far surpass anything built in the past.

For the amateur or professional builder, then, who is contemplating building a one-off design, possibly with the intention of taking a mold off the finished boat for mass-produced fiberglass construction, wood is still one of the best materials to use. Wood can now be used more efficiently and "engineered" better because of the adoption of a construction method known as cold-molding or laminated wood construction. The technique of this modern form of construction revolves around the use of one vital material that has done more to revolutionize wooden boatbuilding in recent years than any other innovation—waterproof glue. Originally developed during the second World War and used extensively in the aircraft industry in the building of the wooden Mosquito bomber (De-Havilland Aircraft Co.), modern adhesives have

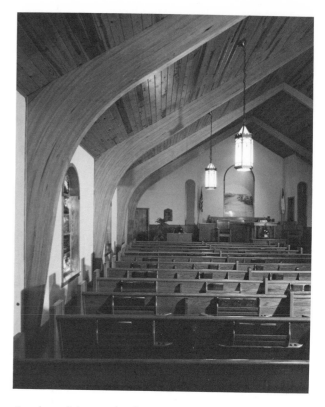

Laminated beams in the West London Baptist Church. (Alder)

been improved and are 100 percent waterproof, remaining that way indefinitely.

There are several types of glues available from various manufacturers. I have found the resorcinol resins and epoxies to be the most satisfactory, each having its own particular advantage. The use of such glues enables the modern builder to join wood strips together permanently to make one-piece structures. The material is thus upgraded in much the same way as occurs when a metal worker welds his metals together without using bolts or rivets.

The technique of improving wood with the use of modern synthetic adhesives is shown in the accompanying photograph of Glulam beams used in high-class building construction. As a young man, I worked in a small factory in Victoria, British Columbia, making similar structures and was impressed by the advantages of this kind of glued construction and the aesthetic beauty of the natural wood finish.

The author's sons cold-molding an 8-foot dinghy with 1/16-inch mahogany veneer.

Put briefly, cold-molding is a process of producing a one-piece curved skin, such as a hull, from thin strips of prepared wood veneers or planks that are glued together. The structure is built up on a curved form or framing so that each lamination or skin has the wood grain running in a different direction. This makes for an extremely strong, light, and stable form of construction. The term cold-molding is derived from the fact that curved structures can be laminated up with glues that cure at room temperature.

Because of the glued construction, cold-molded yachts are usually built upside down—the opposite of the technique used for traditional wooden craft. Much of the structure is built up in position by bending and bonding material

to the required shapes rather than by sawing them out of the solid or by steam bending. This results in lighter work for a builder who is shorthanded and does not require heavy machinery for forming the basic shapes.

There are many different forms of cold-molded construction that have been and are being used by various boatbuilders around the world; yet the basic principle of gluing thin laminates together remains the same, the end result being a superior wooden hull that does not require caulking to make it waterproof.

Although the term cold-molding is relatively recent, the technique itself was realized thousands of years ago by early Chinese craftsmen who developed the principle of laminating timber together to make stable wooden bases for

5

delicately enameled boxes and lacquered furniture. These early craftsmen used gelatine glues made of animal waste. Several hundred years later the ancient Egyptians used similar laminated construction in the manufacture of mummy cases. Some of these 3,500-year-old cases can be seen today in various museums around the world, and many of these show how the timber was cut and molded to complex shapes. About the year 100 B.C., the Greek scholar Pliny the Elder wrote that "hooves of bulls and beasts when boiled make a fine glue for veneering." The great 18th-century furniture makers Chippendale and Sheraton knew a thing or two about laminated construction. Many examples of their work reveal that both these men realized that laminating the wood together made it stable, and this was done extensively wherever lack of movement in the materials was of primary importance.

It is obvious from the foregoing that the techniques of cold-molding have been known for hundreds, even thousands, of years, and yet the method has not been used for the construction of vessels for much more than 100 years or so. The history of cold-molded yacht construction, as I know it, began in Auckland, New Zealand, during the late 1870s through the efforts of two men who are recognized today as being the founders of the yacht-building industry in that country.

Charles Bailey, born in Auckland about the year 1843, ran away from home at the tender age of 12, and after making a living at various jobs, eventually learned the trade of boatbuilding. By 1872, with much experience behind him, he set up his own firm, which was to turn out some of the finest power and sailing vessels ever constructed.

Robert Logan was a remarkable Scottish boatbuilder and designer who emigrated to New Zealand in 1874. He arrived in that country at a time when big yacht racing was commencing. Realizing the opportunities and the demand for yacht building, he turned his knowledge and skill in that direction. Logan worked for four years in the boatbuilding yard of a Mr. Niccol

before founding his own business in 1878 at Devonport, New Zealand.

Both Bailey and Logan used a multi-skin laminated form of construction, known as the three-skin diagonal principle, to build a wonderful variety of vessels using the excellent kauri pine native to the area. This form of construction was not unknown in New Zealand before Logan went out to that country, but it is generally recognized that he was primarily responsible for the use of this method for the construction of racing yachts.

It is probable that Logan had worked in Scottish shipyards building some of the wooden tea clippers that were constructed during the mid-1800s and he may well have picked up this technique there. The 563-ton clipper ship *Vision* built in Aberdeen, Scotland, in 1854 and measuring 170 feet overall with a beam of 27 feet 6 inches, was built with four skins of larch planking, one laid vertically between the frames, two double diagonal. Each of the inner skins was two inches thick, and the outer fore-and-aft skin was 4-1/2 inches, making a total planking thickness of 10-1/2 inches. Samuel White of Cowes, used this form of construction for smaller vessels. The royal yacht *Victoria and Albert II* was also built in this manner in 1855, so it seems likely that Robert Logan was fully experienced in this type of construction before going out to New Zealand.

The one basic ingredient lacking in Logan's technique (and Bailey's as well) was still 75 years in the future, for there were no suitable adhesives to bond the planking laminations together. Nails and copper rivets were used instead. In the absence of waterproof glue, the clipper ships had been made watertight by one or two layers of tarred felt sandwiched between the layers of planking. The planking of smaller craft was frequently made watertight by placing varnished or paint-soaked muslin or canvas between the skins, which were held together with nails and copper rivets. Bailey and Logan used red lead in between their skins and caulked the final, longitudinal skin.

Due to the wonderful examples of wooden

A cold-molded 47-foot ketch built by the author and Dick McIlvride in New Zealand.

vessels built by Bailey and Logan, the triple-skin laminated construction method remained the standard technique for yacht building in New Zealand until the advent of waterproof glues in the early 1950s. The transition to cold-molding was therefore a very easy one for some New Zealand builders to make. One of the most noteworthy of these builders was Max Carter of Auckland, who went on to build a series of magnificent yachts that were outstanding in a country that has a long history of fine craft.

Other builders overseas had begun to build by the laminated wood form of construction using the new war-developed glues. One of the first of these was the Luders Yacht Building Corporation, an American firm, which produced two 40-foot laminated wood sloops to their own designs as early as 1943 and 1944. These boats were slightly smaller than a 6-meter design and were built very lightly even by today's standards, having planking laid up from five layers of 1/8-inch mahogany. During the late 40s and early 50s, the Luders yard also used this method to build a number of the popular Luders

16 class. In Britain, the Fairey Marine Company (a division of Fairey Aviation) near Southampton, England, built a series of laminated wood vessels after World War II. Mass production techniques were used so as to compete successfully with other builders and methods.

Both the Luders and Fairey operations used a process known as hot-molding. The glue had to be heated in order for it to cure. In addition, a great deal of pressure was needed to ensure that there was a good bond between the various layers. This necessitated the use of certain specialized procedures. After planking was completed, a large, airtight bag was fitted over the complete boat and mold. A vacuum was then drawn into the bag to supply uniform pressure over the entire surface of the shell. After the vacuum bag was applied, the whole assembly was placed into a special oven, known as an autoclave, where it remained until the glue was cured.

Before such methods could become established, however, this construction method was pushed into the background by another

7

one that was directed toward mass production—fiberglass.

Despite its unsuitability for mass production in the face of competition from fiberglass, laminated wood construction continued to be used for one-off vessels. Wilf Souter's yard at Cowes, Isle of Wight, turned out many high-class ocean racing yachts over the years. Several large vessels designed by noted naval architect William Garden were built in Seattle shipyards in the mid-1950s. During this time, glues improved, curing at room temperature instead of needing to be heated. Cold-molding had become a reality.

Today, with modern adhesives greatly simplifying the process, cold-molded construction is achieving more and more popularity. Taking advantage of the favorable strength-to-weight ratio of the method, many ocean racing yachts are now built to some form of cold-molded construction, possibly two of the best known being *Windward Passage* and *Golden Dazy.*

In sum, the advantages of cold-molded construction for the custom builder—both amateur and professional—are many. Lumber required is in small sizes, which are more readily available and quickly seasoned. The smaller sizes make it easier for one man to handle and do not require large bandsaws and other heavy machines to shape the various members. Expensive fastenings are greatly reduced by the use of waterproof glue; most of the framing material normally discarded with other construction methods is built into the hull, so that there is a minimum of waste. Planking material, being considerably shorter, does not require butt blocks and subsequent caulking; the completed hull is a one-piece unit *that is considerably stronger for its weight than traditional wooden construction and some of the other materials currently popular.* The practice of using steam boxes and attempting to force heavy frames into unnatural bends is also unnecessary.

Cold-molding is a process that can be used by both amateur and professional boatbuilders, and both can benefit in full measure from the procedures detailed in the chapters that follow. Some of the techniques mentioned in this book have the professional builder in mind and thus might not necessarily reflect the very latest in construction methods. The professional builder is limited to proven building practices that are economically feasible: if too much time is spent on experimenting with some particular part of the job, he could be out of pocket, whereas the amateur builder might not have to be particularly concerned with the amount of time he spends. For this reason the talented amateur builder is often capable of turning out exquisite work.

There is a misconception prevalent among many boating people that cold-molding is a difficult form of construction and that once damaged, a cold-molded yacht is very difficult to repair. It is my intention to explode those myths, for cold-molding is just a different way to build—it is no more difficult nor any easier than any of the other methods of boat construction. It requires the same care and patience and skill as other techniques—plus a knowledge of the procedures, which I trust you will find in the following pages.

Any important undertaking in life has similar requirements if it is to be brought to a successful conclusion. So do not be discouraged, read on, and happy boatbuilding.

2

Plans

The selection of a suitable design for your dreamship will probably not be easy. For the inexperienced boat enthusiast, this can be an elusive, complex, and difficult process. Advice from knowledgeable sailors will often add to the difficulty, as most people who own boats have very definite and often conflicting ideas on what is right or wrong with a particular design. As with most things in life, it is not easy to gain experience without becoming involved. Obviously, the best way of acquiring the necessary know-how is to try to do some practical boating in a variety of craft whenever possible.

The sea is an unrelenting teacher and should not be taken lightly: the quality of many mass-produced stock boats would change dramatically if their designers and builders had to go offshore in those creations. The current trend of instant knowledge that can be dispensed as easily as making coffee does not apply to matters concerning the sea, and anyone who thinks differently is in for a surprise.

We have to learn to walk before we learn how to run, so before setting off to go deep-sea cruising in your own boat, it's best to gain some local experience first. This is particularly true in the selection of a design to build to if you have never built a boat before and have little ex-

perience with tools. It is unwise to entertain ideas about building a large offshore cruising yacht, even though advertisements in boating magazines may promise to show how to build their designs in little time. My advice would be to build a smaller boat first, perhaps a dinghy or runabout that will allow you to obtain some skills with minimum expense. In backyard lots there are hundreds of half-finished hulls that will never be completed because their builders did not realize the magnitude of the task.

The selection of a design should be made with this thought in mind: Do I have the stamina and will to see the job through? Thousands of amateur builders around the world have demonstrated that relatively inexperienced people have built most successful vessels with their own hands, but don't think for a moment that it was always easy. They had to spend many hours and much hard work to finish their craft.

Even with some experience it is sometimes difficult to see or accept the poor features of a boat when you have fallen under the spell of her general appearance. Boats are rather like women in this respect—a good-looking woman may be a joy to look at, but her beauty is no guarantee that she will be easy to live with. How large a vessel do you need, and what type? What do you intend to do with the boat and how many persons will it take to operate the vessel in a seamanlike manner? These are all questions pertaining to the choice of a design and should affect your ultimate decision.

Having acquired some experience in ocean voyaging, I am dismayed at the designs being offered as suitable for offshore cruising. Too often one sees glaring faults: exposed cockpits with poor shelter; impractical interior arrangements (such as a dinette with athwartship seating); transverse bunks; galleys that would be almost useless at sea with the boat heeled on one tack for days on end; lockers that will shower their contents when the doors are opened; self-opening drawers with a mind of their own; bunks that are too short or narrow; the lack of provision for stowage for a dinghy, adequate ground tackle, sail bags, stores, and all the equipment such as charts and navigational gear required for offshore cruising.

Frequently the only way to obtain a design that meets your requirements is to get a naval architect to produce a custom design; his task in producing a design that will suit both you and his own conscience is often difficult. Most boating people feel they can improve on the work of the naval architect, and sometimes, though very rarely, this is so. This does not mean that the plans must be followed to the last letter, but changing shapes and weights and sizes of various structural members is taboo for the inexperienced layman and can result in all kinds of unnecessary problems and possible ruination of a good boat.

It must be realized that there are many facets to a design and that few men are master of them all. It would take several lifetimes for the average person to acquire the complete experience and knowledge to qualify as an expert in the trades and skills required to produce the completed vessel. It is important, therefore, that the builder, owner, and designer recognize their own limitations.

Your choice of a stock design or a new one may be made according to various circumstances—a good designer may live nearby, for example, which has the advantage that he may be consulted for advice during construction. He also may have produced a design you find particularly attractive, and with certain modifications this may suit your needs.

Quite obviously, a stock design will cost less than a custom one—it already has a track record and any faults or problems with previous boats are known and can be corrected. Stock plans are often drawn up for stock people, however, and a great many boating people are individualists who cannot bear being average. For these people who wish to express their own ideas and concepts, a custom design is the only way to go. Fees for custom service vary, of course, but they are generally between 7 percent and 15 percent of the estimated building cost in a professional yard. Individuality doesn't come cheaply. Sometimes a designer will agree to produce a set of plans for a flat fee in much the same way that a builder may quote on the building costs. Frankly, this is a two-edged sword, for most professional naval architects and builders know fairly accurately what their costs are going to be, and restricting the work on the plans to meet a contract price does not always benefit the owner.

During the course of my life around boats, I have met many yacht designers, some of whom have become personal friends and whose work I greatly admire and respect. I am indeed grateful to some of these men who have allowed me to reproduce in this book samples of their work that I have selected as good examples of their own particular styles and ideas. In the following pages you will find an assortment of designs, each having its own character and function. None of them could be called stock boats, although in a couple of cases an additional boat has been built to the same plan. They are not the types of boats one would choose to build as a first-time effort, yet they all have something in common: they were designed to be built in wood and in some cases to be of cold-molded construction. The men whose work is shown here have had years of experience, and some have hundreds of other designs on file that are

The Giles-designed cutter Treasure, *owned and built by the author.* (Denny)

available to those interested in obtaining either stock or custom plans.

LAURENT GILES & PARTNERS

The firm of Laurent Giles & Partners needs little introduction. Founded by Jack Laurent Giles in the early 1930s, the firm has designed some of the great yachts built in British and European yards. Although I had met Jack briefly for the first time in 1957 during my circumnavigation in *Trekka*, and had corresponded with him during the planning of the little vessel, it was not until I went to England in 1962 to build *Treasure* to his designs that I got to know him and his partners well. The little bow-shaped window of his office on the cobbled street of Quay Hill in Lymington, England, displayed a model of one of his designs—his partner Humphry Barton's little Vertue 35. Noted mainly for the seakindly ocean-cruising vessels he drew, Jack Giles was also very active designing racing yachts and motor yachts of the highest caliber. His designs had a classic line that was unmistakable, yet he was bold and imaginative enough to adopt new ideas and concepts and to exploit ruthlessly the gaps in the rating rules governing yacht racing.

A pioneer of cold-molded construction methods, L.G.& P. showed what could be done when wood was engineered intelligently. Adopting techniques used in the aircraft industry, the firm was responsible for the brilliant construction methods used in ocean-racing yachts such as *Myth of Malham* and *Stormvogel* and the fantastic *Blue Leopard*, a 111-foot cruising ketch

whose drawings are included in this book.

To those of us who have been fortunate enough to own one of his designs, Jack will be remembered most for his fine deep-sea yachts that have made many successful world voyages. The plans of *Treasure* and her sister *Sunrise*, which I built for Ron Libkuman in Honolulu over a three-year period, are included here, and many of the photos and diagrams within these pages are of these two vessels.

Although Jack Giles died some years ago, he will always be remembered with affection by yachtsmen around the world. I am indeed grateful to the surviving partners in the firm for allowing me to reproduce these drawings.

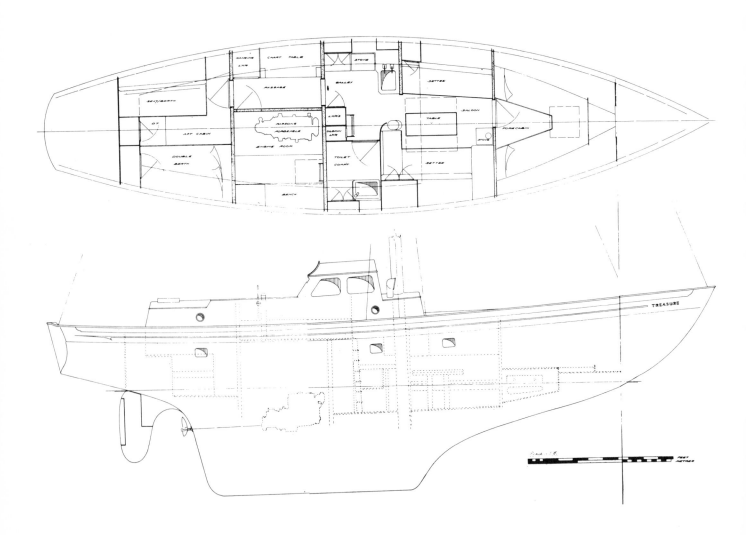

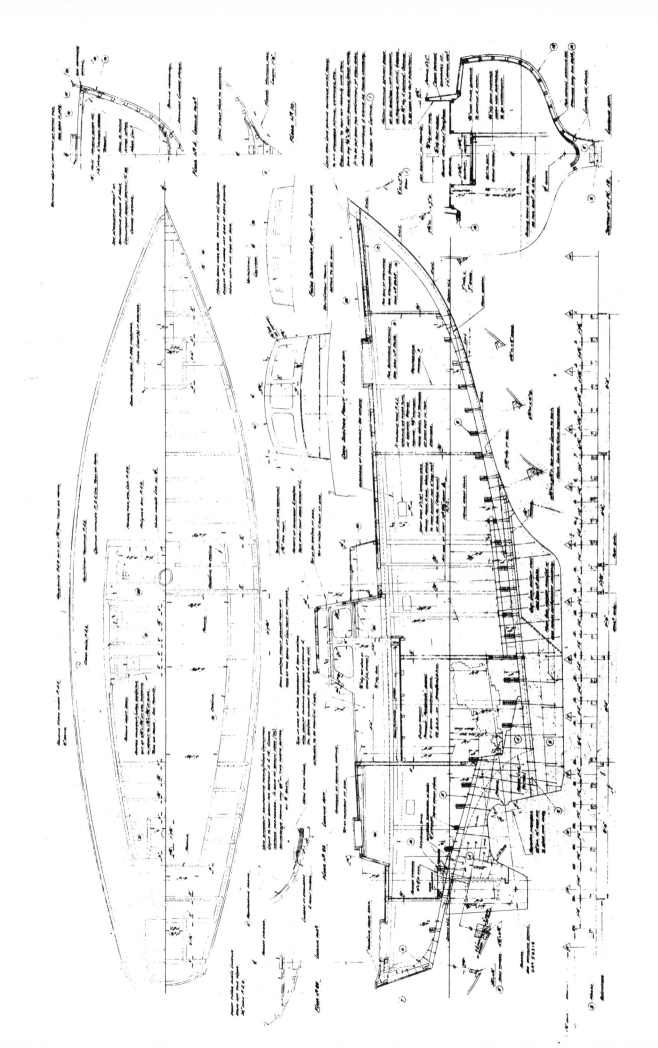

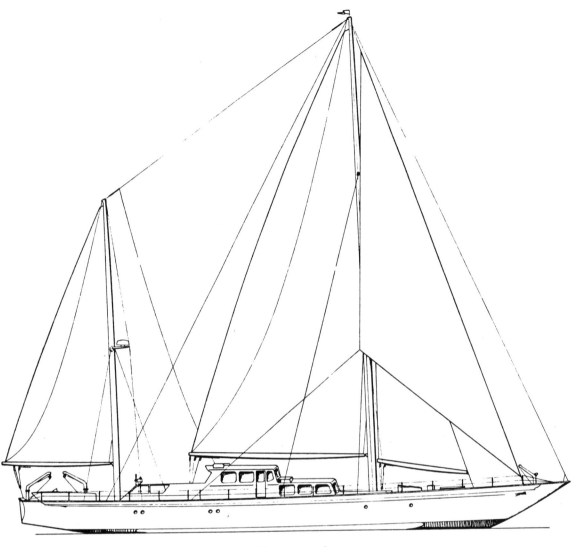

Blue Leopard

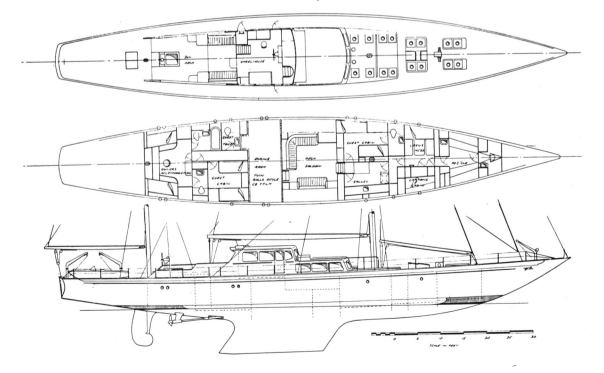

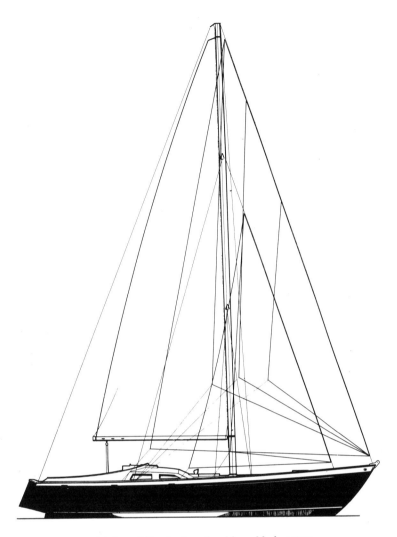

44-foot Giles-designed cold-molded cutter.

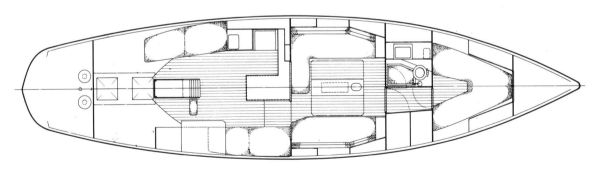

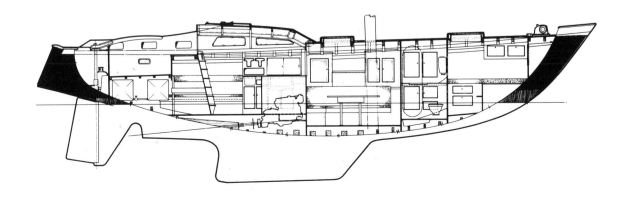

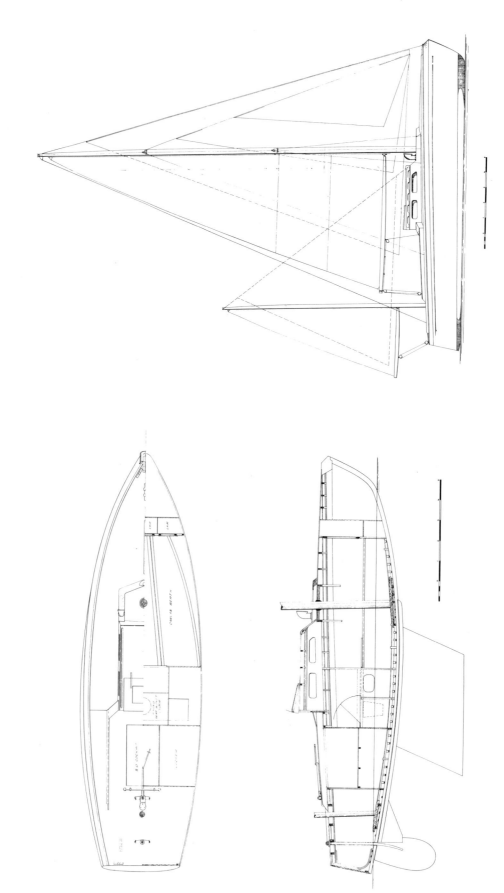

Arrangement and sail plans of Trekka.

JOHN SPENCER

John Spencer, the well-known Auckland, New Zealand, designer and builder, is the foremost authority on plywood hull construction and has been designing and building this type of hull since the late 1940s, when waterproof plywood first became available in New Zealand. He has kindly allowed me to reproduce some of his work in this book.

The advantages of waterproof plywood quickly became apparent for 12- and 14-foot centerboard sailboats, as none of the restricted classes had minimum weights. John's boats, either planked with 4 mm. plywood or cold-molded of 2 mm. veneer, were in many cases half the weight of previous planked hulls, although other builders were producing fairly light clinker-planked hulls using the same waterproof plywood. One of John's earliest designs was the 12-foot Cherub, which now has fleets in Britain, Australia, and New Zealand. The original boat, now over 25 years old, is still in sailing condition, a testimony to his skills and the durability of glued construction.

With better quality marine grades of plywood available in the mid 1950s, it was a natural progression for John to design and build small keel yachts. John's real talent is his ability to design light, strong hulls simply. Whereas other designers were already using plywood, particularly E.G. van de Stadt in Europe, in most cases their construction methods were inherited from earlier traditional planked sharpies not really suited to plywood and glued construction. Some of those early small keelboats from John's de-

The Spencer-designed ocean racer Buccaneer *under sail in Auckland, New Zealand. (Sea Spray)*

sign board used plywood of 8 mm. reducing to 7 mm. thick. Then he did a 35-foot keelboat using two skins of 4 mm. plywood laid across the stringers instead of longitudinally. This boat set the stage for all John's future designs. Although he feels that plywood is stiffer than cold-molded construction, to my mind his boats are essentially cold-molded using wide plywood strakes for the planking instead of narrower solid strips.

For a while John built several high-speed powerboats using similar construction techniques, and by cutting the plywood into 12-inch-wide strips with the grain diagonal, he was able to obtain considerable compound curvature in the flared bows. Soon after this he built *Infidel* (now *Ragtime*) for Tom Clark, and shortly afterward a 45-footer named *Sirius*, which was followed by a 40-footer in which he

designed rounded topsides with a soft chine that had several beneficial effects. Apart from better appearance, the rounded topsides gave increased space inside the hull and stressed the ply, which increased stiffness. *Buccaneer* and *New World* followed, being planked up with 3 skins of 9 mm. plywood for *Buccaneer* and 6 mm. for *New World.* Recent designs from John's board are several half-ton and three-quarter-ton boats.

Wherever it's possible to save weight by using plywood, John uses it; and much of the structural members such as cockpit sides, cabin tops, and cabin sides are either laminated into position or on molds before being fitted into the boat. The drawings reproduced here show the simple yet brilliant construction techniques that are so typical of John Spencer's work, and I am indeed grateful for the opportunity to include this material.

Below and opposite: *Plans of* Buccaneer.

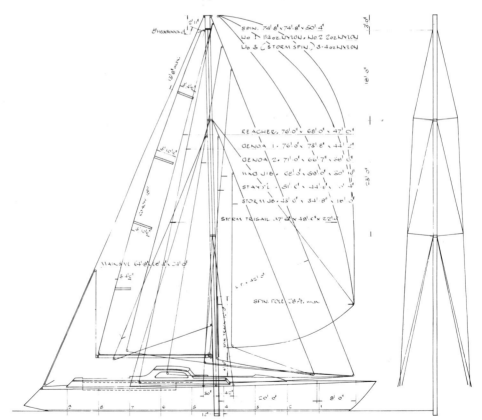

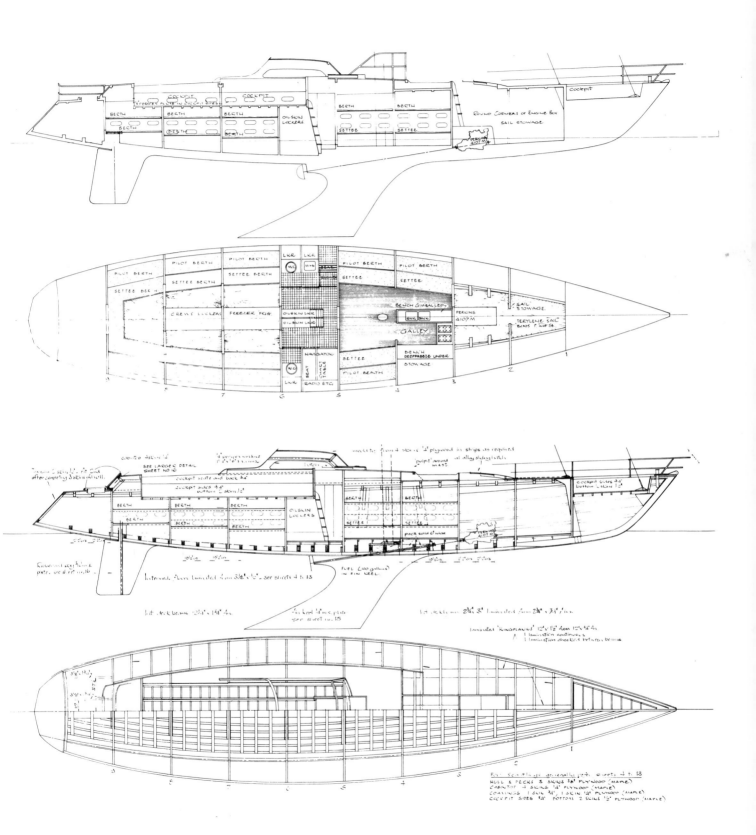

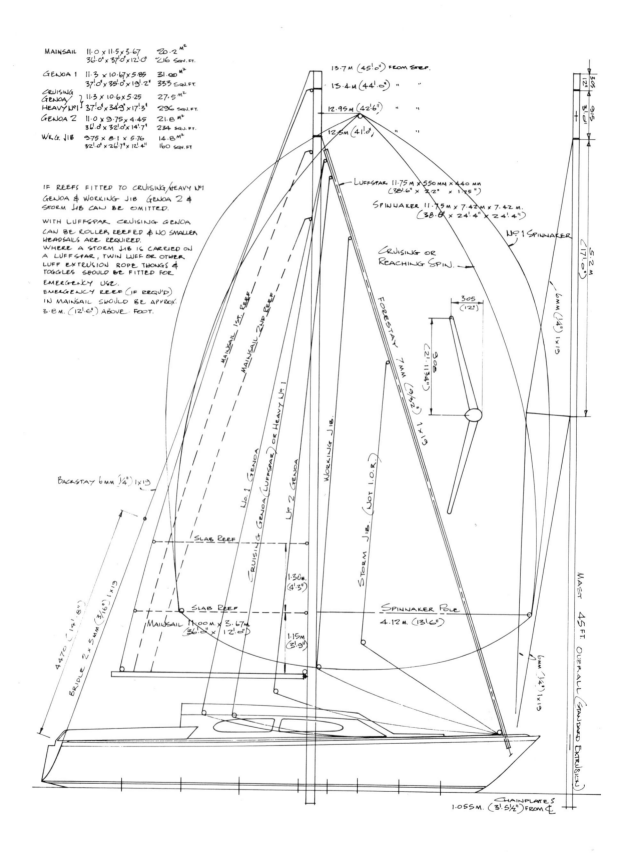

MAINSAIL 11·0 x 11·5 x 3·67   20·2 M²
          36·0' x 37·0' x 12·0' 216 SQU. FT.

GENOA 1   11·3 x 10·67 x 5·85   31·00 M²
          37·0' x 35·0' x 19'·2" 333 SQU. FT.

CRUISING }
GENOA   } 11·3 x 10·6 x 5·25   27·5 M²
HEAVY Nº1   37·0' x 34'·9' x 17'·3' 296 SQU. FT.

GENOA 2   11·0 x 9·75 x 4·45   21·8 M²
          36'·0 x 32'·0 x 14'·7' 234 SQU. FT.

WK.G. JIB 9·75 x 8·1 x 5·76   14·8 M²
          32'·0' x 26'·7' x 12'·4" 160 SQU. FT

IF REEFS FITTED TO CRUISING/HEAVY Nº1
GENOA & WORKING JIB GENOA 2 &
STORM JIB CAN BE OMITTED.

WITH LUFFSPAR CRUISING GENOA
CAN BE ROLLER REEFED & NO SMALLER
HEADSAILS ARE REQUIRED.
WHERE A STORM JIB IS CARRIED ON
A LUFFSPAR, TWIN LUFF OR OTHER
LUFF EXTRUSION ROPE THONGS &
TOGGLES SHOULD BE FITTED FOR
EMERGENCY USE.
EMERGENCY REEF (IF REQU'D)
IN MAINSAIL SHOULD BE APPROX.
3·8 M. (12'·6") ABOVE FOOT.

13·7M (45'·0") FROM STEP.
15·4 M (44'·0) " "
12·95M (42'·6") " "
12·5M (41'·0) " "

LUFFSPAR 11·75 M x 550 MM x 440 MM
(38'·6" x 2'·2" x 1'·75")

SPINNAKER 11·75M x 7·42M x 7·42 M.
(38·6 x 24'·4" x 24'·4")

Nº1 SPINNAKER

CRUISING OR
REACHING SPIN.

MAINSAIL 1ST REEF

MAINSAIL 2ND REEF

FORESTAY 7MM (9½") 1x19

Nº 1 GENOA

CRUISING GENOA (LUFFSPAR) OR HEAVY Nº1

Nº 2 GENOA

WORKING JIB.

STORM JIB. (NOT I.O.R.)

305 (12")

(21·1134") 300

6MM (¼") 1x19

5·2 M (17'·0")

305
12"
3½(0")
915

BACKSTAY 6MM (¼") 1x19

SLAB REEF

1·30M. (4'·3")

SLAB REEF

MAINSAIL 11·00 M. x 3·67M
(36'·0" x 12'·0")

1·15 M. (3'·9")

SPINNAKER POLE
4·12 M. (13'·6")

4470 (14'·8")

BRIDLE 2 x 5MM (3/16") 1x19

6MM (¼") 1x19

MAST 45 FT. OVERALL (STANDARD EXTRUSION)

CHAINPLATES
1·055M. (3'·5½") FROM ₵

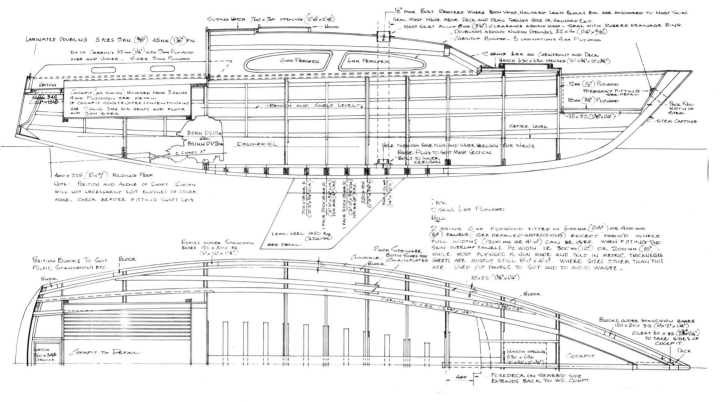

Above, below, and opposite: *Spencer 32 plans.*

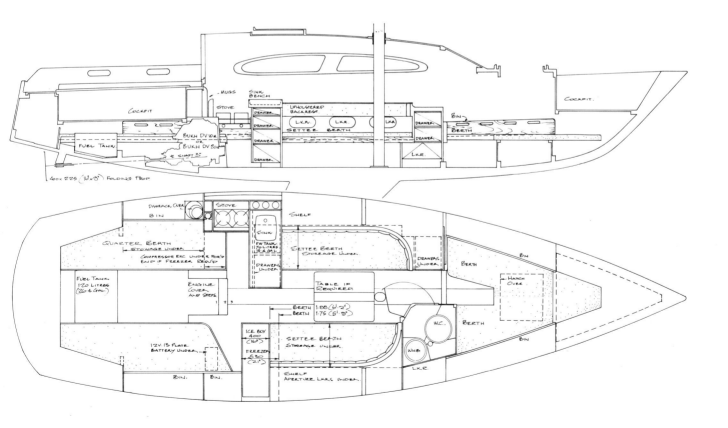

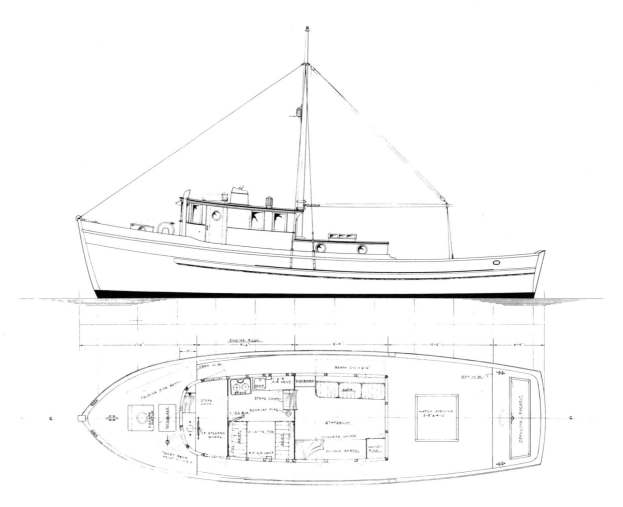

A 44-foot troller-cruiser designed by Frank Fredette.

FRANK FREDETTE

Frank Fredette has been designing and building boats around Victoria, B.C., longer than most people can remember, for as of this writing he is 85 years young. I first got to know Frank in the early 1950s when I was building *Trekka* in Victoria. He was very active at that time, and I remember watching him caulk a new hull that was built to one of his fishing boat designs. A small, wiry man with strong hands and arms from a lifetime of shipwrighting, his pale blue eyes come alight when recounting events of his youth spent in sealing schooners and square-riggers, and one wonders how his slight figure has weathered the years so well.

Frank is a true craftsman of the old school, and there is no aspect of wooden boat construction with which he is not familiar. His knowl-

edge and the skill of his craftsmanship are reflected in his drawings: all the details of the structure are shown on his plans. No one knows traditional wooden construction better.

After going through a great many plans covering a lifetime's work, I have selected three of Frank's designs that to my mind best represent the type of vessels he worked with most. These are the small commercial fishing vessels that are engaged in the salmon fishing industry in the Pacific Northwest. The West Coast troller is a vessel that has to be seakindly to her crew, easily handled, and be able to carry a lot of fish from offshore fishing grounds to the various canneries and freezer plants along this exposed coast. Frank's boats are renowned for fulfilling these requirements; being of moderate beam, they have a gentle motion with easily driven hulls. Construction techniques on these vessels are fairly standard, with the majority of the timber grown in the Pacific Northwest. Framing is usually white oak, and plank fastenings are galvanized boat nails.

The 40-foot troller drawings show a type that is a familiar sight in the many harbors of the British Columbia and southern Alaska coast; the larger 44-foot combination troller is an excellent example of a hull form that has been popular for years in commercial vessels and is being used increasingly in the pleasure-boat market. What a fine cruiser this design would make with perhaps the addition of a flying bridge.

The smaller 34-foot gillnetter I could not resist. This vessel was designed to fish out of the Columbia River in Oregon, so shallow draft was necessary. The hull form is particularly pleasing,

and this type of boat would also make a fine pleasure craft, though the house top and deckworks would need to be reworked.

You will note that these vessels have been drawn with the bow to the left instead of the right, which is the usual practice. This is because Frank is left-handed, a fact that was frequently appreciated by his fellow shipwrights when there was an awkward job that right-handers were having difficulty with.

Frank Fredette will be remembered as long as his boats ply the waters of the coast he knows so well. I only wish more space were available in this book to include some of the lovely schooners and ketches he has designed and built during his lifetime.

44-foot troller-cruiser lines.

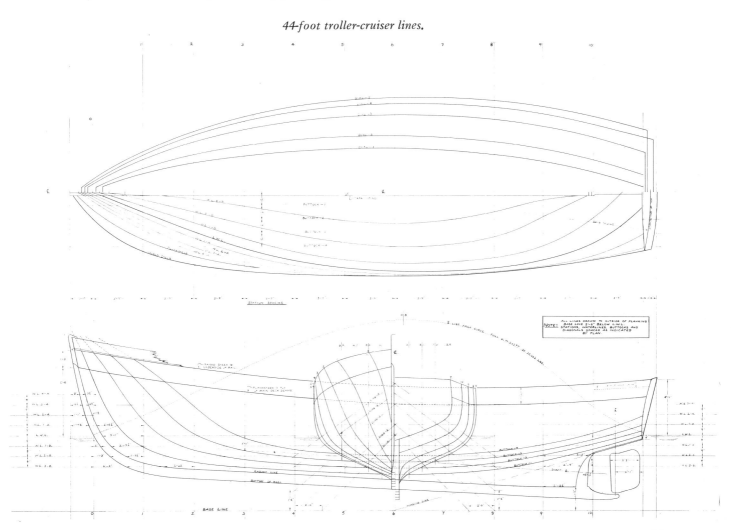

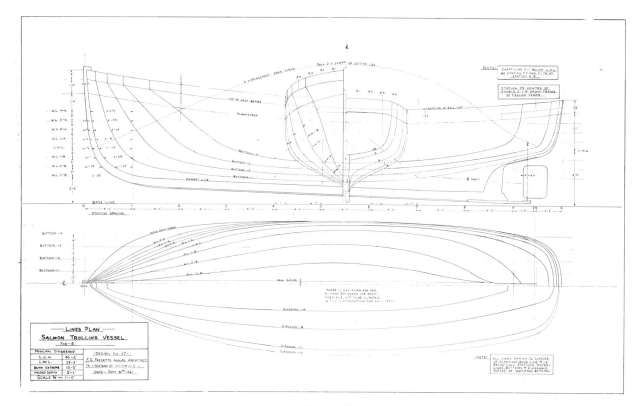

40-foot troller.

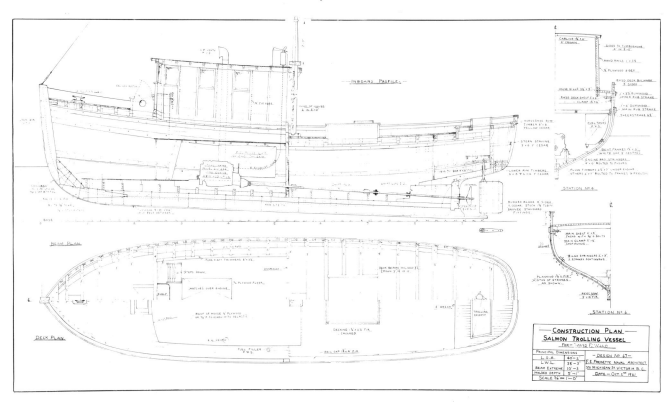

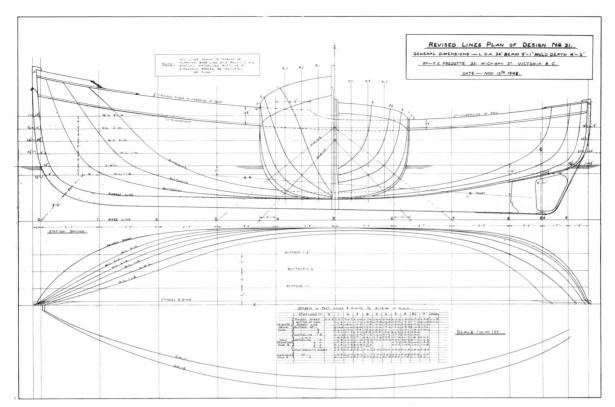

34-foot gillnetter.

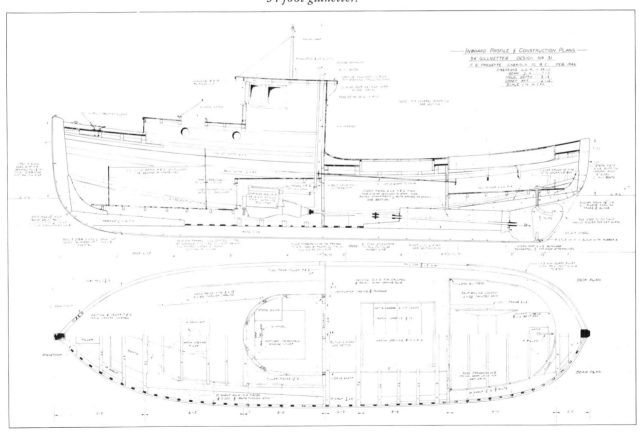

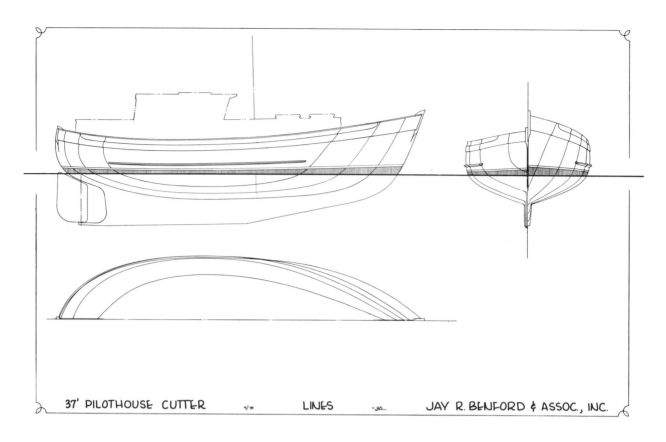

37' PILOTHOUSE CUTTER   LINES   JAY R. BENFORD & ASSOC., INC.

JAY R. BENFORD

Jay Benford is a young designer who has made a name for himself in recent years for the salty cruising boats, both power and sail, that have come from his drawing board. With an office at Friday Harbor in the heart of the San Juan Islands in Washington State, Jay is an active participant in the boating scene and is very familiar with the conditions prevalent in this area.

Early in 1977 I was approached by Hal Cook to build a new vessel, and the design chosen was Jay's 37-foot pilothouse motorsailer. This particular boat is an interesting concept for an area that experiences a great variety of conditions. The waters of southern British Columbia and northern Washington State are subject to strong tidal action, with considerable floating debris from the region's logging industry. Winds are generally light, and the green timbered hills and mountains are frequently obscured by clouds, as this is a wet climate (which is not always appreciated by boating enthusiasts in exposed cockpits). The concept of the design

takes these points into account, for *Corcovado* has a pilothouse with enclosed steering and controls and plenty of power for the often-windless conditions prevalent in these waters.

The lofty cutter rig of *Corcovado* is very efficient, enabling the hull to be driven easily. A Hundested variable-pitch propeller allows the blades to be feathered when the boat is under sail. The original plans had been drawn up for traditional carvel planking, but they were adapted by Jay and myself for glued cold-molded construction. This helped considerably in reducing the overall weight of the structure. These savings were used to increase the weight of the ballast keel, which is an 8,500-pound lead casting. The hull was laid up of three diagonal skins of 5/16-inch-thick Alaska yellow cedar over 1-1/2" x 2" Douglas fir stringers on 9-inch centers. The entire surface is sheathed with Dynel and epoxy.

Corcovado was launched in September 1979 and has proved to be an excellent little ship for these northwestern waters. The hull form gives good stability and a surprising amount of accommodation space below.

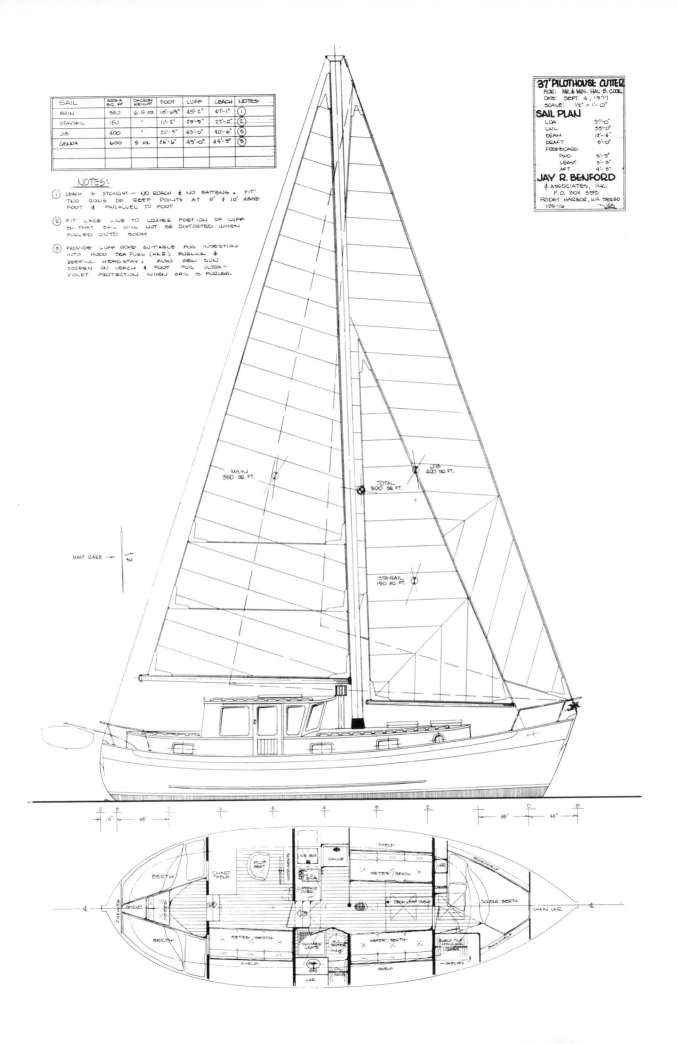

SAIL	AREA SQ. FT.	DACRON WEIGHT	FOOT	LUFF	LEACH	NOTES
MAIN	350	6.5 OZ.	18'-6½"	45'-2"	47'-1"	①
STAYSAIL	150	"	11'-2"	29'-9"	27'-0"	②
JIB	400	"	20'-3"	49'-0"	40'-6"	③
GENOA	600	5 OZ.	26'-6"	49'-0"	45'-3"	③

NOTES:

① LEACH 'S STRAIGHT — NO ROACH & NO BATTENS. FIT TWO ROWS OF REEF POINTS AT 5' & 10' ABOVE FOOT & PARALLEL TO FOOT

② FIT LACE LINE TO LOWER PORTION OF LUFF SO THAT SAIL WILL NOT BE DISTORTED WHEN FURLED ONTO BOOM

③ PROVIDE LUFF ROPE SUITABLE FOR INSERTION INTO HOOD SEA FURL (MK.II) FURLING & REEFING HEAD STAY. ALSO SEW SUN SCREEN ON LEACH & FOOT FOR 'ULTRA-VIOLET PROTECTION WHEN SAIL IS FURLED.

MAIN 350 SQ. FT.

JIB 400 SQ. FT.

TOTAL 900 SQ. FT.

STAYSAIL 150 SQ. FT.

MAST RAKE

37' PILOTHOUSE CUTTER
FOR: MR.& MRS. HAL B. COOK.
DATE: SEPT. 4, 1977
SCALE: ½" = 1'-0"
SAIL PLAN
LOA   37'-0"
LWL   33'-0"
BEAM   12'-4"
DRAFT   5'-0"
FREEBOARD:
   FWD.   5'-9"
   LEAST   3'-3"
   AFT   4'-3"
JAY R. BENFORD
& ASSOCIATES, INC.
P.O. BOX 399
FRIDAY HARBOR, WA. 98250
125-16

SHELF
ICE BOX
RANGE
PILOT SEAT
CHART TABLE
BERTH
INSTRUMENTS
CUPBOARD OVER
SETTEE/BERTH
LKR.
BOOKSHELF
SHELF
SHELF
DROP LEAF TABLE
DOUBLE BERTH
CHAIN LKR.
SETTEE/BERTH
SHOWER GRATE
W.C.
SETTEE/BERTH
SHELF FOR HANGING LOCKER
SHELF
LKR.
OIL TANK
SHELF
SHELVES
BERTH

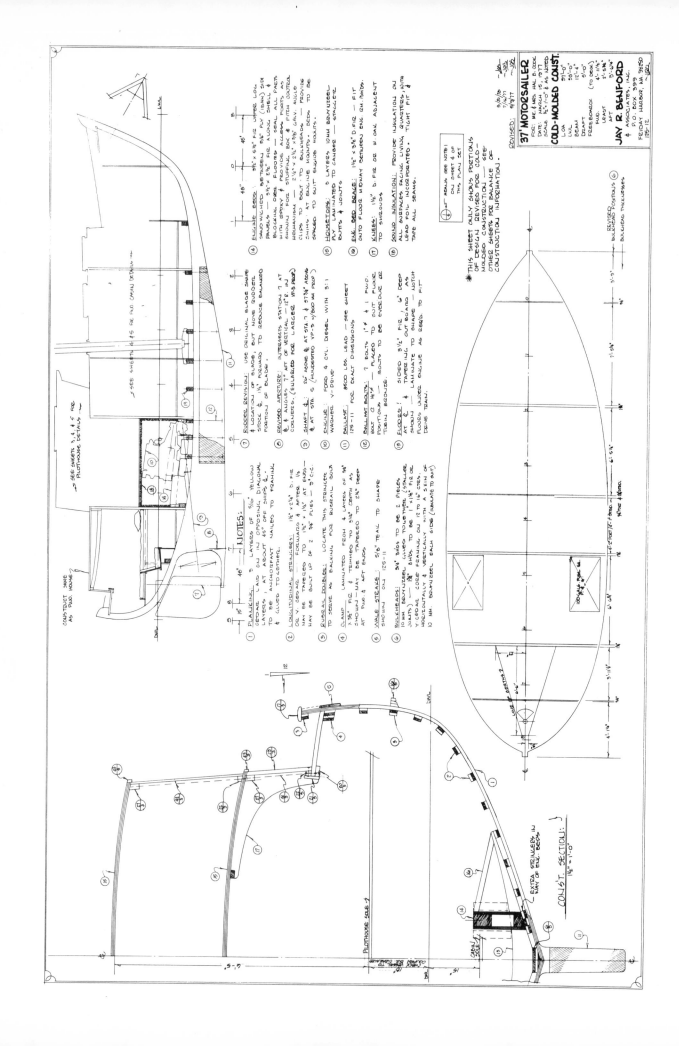

WILLIAM GARDEN

Bill Garden is one of the world's most successful designers, and if I had to choose the most prolific designer, it would be Bill. With a lifetime of boating and designing behind him, this man knows what he is talking about. A Seattle man, Bill moved his family and business to Victoria, British Columbia, some years ago. His charming office is situated on a small island near Sidney, British Columbia: there are drawings, photos, and mementos of a lifetime's work present and the atmosphere that prevails gives one the feeling that he has enjoyed every minute of it.

Bill is one of those few people who seem to be able to design anything and produce a boat that is exactly what the customer wanted. Because of this, I find his work particularly interesting, as it is impossible to fit it into a set category. Most designers, like builders, have some particular style they follow, and their work tends to be variations of a similar theme. Not so with Bill Garden. His work has tremendous variety, ranging from commercial to pleasure craft, sail and power, traditional, heavy to super-light displacement. For people like myself without the openness of mind that Bill has, it is sometimes difficult to understand how he can draw such dissimilar concepts.

Although Bill was well known in the Seattle area in the 1950s, particularly for some of the cold-molded canoe-like hulls such as his own *Oceanus* and *Zia,* he became most familiar to the general boating public for his salty clipper-bowed ketches, hundreds of which have been produced in Oriental yards.

When I approached Bill for two of his designs to include in this book, I asked him if he had any particular favorite. He smiled and shook his head—"I like them all"—which did not make my choice any easier! In selecting *Oceanus* and *Claymore,* I have chosen two rather extreme vessels. There are certain similarities in the designs, as both are very easily driven hulls requiring comparatively little power to move them along at hull speed. Both these vessels use cold-molded construction methods, a technique

Bill is well familiar with. In a world of dwindling energy resources, both these boats represent to me a concept of the future and show the freedom of expression that is so much a part of this man's work. I know many readers will enjoy poring over these drawings.

Below: Oceanus, *designed by William Garden. (Krantz)* Overleaf: *Lines and sail plan of* Oceanus.

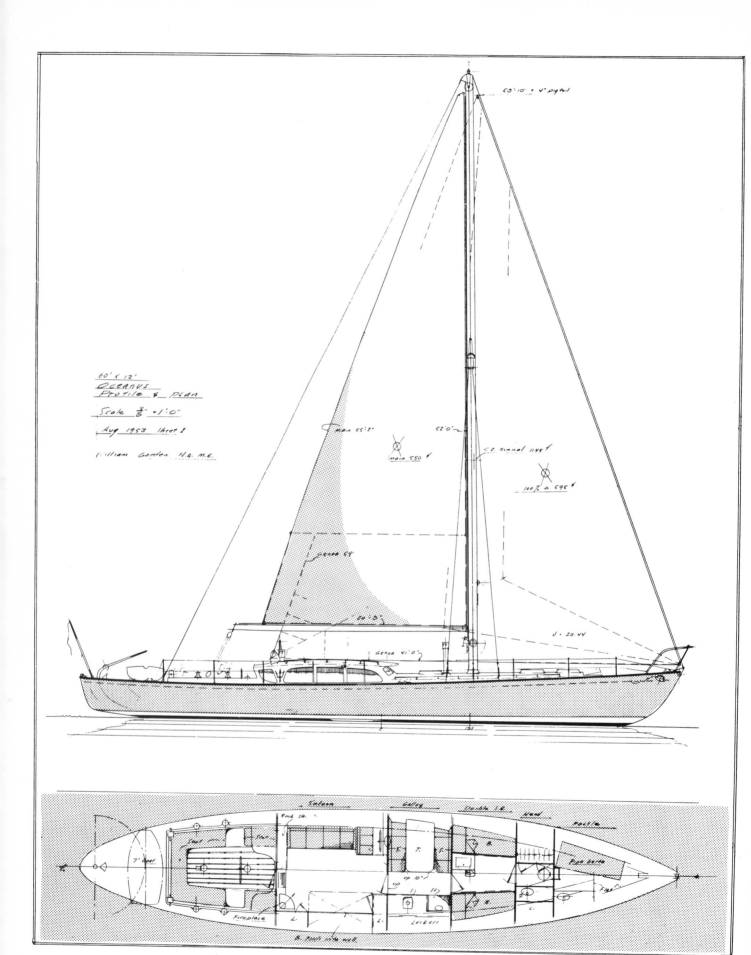

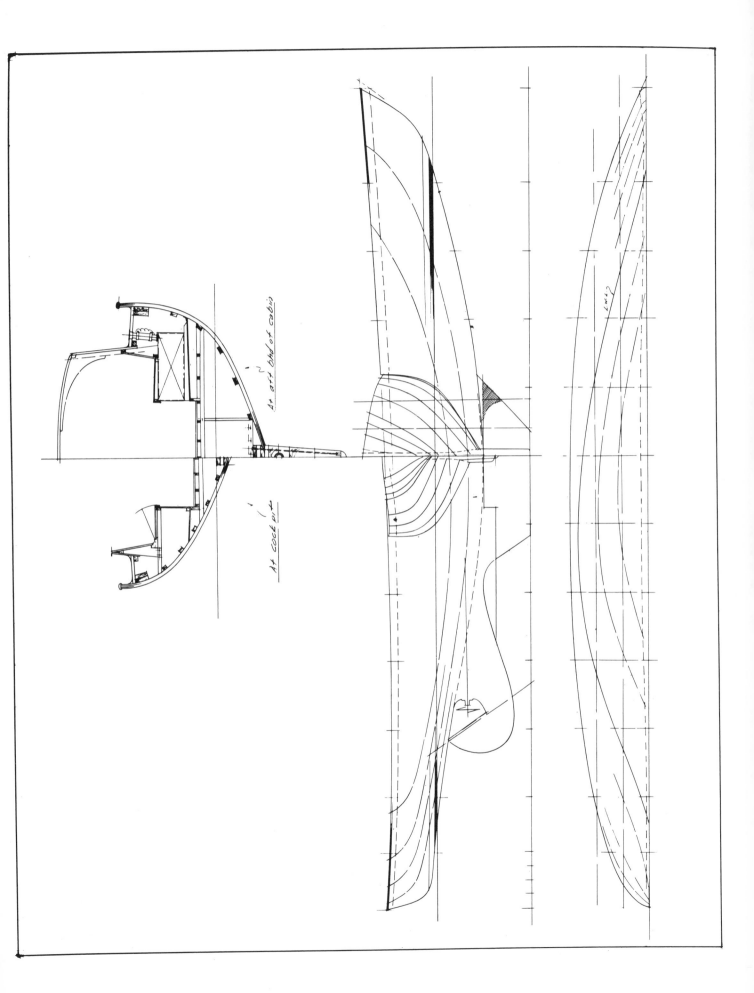

At aft bhd of cabin

At cockpit

Above: Claymore *underway*. Below and opposite: *Plans of* Claymore

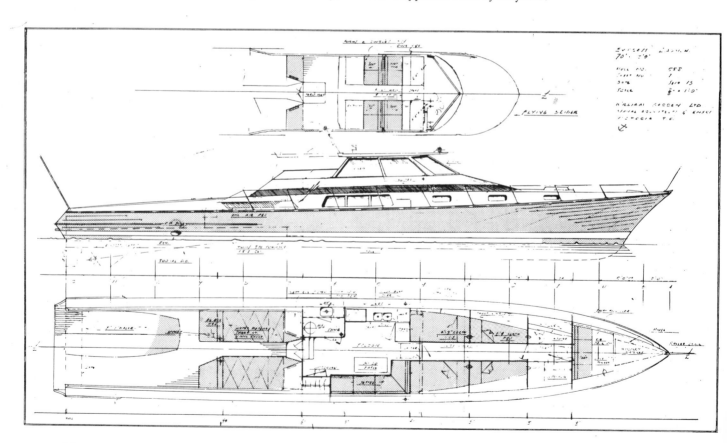

32

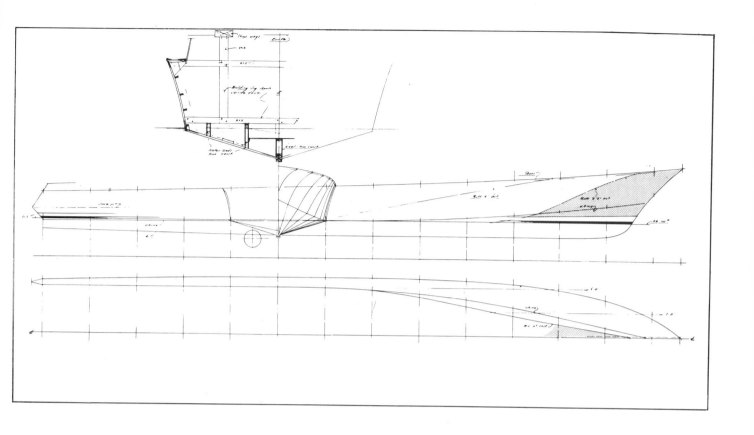

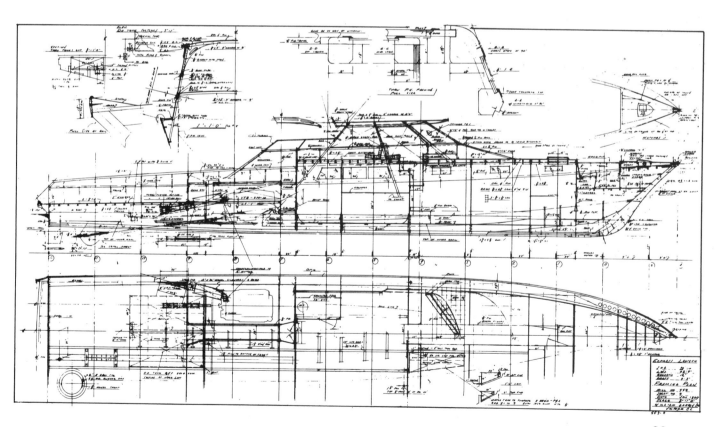

33

The 47-foot ketch Kailda *built by the author in Honolulu to an E.R. Simmerer design. (Bartlett)*

E.R. SIMMERER

Kailda was the last design from the drawing board of the late Ernie Simmerer, who designed her for his own use, which makes her particularly interesting. I was engaged to work on and direct *Kailda*'s construction at the yard of Hawaiian Tuna Packers at Kewalo Basin, Honolulu, a firm with plenty of experience in heavy fishboat construction but no previous experience in building a sailing yacht.

It was an interesting assignment, as most of the staff were of Japanese ancestry, and I learned what fine craftsmen some of those men are. Sadly, before the project was completed, Ernie died, but *Kailda* was gradually completed by his widow, Betty, and a photo of *Kailda* under sail appears above.

Ernie Simmerer grew up in Seattle, Washington, and was trained as an electrical engineer. His love of boating and talent for design work resulted in his designing the 42-foot schooner *Kitone,* which he sailed to Mexico and the South Seas before finally settling in Honolulu.

During the years he lived in Honolulu, Ernie designed many different craft, commercial and private, both power and sail, and his designs are well known for their staunch, wholesome characteristics. His boats were usually heavy and they did not come apart in the boisterous conditions present around the Hawaiian Islands. The lines of *Kailda* show an easily driven hull form with fairly traditional sections. She was planked with 1-3/8 inch Douglas fir carvel planking over oak frames, and there were few hard bends in any of the structure except a few frames toward the stern that had to be laminated.

Kailda is the type of honest cruising boat we seldom see today, since this type of vessel unfortunately requires a lot of man-hours to complete. But the design is well suited to the skilled amateur builder, although I would prefer cold-molded construction to the carvel planking as that was specified.

Even so she is a fine vessel and I am indebted to Mrs. Betty Simmerer for the use of these plans.

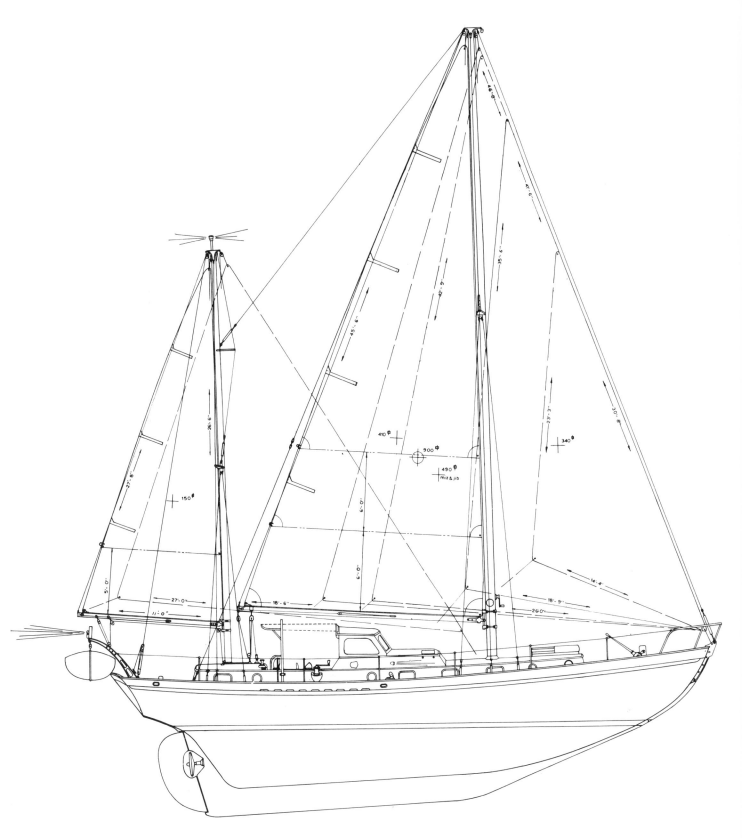

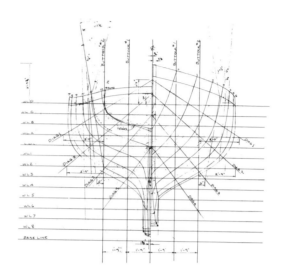

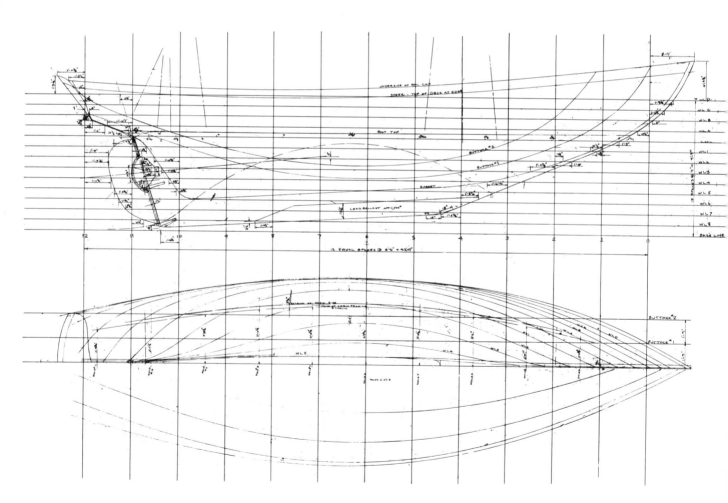

3

Tools and Equipment

To build any kind of boat requires the use of a number of tools, so before we get down to actual construction, it would be good to consider what kind of equipment is required to build a modern wooden yacht.

Anyone who has seen the tool kits of old-time craftsmen marvels at the number and variety of tools these men used. Broadaxes, adzes, and slicks are tools that require skill and respect—or either job or operator is in for a rough time.

One of the good things about cold-molding is that many tools that are used extensively in other forms of wooden construction are not necessary, since few parts of the vessel will be cut out of large, solid members. It is considerably easier to build these up out of smaller pieces and glue them together, and this also has the benefit of making these members more stable and strong and less likely to warp, shrink, or check.

Naturally enough, the amount of tools and equipment you will need depends very much on the size of vessel you intend to build. If your project is relatively small, such as the building of a light plywood runabout or sailing dinghy, you will need only a few hand tools, with perhaps the aid of an electric drill. But for larger vessels, which will involve many more hours of work,

you will only cheat yourself by limiting your tool kit.

Good interior joinerwork requires the use of many tools you can possibly do without for the basic construction of the hull itself. If, however, you intend to complete the boat, it's foolish economy to limit your tool inventory, because there are many tools that will save you untold hours of hard labor.

It is becoming increasingly difficult for the young professional builder to obtain high-quality hand tools. Most of the manufacturers who used to produce tools that were well made and of good quality have either gone out of business or now make a selection of rubbish that is deemed suitable for the "home handyman," whomever that is supposed to mean. Tools that were made with thought and pride, that had rosewood handles which actually fitted the hand, with good balance, brass fittings, and polished steelwork—these kinds of tools were a joy to use and would last a professional for life.

There are still a few dealers left who supply fine tools, which are usually made in Europe and Japan: if your project is going to be a large one, it might be worthwhile to buy some of these better tools rather than frustrate yourself trying to use the pathetic substitutes usually offered in neighborhood hardware stores. On the other hand, many of these same hardware stores offer a variety of portable power tools, many of which are excellent and can save you a lot of unnecessary work.

Since we have to start somewhere, it might be good to consider a hypothetical basic kit of hand tools for building an average cruising boat of about 35 feet, if there is such a thing.

SAWS

A good crosscut saw about 26 inches long and with 10 teeth to the inch will be used frequently for all manner of jobs. Get one with a comfortable feel to the handle, which should be well secured to the blade with at least four stud fastenings. Beware of plastic handles; some are easily broken and almost impossible to repair.

Later, when doing cabinetwork and fitting out the interior, you will need a tenon or backsaw about 12 inches long and with about 12 teeth to the inch. Good makes to buy are Disston-Atkins, even some of the better Sears Craftsman brand, and the British Spear & Jackson. One of the best brands available is the elephant trademark of W. Tyzack, Sons, and Turner of Sheffield, England. Two saws are a minimum, and you will probably need a coarser-cutting handsaw if power tools are not used.

PLANES

Probably the most useful general-purpose plane in your kit would be what is known as a jack plane. They are made in both wood and steel, each type being extremely useful. For cold-molded work, however, I would recommend a No. 05 Record Brand plane made by C. & J. Hampton of Sheffield, England, a company that still makes an excellent selection of quality steel tools, particularly hand planes. The balance and finish of these tools are still good, and it's doubtful if you will find any planes to match them. A Record No. 077A rabbet plane and a

small block plane are very useful tools during the planking operation. If you can afford it, a compass plane, which allows the sole to be adjusted for planing concave and convex surfaces, is also a fine tool. Spokeshaves with rounded or flat faces for shaping tighter curved surfaces are also available in the Record brand and are always in use during the finishing work.

CHISELS

A variety of chisels is necessary for notching and chopping out to allow the various construction members to interlock. My basic choice would be 1/4", 3/8", 1/2", and 1", but once again the quality of chisels available today is but a shadow of those of the past.

By far the best chisels I have used in recent years are some that are made in Japan. Sensibly designed, with wooden, socketed handles slightly offset and hollow-ground faces, these chisels are strongly made with superb steel. In fact, many of the hand tools used in the Orient are well made, but Westerners usually find it difficult to adopt a completely different approach in using them by pulling planes and saws on the cutting stroke instead of pushing.

OILSTONE AND SHARPENING

To keep your chisels and plane irons sharp, you will need a good oilstone. These vary considerably in price, but a good artificial stone at moderate cost is made under the India brand. Get a combination stone with coarse cutting on one side and fine on the other. The size most professionals use measures 8 inches by 2 inches. As stones are usually supplied in a cardboard container, it is necessary to provide a wood box to protect them as they are quite brittle and easily broken if dropped. It is usual to make a box by hollowing out a solid piece of hardwood, such as teak, to fit the stone. This can be done with mallet and chisel, and the stone is set just over halfway into the wood. A lid made the same way will protect the surface of the stone when not in use. To stop the box from sliding about when sharpening a tool, it is customary to drive a small nail into each bottom corner of the base, and cut the heads off so that they project about 1/16 inch. A new oilstone will soak up quite a bit of oil when first used; it is good practice to place the stone in a container of light machine oil for a day or two to allow it to absorb as much as possible.

When sharpening, make sure the stone is level and at a convenient height, such as on a table or bench. Grasp the chisel or plane cutter firmly in the right hand, using the middle and index fingers of the left hand to steady the tool. Concentrate on holding the tool at a steady angle, avoiding a rocking motion but using the full length and surface of the stone. Keep the surface well lubricated during sharpening and examine the edge of the tool frequently to see how you are progressing. Remember the old adage: "If you can see the edge, there isn't one." On a wide cutter such as a plane iron, it will be possible to note a dull appearance at the cutting edge of a blunt tool. However, during sharpening you will notice that the stone is gradually cutting away the metal behind the edge until the dull section has disappeared. At this stage, turn the cutter over, and holding it face down and completely flat, give it a few rubs to remove the "feather edge." Test the edge by carefully moving your thumb *across* rather than *along* the edge. If sharp, it will tend to grab the skin rather than just slide across. The important steps in sharpening are: (1) to place the stone at a convenient height, such as on a bench or table, (2) to have the stone level and firmly placed, and (3) to sharpen the tool at the correct angle and concentrate on holding that angle.

When the sharpening of plane irons has been completed, tilt each corner of the iron to cut away the metal, which otherwise would leave ridges on a planed surface. Quite often, however, a used stone is slightly concave and leaves a rounded cutting edge, which does not require this treatment. An old, worn stone can fre-

quently be rejuvenated by cutting it down on a level cement floor. Use plenty of water and rub the surface of the stone against the cement. If the cement has been made with a sharp sand, it will cut the stone down quickly.

Every so often it will be necessary to remove much of the steel behind the cutting edge. This operation is known as "grinding" and was accomplished in the past by use of a wheel-shaped grinding stone that had its lower half submerged in a box filled with water. A handle or pulley on the side revolved the stone and the water lubricated it, preventing the temper of the cutter from being lost by excessive heat. Today those grinding stones are less common, so you will probably have to use a modern high-speed grinder, which requires careful use if the cutter's edge is not to be "burned" and the temper lost. A small, electric-powered grinding wheel should be set up handy to the workbench. Set a pail of water close beside so you can dunk the tool into the water regularly and cool it. Most tools are sharpened to about a 25-degree angle on the oilstone, so it may help the novice to cut a small piece of plywood to that angle to accustom himself to holding the tool at this angle. On the grinder it is frequently possible to set a guide on which to rest the tool during the grinding operation, but because many cutters and chisels are tapered in section, you many have to adjust this guide when grinding different tools. An angle of between 15 and 20 degrees is usual, and you should grind away enough metal until approximately a 1/16-inch edge remains. Further grinding will almost certainly result in burning, and the tool then will not hold an edge.

Sharpening tools is a common enough job for a woodworker, and a novice will soon acquire the necessary skill with practice. If I have digressed somewhat from the subject of a basic toolkit, it is because so many inexperienced people attempt to work with blunt tools, which often are far more dangerous than sharp ones.

A note of caution on the use of grinding wheels: always use safety goggles to protect the eyes from minute particles of steel.

SQUARES AND BEVELS

Your kit should have a large, flat steel square known as a roofing square. They measure 16 inches by 24 inches in the U.S. and are sometimes 18 inches by 24 inches in Europe. This is a good tool for marking out during lofting and on sheets of plywood, where other types of squares do not lie flat. Another very handy marking-out tool is a small 12-inch adjustable combination square, which will also mark out 45-degree miters and sometimes has a glass level built into the handle. The quality of these tools will also vary, so before buying them, it is best to check whether they are indeed square. By drawing a vertical line from a straightedge and reversing the square onto the other hand, it is possible to see if there is any apparent error.

You will also need a couple of adjustable bevel gauges, 8 inches being a good size. These are used to mark many of the bevels required in fitting various members into position, and to pick up important bevels from the lofting itself.

HAMMERS

A hammer is an essential tool in any kind of wooden construction where fastenings are used, and in cold-molding you will need more than one.

Claw hammers are the best choice, particularly during lofting and planking, where nails frequently need to be withdrawn. For this reason a strong, modern handle of either steel or fiberglass, which is cushioned with a covering of rubber, will be less prone to breakage and kinder to elbow joints. I have found that when planking day after day, a 20-ounce hammer is too heavy and can result in a condition similar to tennis elbow. This is painful, and the best cure is rest, which usually is not practical when you have a job to do. While a 16-ounce hammer does not have the power of the larger one, it is quite adequate for driving nails less than 1-1/2 inches long for planking. A small sledgehammer is required for driving larger fastenings and bolts,

or for use as a dolly to back up material such as stringers when planking is being nailed to them.

Don't get a sledgehammer that is too heavy, for you will frequently be working alone and need to hold up the sledge in your left hand while driving a nail with your right (assuming you are right-handed).

MISCELLANEOUS TOOLS

There are several small tools required in boatbuilding that are seldom mentioned but continually used and frequently carried in a pocket or bib apron. A measuring tape, of course, is essential and is in constant use. Some of the larger sizes are heavy and bulky, so a 10-foot 1/2-inch-wide tape is my choice. When marking out, you usually hold the tape in your left hand and a pencil in the right. As a result, it is frustrating to find the numbers on the tape upside down, so it is good to have the kind of steel tape that has markings reversed, which frequently prevents stupid and unnecessary errors.

Nail sets or punches are also used frequently. It's worthwhile having one of the mechanic's type, which has a larger shank than the normal carpenter's punch—fastenings are sometimes driven into counterbored holes, and the shorter punches are considerably more painful to use.

There are several other small hand tools used by the wood boatbuilder that will be necessary, particularly during the interior finish work. These tools include a marking gauge, dividers or a scriber, a carpenter's spirit level about 24 to 30 inches long, and a good pair of pliers, or end cutters to remove some of the nails you will undoubtedly encounter when notching out parts of the structure for additional members.

DRILLS AND AUGERS

A would-be boatbuilder faces a daunting prospect if he proposes to drill all the necessary holes by hand. Certainly one of the greatest aids to the builder is a power drill using modern drill bits. These bits bore complex-shaped holes that fit the fastening precisely. In addition, they counterbore, enabling the fastening to be covered by a wooden plug. This saves countless hours of needless work. Depending on the size of the vessel, you will probably need more than one of these laborsaving tools. Pilot holes for small nails and screws will require a fairly high-speed drill of about 2,000 revolutions per minute (RPM), with a minimum chuck capacity of 1/4 inch.

Larger fastenings, such as bolts and drifts, require holes that are sometimes in excess of 36 inches long. A 1/2-inch drill with a speed of about 400 RPM is a good all-around drill. The most common bits used are machine twist drills with extensions welded to them and turned down at the inboard end to 1/2 inch in diameter so as to fit the drill chuck. These bits frequently can be found inexpensively in secondhand stores; they are less prone to damage if you should strike a fastening than if you were using wood augers.

POWER TOOLS

Portable power tools will save a tremendous amount of useless labor when the vessel to be built is of any size, so it is worthwhile to consider which type of tools will be most useful in this respect.

Unless the builder has access to heavy equipment, it is assumed that the sawmill will deliver the lumber required already broken down to size without the need for resawing or planing. Material for framing and planking will obviously have to be cut as required, but it should not need to be reduced in thickness, so several large machines that always have been considered indispensable for traditional wooden construction are not required.

Next to the electric drill in usefulness is the portable saw, usually referred to as a "Skilsaw," regardless of make. A 7-inch saw blade is a good size, as it will cut material a full 2 inches thick yet be light enough to handle with one hand.

That, incidentally, should be the criterion, because much of your cutting will be done with one hand, and the saw should be well balanced so as to allow you do to this. A tungsten carbide-tipped blade will save much resharpening when ripping planks, particularly in teak and other hardwoods, but crosscutting requires fine, even teeth to avoid splitting.

A good jigsaw will do many jobs that a band saw is used for, plus some that a band saw cannot do. When cutting out curved shapes in plywood for bulkheads, etc., it is much easier to use this useful tool than to handle large sheets of plywood on the table of a band saw.

The portable power plane is the modern adze. This excellent tool has a multitude of uses, from planing scarfs in lumber and plywood to shaping off deadwood and even lead keels. I would have no hesitation in choosing it over a power jointer, or buzzer as it is sometimes called. Several makes of power planes are available, but these are generally expensive, so your budget will have to determine which one you purchase. Check whether a sharpening kit can be purchased for the blades—on some planes it's necessary to have cutters sharpened professionally, which is inconvenient and expensive. The chip deflector of the plane should be reversible, allowing chips to be ejected on either side; with some models, the chips are thrown into the operator's face when planing a vertical surface. Some makes are awkward, heavy, and often bulky, and even the strongest pair of arms will soon tire when these models are used in awkward positions.

A tool that is a great help during finishing work is a router. This high-speed machine uses a variety of cutters and is a small version of the shaper or spindle. Used for grooving, rounding edges, cutting dadoes, etc., this is a very versatile tool.

There are a variety of machine sanders on the market, and each has some particular virtue. However, if the choice has to fall on one, by far the best for cold-molded construction is a high-speed soft-pad sander. My choice is the Black and Decker 4043 Model 3000 RPM. This is a well-balanced professional tool that is used with

A homebuilt shed can save a lot of rent.

a soft pad disc to which sandpaper is applied with a special adhesive. This machine, used for sanding a hull smooth, working fiberglass, or finishing cabinetwork, will save you countless hours of labor.

Of the nonportable power tools, a table saw is probably the best, but in my opinion, a good portable saw is a better choice. Table saws vary considerably in size, but a 10-inch saw of the type many building contractors use on job sites is ideal. These are sometimes listed for sale in the want ads in local newspapers—they can be bought at most reasonable prices and sold once the job is done.

A jointer (sometimes called a buzzer) is another useful machine that usually has three knives in a revolving cutting head. These machines have planed countless fingers off the unwary over the years. Of all power equipment, it pays to treat jointers with particular respect.

Band saws that were so necessary in traditional boatbuilding are little used with laminated construction. A small band saw can be handy for cutting beadings and moldings during the finishing work, but some of the previously mentioned hand tools will be of more general use.

WORKBENCH AND WORKSHED

Several other items of equipment are required for building a boat whether using the cold-molded method or not. It's worthwhile building a workbench and fastening a decent woodworking vise to it. Benches vary in height from 30 to 36 inches and should be at least six feet long. There are various designs of benches, which are usually dictated by the space available and the materials at hand. You will likely be using the vise to hold quite long pieces of lumber, such as planking strakes, so you will need some method of holding up the end of the material. This can be done with a wooden peg, which is placed in one of a series of holes drilled into a vertical post, such as a leg, fixed at the end of the bench between the top and the floor. The vise is normally mounted at the left end of the bench as you face the front. Hardwood cheek pieces of heavy plywood are fastened to the inside of the steel jaws of the vise to protect the lumber while it is being worked. Because the vise is used so much for holding lumber while being planed, it is helpful to make the whole bench more rigid by splaying the legs out at each end instead of making them vertical.

You will also need at least two strong sawhorses about 24 inches high on which to rest planks as they are cut. These can be made light yet strong by using 2 x 4's for the tops and notching 2 x 3 legs into the tops. A 1/2-inch plywood gusset fastened to the tops of the legs at each end immediately under the 2 x 4 top will give good support. There are quite a number of angles to cut when making these horses, so it is an excellent exercise for a novice. Sawhorses will suffer much rough treatment, being used frequently to support staging, so it is important to make them well. The addition of glue to the joints also stops racking.

The choice of a suitable workshed is often difficult for the amateur builder, yet today it is seldom necessary to build close to the water due to the availability of modern moving equipment. So there is considerably larger scope in the choice of location. In any event, with limited time because of regular work, it is often impractical for some builders to use facilities very far from home. Frequently it is difficult to erect a workshed in the back garden because of building restrictions, yet this is by far the best solution for the average person. The type of shed required can be built at very little cost when compared with the alternative of paying rent. One possibility is to seek out contractors who specialize in demolition work—they frequently have secondhand lumber and roofing at a fraction of the cost of new material. Depending on location, it may be necessary to provide lights or heat, particularly if working evenings, for although building a boat is an interesting and pleasurable project, it is also a lot of hard work. Some attention to the comforts of the building shed will be greatly appreciated in the weeks and months ahead; it pays to provide yourself with the best facilities possible if faced with a long job.

4

Materials

In the first chapter I mentioned some of the materials available to the modern boatbuilder. Perhaps we should consider the question of lumber first, as this is one of the major initial expenses of construction.

Wooden vessels are built of many different types of lumber. Although some types have better qualities than others, the deciding factors in choosing lumber are usually availability and price. In traditional carvel construction, a great amount of hardwood is required in the structural members (keel, stern, frames, etc.) to hold the fastenings. The framework of the cold-molded boat, however, does not depend entirely on the ability of the lumber to hold fastenings well, and many woods hitherto considered unacceptable for framing are in fact excellent for cold-molding. Softwoods generally glue better, are lighter, cost less, and are usually more available, so don't think you have to conform to the traditional choice.

Every country has its own native woods, many of which are quite suitable for yacht construction. The forests of Europe and Asia had supplied shipbuilding lumber for centuries before the great wealth of the Americas was discovered. Present-day Australian and New Zealand boatbuilders use locally grown timbers

that are unknown to other parts of the world, and these same builders are often unaware of the lumber types grown in parts of North America or Africa. But the same basic techniques of construction can be used, and a well-built wooden boat will last a lifetime, whether it be built of kauri pine, teak, African mahogany, or Alaska cedar. The important factor is the skill of the craftsman who builds the vessel and how well he does his work.

In recent years, lumber dealers have imported many different kinds of woods, mainly from tropical areas such as South America and some of the Pacific islands. Most of the woods have exotic-sounding names, and little is known of their characteristics except by those who have used them. It pays to investigate these woods, many of which are of excellent quality and reasonably priced.

CONSIDERATIONS IN WOOD SELECTION

There are basic characteristics of wood as a construction material, that must be considered in each individual wood before it is chosen as being suitable for use. These may be summed up as follows, though not necessarily in this order.

1. *Decay resistance.* While still important, this factor can be greatly assisted with the use of modern preservatives, which may be applied by brush or spray. This is often done by lumber dealers in special tanks that allow the wood to be pressure-treated, thus obtaining maximum penetration of the preservative. Wood treated this way often comes with a guarantee of its durability, and several of the large lumber companies have trade names for their process.

2. *Stiffness.* Generally, the hardwoods are stiffer than the softwoods. The choice between the two types is not always easy, as the hardwoods generally weigh more but have greater strength, allowing for thinner structures. When almost every structural member in a yacht is curved, the degree of stiffness becomes an important consideration, particularly for planking, which may or may not be supported by adequate framing between bulkheads. Quite obviously, some woods offer better weight/stiffness ratios than others. Designers are always looking for materials with superior performance and it is a tribute to wood that its fine qualities in this respect can still match many of the so-called wonder materials, which are often very expensive.

3. *Ability to hold fastenings.* In the past, with traditional construction methods it was most important that certain structural members be made of woods that could hold fastenings well. The backbone structure and transverse framing of vessels were usually of hardwoods that would hold tapered nails and spikes driven into them.

The use of waterproof glues to bond planking to such members has changed this practice somewhat, and keels and transverse framing in the form of bulkheads are often of softwoods, which are lighter and generally glue better than hardwoods. Modern fastenings, such as the barbed ring nails and screws, combined with suitable adhesives, provide permanent joining of material.

4. *Stability.* Due to changing moisture content, all woods expand and contract. The greatest movement is along the annular rings, which is why plain-sawn or flat grain lumber is not as stable as vertical-grain or quarter-sawn material.

With laminated techniques, however, flat-grain stock is often a better choice, as any such movement is "locked up" by the waterproof barrier of the glue line, most exposed material being vertical grain on the sides. For laminated keels, stems, deck beams, engine beds, etc., flat-grain stock is a better choice, particularly if these members have to be laminated to curved shapes. Plain-sawn lumber generally costs considerably less than quarter-sawn, which generates a lot more waste and labor in breaking it down from the log. If planking a vessel with several skins or laminations, it is worth picking out the best stock for the inner and outer skins, using the flat grain and any poorer quality material for the inside or core skins, where they will be locked up with glue.

5. *Weight.* As mentioned earlier, hardwoods generally weigh more than the softwoods. The accompanying section includes the weights and uses of some popular construction woods and will give some indication of the differences. (*See also* Appendix.)

With so many types of wood available, it is often difficult to decide which material best suits the needs required of it. Hardwoods are best used for structural members that support heavy loads such as mast steps, transverse floor timbers that may also carry keel bolts, and other important tie rods, bolts, etc., where extra strength is required. They also resist abrasion when used for rails, beltings, and guards. Unfortunately, due to their density and certain natural oils, some hardwoods offer poor gluing characteristics, and this must be weighed against the advantage of superior strength.

The ability of a wood to be glued successfully should be one of the chief reasons for its selection. With the above considerations in mind, the amateur or professional builder usually has many different options to choose from. He should evaluate them carefully to see which particular wood is the best choice for his requirements.

Possibly the most common lumber available

in the world today, due to the huge logging industry in North America, is Douglas fir, sometimes called Oregon pine. This material, if of good quality, is quite suitable for the entire hull. Alaska yellow cedar is another fine lumber that could be used for this purpose. Western red cedar, though soft, is durable, glues well, and is an excellent choice for planking.

Woods such as white cedar, cypress, white pine, and longleaf yellow pine (pitch pine), which grow in the eastern and southern states, are also good choices. They are easily worked and have a straight, even grain when cut from good quality logs. For structural members such as laminated floors, knees, and frames, white ash, rock elm, and white oak are fine woods, being hard and tough, yet able to bend easily and take glue well.

In the past, great emphasis was placed on the need for obtaining only the best air-dried lumber, but the chances of finding that kind of material today are almost nil. There are, however, many lumberyards that can supply good-quality kiln-dried material, which is excellent for the purposes of cold-molding.

To glue lumber together reliably, it is important that the moisture content of the wood be within acceptable limits—between 12 percent and 15 percent is normal. Since most of the lumber required in cold-molding is in small sizes, the material will soon after delivery adapt to the local average conditions, thus becoming stable and unlikely to twist and check, as so often happens with large balks.

The accompanying illustration from the U.S. Forest Service shows the typical movement or shrinkage that occurs in lumber due to changing moisture content. Maximum shrinkage occurs along the lines of the annular rings about twice as much as across the layered rings, which is why boat lumber normally is cut with vertical grain or is rift sawn, also known as quarter sawn. Unfortunately, this method of breaking down the log to usable lumber is somewhat wasteful, and this factor makes vertical-grain stock generally more expensive.

While on the subject of lumber, I should

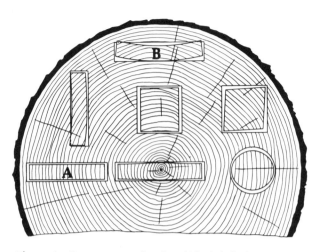

Figure 1. *Quarter-sawn lumber (A) shrinks less and with less distortion than flat-sawn lumber (B).*

advise that it ought to be stored carefully, which will also aid further seasoning. Stack the material with a damp-proof covering underneath the pile and fillets between the layers. Keep the wood dry and straight and avoid storing it where it will be subjected to extreme temperature changes, as in sunlight. With some hardwoods, it is good to seal the end grain of the boards by applying paint or sealer, which will prevent rapid moisture loss and consequent splitting.

LUMBER SIZES AND SHRINKAGE

The timber producers of the world often have different methods and techniques for cutting and marketing their hardwoods and softwoods. This is understandable when one considers the giant automated mills of the Pacific Northwest and compares this type of operation to some of the small sawmills situated along riverbanks in the far-off tropical regions of Africa, South America, and Southeast Asia.

To understand some of the confusion in lumber sizes between hardwoods and softwoods, it may help if we compare the production of the two types.

In North America most of the lumber marketed is softwood, and this is sawn to a nominal size. For example, a 1 x 6 is cut 1 inch thick and 6 inches wide, so we are able to buy uniform quantities of 1 x 6's or 1 x 8's, as the case may be.

From the sawmill, the lumber is either taken to a drying kiln and dried or stacked for air-drying. In the case of kiln-drying, with clear stock the moisture content is usually reduced to about 8 percent. As a result of drying, the piece that was 1" x 6" now measures 15/16" x 5-3/4" or slightly less, but it is still called 1 x 6. When this piece of material is planed on all four sides, the size of it has been further reduced to 3/4" x 5-1/2", but it is sold as a 1 x 6.

In measuring softwoods, a standard rule is used and only a small tolerance over and under the nominal size is allowed. Some countries use this method on both softwoods and hardwoods, but they generally cut oversize to allow for shrinkage.

Most hardwood mills are small and use a different method in sawing than do softwood mills. In softwoods, large timbers called cants are fed through the "gang" saw, which cuts many boards uniformly at one time. Hardwood, however, is usually cut by revolving the log and removing the clear material from the outside, leaving the centers in small timbers and blocking. In doing this, the hardwood man cuts his boards as wide as possible and usually does not square the edges unless it is to remove excessive bark and sapwood. This results in boards that could be any width and thickness. There is no defined size of 1" x 6" or 1" x 8", and as a result they use a different type of measurement rule. This is called a board measure rule. The rule is divided into lines of figures, with the length of the piece marked first, such as 8', 10', 12', 14', 16'. The graduation on each line represents the board footage of each width. So by taking a 12-foot board and laying the rule across the piece at one-third the length of the board from the narrowest width the board footage can be read at a glance. The wider the piece, the more board footage. The rule applies to one inch only; to get the footage on 2-inch material the

figure is doubled, on 1-1/2 inch material, half is added, and so on.

All hardwood is measured in a green condition, and this footage remains with the board whether it is kiln-dried, air-dried, or left green.

A board measured when green will shrink an average of 7 percent after kiln-drying, depending on the species. The amount of shrinkage after air drying will vary depending on the average conditions relative to humidity and temperature of the locality concerned. Moist climates are less conducive to this method of seasoning lumber than dry ones, and some dense species of lumber will require many months, or even years, to adapt completely to the local conditions. To compensate for shrinkage, extra material must be allowed for. It certainly pays to take shrinkage into consideration when estimating costs of a finished product in hardwood lumber.

The following is an example of the cost for materials and machining of running an amount of hardwood. Boat planking to run 2000 feet, 3/4-inch x 8-foot hardwood surfaced two sides. (All figures are per thousand board foot measure.)

Materials	$600.00
Shrinkage, 7%	42.00
Waste, 20%	120.00
Machining	100.00
	$862.00
2000 ft. x 2 =	$1724.00

The materials cost is obtained from the price list; shrinkage we know is 7 percent or more. With regard to waste, it is a figure that can be obtained only by experience or trial runs. Some woods, such as Philippine mahogany, ramin, and the lumber from large trees, have very little waste, whereas other hardwoods have a high waste factor. Much will depend on the sizes required and the way the builder utilizes his materials.

The above is a very brief coverage of a large subject, but I hope it will help you to understand the problems of estimating quantities, so that you can arrive at reasonably accurate cost estimates for your boatbuilding woods.

SUITABLE WOODS

To help the would-be boatbuilder choose lumber for his project, I have drawn up a list of various woods, followed by a description of each one. In compiling this information, I have gone through many publications and books, as well as drawn upon my own experience. Most of these woods are described in relation to their use for boat-building rather than for general construction use. Consequently many common species have not been included here, because they are not generally suitable for yacht construction. For example, I have excluded the most common wood cut in New Zealand today, the remarkable pine, also known as Monterey pine (*Pinus insignus;* also *Pinus radiata*), which was first introduced to New Zealand in 1860. The trees were indeed remarkable because of the speed of their growth. Several forests of this species were planted, and it has been the main lumber used in the building construction industry for several years. Because of its quick growth, however, it is soft and has many knots. Compared with other available woods, it is a poor choice for boat-building.

Many other species have been omitted because of the lack of detailed information. Several excellent woods that I have used in South America and South Africa are not represented because of the difficulty in obtaining accurate technical information. For this reason, it pays to investigate native woods grown in your locality that may be not only suitable but even superior to species imported from other regions.

For those interested in learning more about the specifications and qualities of available woods, many countries have Government Forestry Services that will, upon request, send detailed literature on their particular species.

LIST OF SUITABLE WOODS FOR BOATBUILDING

ABURA
AFARA LIMBA
AFRORMOSIA
AGBA
RED ALDER
ANGELIQUE
APITONG
AMERICAN ASH
EUROPEAN ASH
BALSA
EUROPEAN BEECH
YELLOW BIRCH
BLACKBUTT
ALASKA YELLOW CEDAR
SPANISH CEDAR
WESTERN RED CEDAR
WHITE CEDAR
COACHWOOD
BALD CYPRESS
ROCK ELM
DOUGLAS FIR
WHITE FIR
GABOON
GREENHEART
WESTERN HEMLOCK
IROKO
IRONBARK
ISHPINGO
JARRAH
JELUTONG
KARRI
KOA
EUROPEAN LARCH
WESTERN LARCH
LIGNUMVITAE
AFRICAN MAHOGANY
HONDURAS MAHOGANY
PHILIPPINE MAHOGANY
EASTERN HARD MAPLE
MERANTI
RED OAK
WHITE OAK
OBECHE
EASTERN WHITE PINE
KAURI PINE
MALAYAN KAURI PINE
PARANA PINE
SOUTHERN PINE
WESTERN WHITE PINE
RAMIN
REDWOOD
SPOTTED GUM
EASTERN SPRUCE
SITKA SPRUCE
TEAK

ABURA
(*Mitragyna* spp.)

Average weight at 15 percent moisture content—36 pounds per cubic foot
Durability—not resistant
Source—Tropical Africa

Abura is a pale reddish to light brown wood with a fairly fine, even texture. The grain is slightly interlocked and the wood works fairly easily, taking glues and stains well. Abura may be used as an alternative to softwood, but it needs to be treated to make it suitable for much marine work. The wood is of medium hardness, and fastening holes should be pre-drilled to avoid splitting the material.

AFARA LIMBA
(*Terminalia superba*)

Weight at 15 percent moisture content—35 pounds per cubic foot
Durability—not resistant
Source—Tropical Africa

Afara limba grows in west central Africa and the Congo region and is considered an abundant species. The wood varies in color from a gray white to a creamy brown and may contain dark streaks. This light-colored wood is considered important for the manufacture of blond furniture. The wood is generally straight-grained and of uniform but coarse texture. It seasons easily with little shrinkage and is stable.

Afara limba works easily and glues well. It is not very durable and requires preservative treatment when used in exposed conditions. While it generally needs filling and staining before varnishing, it is a good general-purpose wood when used for interior work.

AFRORMOSIA
(*Afrormosia* spp.)

Average weight at 15 percent moisture content—44 pounds per cubic foot
Durability—very resistant
Source—West Africa

Afrormosia, also known as Kokrodua, is an excellent quality wood having many desirable features. The wood has high strength, natural durability, and good dimensional stability. It is being used by yacht builders and furniture manufacturers as a good alternative to teak, although, aside from its dark brown color, it differs from it in many respects.

Afrormosia is grown in the semideciduous forests of the Ivory Coast, Ghana, Cameroun, and Congo. The tree is large, reaching a height of 160 feet and a diameter of four to five feet. Some of the larger trees are free of branches for 100 feet.

Afrormosia is widely used in European boatyards because it is readily worked with both hand and power tools. It glues quite well with resorcinol glues, lacking the oily, waxy feel of teak. The wood has a grain that is finer and of a more uniform texture than teak, but it can be used for much the same purposes—planking, brightwork, and interior joinery.

AGBA
(*Gossweilerodendron balsamiferum*)

Average weight at 15 percent moisture content—32 pounds per cubic foot
Durability—resistant
Source—Tropical Africa

Agba is a large West African tree that grows in the tropical rain forest areas of southern Nigeria, French Equatorial Africa, the western Congo, and Cabinda. Agba frequently attains a height of 200 feet, with a diameter of seven feet. The trees are straight and cylindrical and the lowest branches may be as high as 80 to 100 feet above the ground.

The milled lumber is generally a uniform light brown in color and straight-grained without figure. It glues well, is easily worked, and is a good choice for a variety of uses in boat construction, such as planking, joinerwork, etc. The wood is very resistant to decay by both white rot and brown rot fungi, possibly due to a certain amount of natural gum contained in the trees.

RED ALDER
(Alnus ruba)

Weight at 15 percent moisture content—31 pounds per cubic foot

Source—western Canada, northwest United States

Red alder grows along the Pacific Coast of North America between Alaska and California and is cut commercially along the coasts of Oregon and Washington. It is the most abundant hardwood of this area.

The wood of red alder varies in color from almost white to a pale pinkish brown and has no visible boundary between heartwood and sapwood. It is moderately light in weight, intermediate in most strength properties, but low in shock resistance.

Red alder is a fast-growing tree and is generally straight-grained. The wood works easily and glues well, being quite stable when dry, with little shrinkage. Many different wood finishes can be obtained by using the mild grain as a base.

Because of the difficulty in obtaining clear stock, most red alder is sold as material suitable for kitchen cabinets, moldings, small turnings, core stock, and light furniture. It is a lumber suitable for most interior use, but it is not considered durable; consequently, it needs protection with preservative treatment.

ANGELIQUE
(Dicorynia guianensis)

Average weight at 15 percent moisture content—47 pounds per cubic foot

Durability—very resistant

Source—South America

Angelique is a fine tropical hardwood that grows on high ground not subjected to flooding along the banks of the Rio Negro River and its tributaries in Brazil's Amazonas Territory. It is being marketed under the name of Guiana teak, and its chief use at present is in the building industry, where it is used for flooring in heavy traffic areas, such as banks, hospitals, hotel lobbies and dance floors.

The wood varies in color between different trees and looks somewhat like a cross between teak and mahogany. This wood is a good boatbuilding material, being suitable for planking, decking, framing, and underwater members, but due to its silica content, it is hard on tools. Carbide cutters provide the most effective way of working the material.

Angelique is hard and holds fastenings well. There is little information on its gluing characteristics, but with modern adhesives, this should present no problem.

APITONG
(Dipterocarpus grandiflorus)

Weight at 15 percent moisture content—44 pounds per cubic foot

Durability—resistant

Source—Philippines

Apitong is the most common structural timber of the Philippines. The principal species are Apiton panau *(D. gracilis)* and hagakhak *(D. warburgii)*. All members of the genus are timber trees marketed under the name of apitong. Other important species of the genus *Dipterocarpus* marketed are *keruing* in Malaysia and Indonesia, *yang* in Thailand, and *gurjun* in India and Burma.

The wood is light to dark reddish-brown in color, comparatively coarse to fine textured, straight-grained or very nearly so, and strong, hard, and heavy. The wood is characterized by the presence of resin ducts that occur in short arcs as seen from end-grain surfaces.

Apitong machines well but is hard to work with hand tools. It takes paint and glue moderately well and is a good low-cost choice lumber for many aspects of wooden boatbuilding, being suitable for structural members, keels, stems, framing, rudders, etc. The heartwood is fairly resistant to decay and insect attack but should be treated with preservatives when used in areas susceptible to decay.

AMERICAN ASH
(*Fraxinus americana*)

Weight at 15 percent moisture content—41
  pounds per cubic feet
Durability—not resistant
Source—eastern United States

American ash is usually separated into tough ash and soft ash. The former has a harder texture composed of longer fibers. Ash is a ring-porous wood, and the open pores give the wood a beautiful, full figure. The wood is a creamy white in the spring and a rich brown in the summer. Ash is tough and has high shock resistance, being used mainly for axe, hammer, and shovel handles and sports equipment, such as baseball bats and tennis racquets.

In the marine field, ash is used mainly for oars and paddles, tillers, and boathooks. Small dinghies and canoes are frequently framed with ash. It glues well and makes fine laminated knees and other structural members not subjected to wetting.

EUROPEAN ASH
(*Fraxinus excelsior*)

Weight at 15 percent moisture content—44
  pounds per cubic foot
Durability—not resistant
Source—much of Europe

European ash is similar to its American cousin (*Fraxinus americana*), having a white color with an occasional pinkish tinge. The wood is straight-grained with a somewhat coarse texture, is moderately hard, and has excellent bending qualities. It works fairly easily, glues well, and can be finished smoothly.

Its uses in the marine field are similar to those for American ash, being mainly confined to small components, such as laminated tillers, handles, and decorative trim and beadings, since it contrasts well with darker woods, such as mahogany or teak.

BALSA
(*Ochroma pyramidale*)

Weight at 15 percent moisture content—6 to 11
  pounds per cubic foot
Durability—not resistant
Source—South America

Balsa is widely distributed throughout tropical America, from Southern Mexico to southern Brazil and Bolivia, but Ecuador has been the principal area of growth since the wood gained commercial importance.

Balsa possesses several characteristics that make possible a wide variety of uses. The wood is readily recognized by its light weight, white to very pale color, and unique velvety feel. It is by far the lightest and softest of all woods on the market. Because of its ultra-lightweight and exceedingly porous composition, balsa is highly efficient where buoyancy, insulation, and dampening of vibration are important considerations. The principal uses of balsa are in livesaving equipment, floats, core stock, insulation, sound modifiers, and models; its use as a core stock in ultra-lightweight yacht construction has been notable in recent fiberglass sandwich vessels.

The wood has little strength and durability but readily absorbs resins, particularly when laid up with the end grain exposed, where it has surprising compression strength. It works and glues easily and was once very popular as a material for surfboards.

EUROPEAN BEECH
(*Fagus sylvatica*)

Weight at 15 percent moisture content—43
  pounds per cubic foot
Durability—not resistant
Source—Europe

European beech is a pale-brown to reddish-brown wood that has minute brown flecks that are visible in vertical grain surfaces. The wood has a fine, even texture, being hard and moderately heavy. It glues easily and works to a smooth, clean surface, staining and finishing well.

Generally used for furniture, flooring and plywood, beech is familiar to woodworkers from the wooden planes made by European tool-makers. Beech is not considered very durable but takes preservative treatment easily.

YELLOW BIRCH
(Betula alleghanensis)

Weight at 15 percent moisture content—42 pounds per cubic foot
Durability—not resistant
Source—eastern Canada and United States

Yellow birch is a hard, heavy, uniform, fine-grained wood. The figure is subdued but gives an attractive finish and the color varies from white sapwood to a red-streaked heartwood.

The grain is somewhat curly and needs to be worked with sharp tools. Birch takes glue well and is frequently used in the plywood industry. Its marine applications are mainly in interior finish work. Due to its poor durability, it needs protecting with preservatives in exposed situations.

BLACKBUTT
(Eucalyptus pilularis)

Weight at 15 percent moisture content—56 pounds per cubic foot
Durability—durable
Source—eastern Australia

Blackbutt is one of the most plentiful coastal hardwoods grown in New South Wales, Australia. The trees reach heights of 150 feet and diameters of four feet. The heartwood is a light brown, though material from the Casino Forestry District frequently has a pink tinge. The texture is coarse, but the grain generally straight, although small gum veins are common. The wood is worked easily and bends well, being hard, strong, and tough.

Blackbutt is a good planking material, but like many members of the *Eucalyptus* family, it takes a long time to season and is rather prone to checking if dried too quickly.

ALASKA YELLOW CEDAR
(Chamaecyparis nootkatensis)

Weight at 15 percent moisture content—30 pounds per cubic foot
Durability—resistant
Source—Alaska, British Columbia

Alaska cedar is one of the world's truly fine boatbuilding woods. In its southern locations, the trees grow on the western slopes of the coast range fairly high up, from elevations of 400 feet to 5,000 feet. In the northern areas, however, the trees descend to sea level.

The heartwood is an unmistakable bright, clear yellow with a strong, pleasant odor when cut. It is moderately heavy, strong in bending endwise, compression- and shock-resistant. Uniform density and stability with low shrinkage make this a valuable wood.

Yellow cedar works easily with hand and power tools, it glues well, and it varnishes beautifully. It has a reputation for painting only moderately well, but this may be unjustified with modern paints. Yellow cedar is an excellent choice as a boat lumber—many yachts and commercial craft are planked and decked with it in the Pacific Northwest.

Although the tree looks like a cedar and is so termed, its botanical name shows that in fact it is a cypress. It is one of the few woods that could be used to build an entire vessel, and in this respect is not unlike New Zealand kauri pine.

SPANISH CEDAR
(Cedrela angustifolia)
(Cedrela oaxancensis)
(Cedrela odorata)

Weight at 15 percent moisture content—30 pounds per cubic foot
Durability—resistant
Source—Central America

Spanish cedar or cedro comprises a group of about seven species that are widely distributed in tropical America from southern Mexico to northern Argentina. The wood is more or less distinctly ring-porous, and the heartwood varies from light reddish brown to dark reddish-brown. The heartwood is characterized by its distinctive cedar-like odor. The wood seasons readily. Its strength is similar to mahogany, except in hardness and compression perpendicular to the grain, where mahogany is definitely superior.

Spanish cedar is considered decay-resistant and works and glues well. It is a good boat-building material and is used locally wherever an easily worked, light but strong, durable, straight-grained wood is required.

Spanish cedar and mahogany are the classic timbers of Latin America.

WESTERN RED CEDAR
(*Thuja plicata*)

Weight at 15 percent moisture content—24 pounds per cubic foot
Durability—resistant
Source—seaward slopes in the Pacific Northwest, British Columbia

Western red cedar is a light, strong, durable wood that has won much favor with boat-builders all over the world. It comes in long, clear lengths and has an unmistakable strong, pleasant odor when cut. The only drawback to this fine wood is its natural softness; when used as a planking material, it will take little punishment unless protected by some form of hardwood or synthetic sheathing.

The wood is dark brown in color and glues very well. For light cold-molded construction it has no peer, but it requires care in working because of its softness.

The great canoes used by the Coast Indians of western Washington State and British Columbia were made of this easily worked wood—one of the most notable examples was the modified canoe used by Capt. J. Voss of Victoria, British Columbia, during his world voyage in 1903.

Fortunately, there are still good supplies of this wood available to boatbuilders.

WHITE CEDAR
(*Chamaecyparis thyoides*) Atlantic
(*Thuja occidentalis*) northern

Weight at 15 percent moisture content—22 pounds per cubic foot
Durability—resistant
Source—eastern United States

Both these species of white cedar grow in the eastern part of the United States. Northern white cedar grows from Maine along the Appalachian Mountains and westward through the northern part of the Great Lake states. Atlantic Cedar, also known as juniper, southern white cedar, and swamp cedar, grows near the coast from Maine to northern Florida and westward along the Gulf coast to Louisiana. It is strictly a swamp tree.

The heartwood from both species is similar, being a light brown color and having a very aromatic odor. Though not as strong and hard as the western cedars, it is very light and is often used as a planking material. White cedar is very resistant to rot but is seldom available clear of knots as are the western cedars. Having a good uniform texture, it glues well and is very stable with little shrinkage.

COACHWOOD
(*Ceratopetalum apetalum*)

Weight at 15 percent moisture content—39 pounds per cubic foot
Durability—not resistant
Source—eastern Australia

Coachwood is a rain-forest species reaching a height of 100 feet and 2.5 feet in diameter. The heartwood is pinkish-brown in color, being variable in intensity, and it has a pleasant odor.

The grain is generally straight, with a fine texture, and the wood is relatively easy to work. Coachwood glues easily, holds fastenings well, and seasons relatively quickly. It is used extensively in the manufacture of marine-grade plywood, furniture, joinery, turning, and carved products.

BALD CYPRESS
(*Taxodium distichum*)

Weight at 15 percent moisture content—32
  pounds per cubic foot
Durability—very resistant
Source—southern United States

Bald cypress has a good reputation as a boatbuilding wood; it can be used for many purposes. It grows mainly in the southern United States and is available in wide boards, long lengths, and clear, straight grain. The color of the heartwood varies, ranging from light yellowish-brown to dark brownish-red, brown, or chocolate. The wood is moderately heavy, quite strong and hard, and very durable. Cypress is an excellent general-purpose lumber, being suitable for planking, decking, and exterior and interior joinerwork. It is a popular material with builders familiar with it, but its one undesirable characteristic is its ability to soak up moisture. Provided that the wood is waterproofed, this is no problem, but many craft planked with cypress float considerably deeper than they were ever intended to.

ROCK ELM
(*Ulmus thomasii*)

Weight at 15 percent moisture content—43
  pounds per cubic foot
Durability—moderately resistant
Source—Canada

Rock elm has long been one of the favorite hardwoods of British boatbuilders, although it is grown mainly in eastern Canada and the Northeast of the United States.

Used mainly for framing as an alternative to white oak, rock elm has an amazing ability to bend to almost impossible curves without breaking. The wood is a pale brown color and straight-grained, somewhat similar to ash, with a good texture. Because of its stringy nature, it is difficult to work with hand tools, but it cuts easily with power tools, leaving a good finish that takes glue, stains, and varnish well.

Rock elm was used as a planking material

below the waterline for the famous clipper ship *Cutty Sark*, and I used the same material for the diagonal planking on *Treasure*. It can also be used for laminated knees and gunwales of small craft; it takes steam well, and for my money is a better choice than oak if bending is the chief criterion.

DOUGLAS FIR
(*Pseudotsuga taxifolia*)

Weight at 15 percent moisture content—32
  pounds per cubic foot
Durability—moderately resistant
Source—Pacific Coast North America, mainly
British Columbia

Douglas fir is considered the prime softwood of the world, due to its quantity and the long, large timbers that are available. The wood is variable in color from reddish to yellowish heartwood to an off-white sapwood. It is moderately soft, straight-grained, and strong. It varies in quality due to the difference in the sizes of second-growth trees and prime stock, but good Douglas fir is hard to beat, being easily worked with hand and machine tools. This wood glues well and holds fastenings equally well. For marine work, good vertical-grain fir makes excellent planking and decking and is another of the few woods that could be used for the entire structure, including spars.

As the botanical name implies, it is not a true fir: *pseudo* means false; *tsuga* is Japanese for Hemlock, which adds up to false hemlock. Douglas fir is actually a member of the pine family.

WHITE FIR
(*Abies concolor*)

Weight at 15 percent moisture content—27
  pounds per cubic foot
Durability—not resistant
Source—western United States

Six commercial species make up the western true firs, which are grown in Washington, Oregon, California, western Montana, and northern Idaho: subalpine fir (*Abies lasiocarpa*),

California red fir (*A. magnifica*), grand fir (*A. grandis*), noble fir (*A. procera*), Pacific silver fir (*A. amabilis*), as well as white fir. These western firs are light in weight and soft but firm. There is little distinction between sapwood and heartwood; the color is whitish or light buff. It has a slight disagreeable odor when green, but when dry has little smell or taste. White fir kiln-dries well but is prone to checking if dried too fast. The wood machines well with both hand and power tools and can be glued easily. The grain can be fine to coarse, and as a result, the finish varies as to smoothness. Tools need to be kept sharp to prevent this softwood from tearing.

White fir and its similar species are marketed together, so selectivity is required to obtain good material. It is generally used in building construction for interior finish, sidings, and sash and door stock. Prime stock is suitable as a boatbuilding material if carefully dried. The wood is not considered durable when exposed to conditions fostering decay, so it should be treated with a preservative, which it will accept readily.

GABOON
(*Aucoumea klaineana*)

Weight at 15 percent moisture content—25
 pounds per cubic foot
Durability—not resistant
Source—west Africa

Gaboon, also known as okoume, is found only in west central Africa and Guinea, including Gabon and parts of the Congo. The wood has a salmon-pink color and in appearance looks very much like a light mahogany, but it is not related to that species. The wood is light, works well, and finishes excellently. Gaboon glues well and is popular as a material for plywood and paneling. It offers unusual flexibility in both working and finishing because the color, which is of medium intensity, permits toning to either lighter or darker shades.

Gaboon has long been popular with European boatbuilders, particularly for smaller craft where weight is often a critical factor.

GREENHEART
(*Ocotea rodiaei*)

Weight—approximately 66 pounds per cubic
 foot
Durability—very resistant
Source—South America

Greenheart is essentially a tree from Guyana, although it also grows in Surinam. The heartwood varies in color from light to dark olive-green or nearly black. The texture is fine and uniform.

Greenheart is very strong and stiff; because of its high density, it is difficult to work with hand tools. It cuts quite easily with carbide-tipped cutters and can be finished to a deep, lustrous color that is more impressive than teak and considerably stronger, too. Valuable for maximum abrasion service in commercial craft, greenheart is commonly used for guards, beltings, and rail caps, as well as protective sheathing for bottom planking, keel shoes, etc., due to its resistance to marine borers.

Like some of the Australian hardwoods, greenheart takes several years to season and is generally used before this has been accomplished, which results in consequent shrinkage and unreliability of glued joints.

For mooring bitts, samson posts and the previously mentioned uses, greenheart cannot be beaten, but it is generally suited to commercial craft rather than pleasure yachts.

WESTERN HEMLOCK
(*Tsuga heterophylla*)

Weight at 15 percent moisture content—30
 pounds per cubic foot
Durability—not resistant
Source—Canada, northwest United States

Western hemlock, also known as Alaska pine, Prince Albert fir, Hemlock spruce, and Pacific hemlock, grows throughout the coastal and interior areas along the Pacific Coast from Oregon north to Canada and southeastern Alaska.

The heartwood and sapwood of western

hemlock is almost white with a purplish tinge; the sapwood is generally not more than one inch thick and is lighter in color. The wood contains small, round, black knots that are usually tight and stay in place. When fresh cut, western hemlock has a sour odor, but it is moderately hard and is generally straight-grained, with a medium to fine texture. The wood machines well and is used generally as a construction lumber in the building industry for all but the heaviest applications, making good moldings, sheathing, joists, and studding. Like white fir, it needs careful drying, as it has a large water content. Prime stock looks like Sitka spruce, although it cannot match the strength of that species.

Due to its ability to glue well and its light weight, prime western hemlock is suitable for laminated construction in boatbuilding. It holds fastenings on a par with most softwoods and is generally available. The wood is not considered durable, and like most of the North American softwoods, it should be treated for use in exposed conditions.

IROKO
(Chlorophora excelsa)

Weight at 15 percent moisture content—41 pounds per cubic foot
Durability—very resistant
Source—Tropical Africa

This tough, durable wood is sometimes referred to as African teak, and some of its qualities are not unlike the prized *Tectona grandis* of the Far East.

Iroko is a light greenish-yellow brown when fresh cut, aging to a medium to dark reddish-brown wood, which has an interlocking grain structure that is often difficult to work with hand tools. The wood generally is coarser than teak, and like teak, it glues only moderately well. It is used in European boatyards for much the same purposes as teak—planking and exterior brightwork, decking, and interior joinerwork. It is not an easy wood to plane by hand and it must be worked carefully to obtain a smooth surface. Iroko can, however, be finished well; it can be left bare or varnished, depending on its use.

IRONBARK
(Eucalyptus sideroxylan, E. paniculata, E. siderophloia, E. resinifera)

Weight at 12 percent moisture content— approximately 72 pounds per cubic foot
Durability—very resistant
Source—Australia

Ironbark is a general name given to several eucalyptus species grown principally on the eastern coastal slopes of northern New South Wales and southern Queensland, Australia. As its name implies, it is an immensely strong and very dense hardwood, with an interlocking grain structure that makes it difficult to split.

The wood is a dark purple-red when cut, turning to a deep brown-red with age and exposure. It is used chiefly for the decking and framing of bridges and wharves. Due to its resistance to damage from marine borers, it is also used for pilings in tropical waters.

Due to the density of the wood, it takes a minimum of two years to season even relatively thin material, and like many other Australian hardwoods, it is prone to extensive checking if dried too quickly. Because of its natural resin or gum, ironbark does not glue well, and its chief use in yacht construction is for backbone assemblies, rudders, and shoes. It is often used as mast step material or for floor timbers in carvel construction, being well suited to carrying heavy bolt loads, but it does shrink even when sealed with some of the modern wood sealers. However, for exterior use, such as beltings and guards, ironbark can be matched only by greenheart.

ISHPINGO
(Amburana acreana)

Weight—approximately 43 pounds per cubic foot
Durability—very resistant
Source—South America

Ishpingo is one of the woods that has recently become available from the great forests in the upper reaches of the Amazon Basin in Brazil, Bolivia, and Peru. Wood specimens identified as

Amburana, originating in Pará, Brazil, suggest that the range is much more extensive than the literature would indicate.

Ishpingo trees reach heights of 100 feet and more, with diameters of two to three feet, providing about three 12-foot logs per tree. The wood is a yellowish to light brown with a slight orange cast. The color deepens to a golden brown or light brown when exposed to the air. The grain is interlocked, with the resulting stripe looking narrow on vertical grain surfaces. The heartwood has an oily or waxy feel and a pronounced coumarin odor.

It is reported that ishpingo shrinks very little, and even where sun-racked for air seasoning, the lumber does not warp and shows little if any end or surface checking. It has been compared favorably with teak and has great promise as a boatbuilding wood. Data on gluing ability is not available but it is expected to glue only moderately well because of its composition.

JARRAH
(Eucalyptus marginata)

Weight—approximately 54 pounds per cubic foot
Durability—very resistant
Source—Australia

Jarrah is a wood native to the south coast of Western Australia and is one of the principal timbers of the sawmill industry. The heartwood is a uniform pinkish to dark red, often a rich dark red mahogany hue, turning to a deep brownish-red with age and exposure to light.

The sapwood is pale in color and usually very narrow in old trees. The texture is even and moderately coarse, and the grain, though usually straight, is frequently interlocked and wavy. The common defects in jarrah include gum veins or pockets, which in extreme cases separate the log into concentric shells.

The wood is heavy and hard, possessing correspondingly high strength properties. The heartwood is rated as extremely resistant to preservative treatment due to its density, but it has a good natural resistance to attack from termites and fungal decay. Not surprisingly,

jarrah is difficult material to work with machine and hand tools. It is used mainly for piers, jetties, and bridges and for pilings and fenders in dock and harbor installations.

Jarrah is used for window sills and thresholds in South African housing and is also used on commercial vessels and yachts for guards and capping. I have even seen it used as a decking material, although the owner who laid it maintained that ever since, his vessel has had a straight sheer.

JELUTONG
(Dyera costulata)

Weight at 15 percent moisture content—29 pounds per cubic foot
Durability—not resistant
Source—Malaysia, Philippines, Thailand, Burma

Jelutong is an important species in Malaysia, where it is best known for its latex production rather than its timber. The wood is white or straw-colored and there is no differentiation between heartwood and sapwood.

The texture is moderately fine and even, with a straight grain and lustrous finish when planed. The wood is reported to be seasoned easily, with little tendency to split or warp. Unless stripped and dried soon after felling, however, it will stain. Jelutong is easy to work in all operations, finishes well, and can be glued satisfactorily.

The wood is rated nondurable, but it takes preservatives well and can be used as a good general-purpose lumber mainly for interior use.

KARRI
(Eucalyptus diversicolor)

Weight at 12 percent moisture content—57 pounds per cubic foot
Durability—resistant
Source—Australia

Karri is a very large tree limited to Western Australia, occurring in the southwestern portion of the state. Karri resembles jarrah in structure and general appearance but is usually paler in color and on the average slightly heavier. The heartwood is rated as moderately durable;

because of its density, it is resistant to pre-servative treatment.

Karri is fairly hard to cut with machine tools and really tough with hand tools. It dulls cutting edges more than jarrah does, and is also a difficult wood to glue successfully. Its uses are much the same as for jarrah—heavy construction members, bridges, beams, and beltings. Karri is popular because of its strength and its availability in large sizes and lengths that are free of defects. Like many of the Australian hardwoods of the *Eucalyptus* variety, karri takes years to season naturally, and if dried too fast, develops extensive surface checking and warping and twisting.

KOA
(Acacia koa)

Weight—approximately 43 pounds per cubic foot
Durability—resistant
Source—Hawaiian islands

This fine tropical hardwood is still available in the Hawaiian islands, being used mainly in the manufacture of quality furniture and carved wooden ornaments and bowls. The wood is a rich brown color that is sometimes streaked with black. It has a firm, white sapwood often used for visual effect.

The wood was used by ancient Hawaiians for canoe building, and there are still a few modern replicas being used there today in the sport of canoeing. Several yachts built in Hawaii have been completed with koa interiors. The wood is hard and stable, works relatively easily, and takes glue moderately well. Koa is considered durable and resistant to borer attack.

EUROPEAN LARCH
(Larix decidua)

Weight at 15 percent moisture content—35 pounds per cubic foot
Durability—resistant
Source—Europe

Larch is one of the general-purpose softwoods of Europe, being widely distributed and growing on relatively high terrain. The wood is a light orange to red-brown in the heartwood, normally straight-grained, with medium texture and hardness.

European larch is considered fairly resistant in durability due to its resin content, which sometimes makes it difficult to work with hand tools. Planes in particular tend to "gum up," when used on larch, so they should be lubricated with oil or kerosene occasionally. Generally it glues quite well and holds fastenings equally well. It is very often used as a planking and decking material, principally in commercial craft where scantling sizes are generally heavier.

WESTERN LARCH
(Larix occidentalis)

Weight at 15 percent moisture content—34 pounds per cubic foot
Durability—moderately resistant
Source—northwest United States

Western larch grows inland on the eastern slopes of the Cascade Mountains, generally at altitudes between 1,800 feet and 4,000 feet. The sapwood is whitish to pale straw brown and is rarely over one inch in width; the heartwood is russet to reddish-brown. The wood has a characteristic oily appearance and a greasy feel, yet it glues easily. It does not, however, accept paint too well. It is not an easy wood to work by hand, being rather coarse textured, moderately hard and heavy, but with a straight grain.

Western larch machines readily but is rather prone to split easily if nails are driven close to the end of a board. If prime stock is used and cut with vertical grain, western larch is suitable for much the same purposes as its European cousin—planking, decking, beams, etc.

Although it is a softwood and coniferous, larch sheds its needles in winter.

LIGNUMVITAE
(Guaiacum Officinale)

Weight—approximately 77 to 83 pounds per cubic foot
Durability—very durable

Source—Central America, West Indies, northwest coast of South America, west coast of Mexico

Lignumvitae is one of the hardest, heaviest, and closest-grained timbers known. The heartwood is a dark greenish-brown to black; the sapwood is very sharply defined, being yellowish in color. The grain is interlocked, without a definite pattern, which makes planing difficult.

Lignumvitae has a waxy feel, due to a very heavy resin content; it tests higher than any other wood on impact resistance. Lignumvitae is used for bushings for propeller shaft stern tubes in large ships, but because of its hardness, it cannot effectively be worked with hand tools. It is also used for deadeyes and in some high-quality blocks—also for mallet heads and tool handles. Lignumvitae is a wood for which there is no substitute. When the wood is placed under water, the resin emulsifies and forms a lubricant that will last for several years. Because of this resin, it is almost impossible to glue. Logs are seldom over 18 inches in diameter or over six feet in length.

AFRICAN MAHOGANY
(Khaya ivorensis)

Weight at 15 percent moisture content—34 pounds per cubic foot
Durability—moderately resistant
Source—west central Africa

African mahogany comes from large trees that often have a diameter of up to six feet, with a clean, cylindrical trunk extending 40 to 80 feet above the buttresses, which are sharp but do not extend much more than four to five feet above the ground.

The wood varies from pale pink to a dark reddish-brown, having an interlocked grain pattern and texture similar to that of Honduras mahogany *(Swietenia)*. However, it is slightly coarser and sometimes suffers from a defect known as "thunder-shakes," where the wood appears to have been compressed, causing a break across the grain with subsequent strength loss. African mahogany works easily, bends

moderately well, and, like the other mahoganies, glues exceptionally well.

Because of its wide, clear stock, it is a very popular boatbuilding lumber for planking, beams, superstructure sides, interior joinerwork, and finishing trim. It is, however, only moderately resistant to decay and should be protected with a suitable preservative in exposed locations. Some European builders have experienced a peculiar effect on fastenings when using this lumber for boat planking, reporting that bronze screws were subjected to rapid deterioration not noticeable with other lumbers. My own *Treasure* has the outer longitudinal skin of planking in African mahogany and, with over 12 years of continual service, shows no sign of deterioration. However, in this case the wood is protected by a layer of fiberglass sheathing.

HONDURAS MAHOGANY
(Swietenia macrophylla)

Weight at 15 percent moisture content—34 pounds per cubic foot
Durability—moderately resistant
Source—Central America.

Frequently termed American mahogany, this excellent boatbuilding wood is grown throughout Central American from southern Mexico into South America as far south as Bolivia. *Swietenia* is rated the best of the mahoganies, being generally straighter in the grain with good dimensional stability that allows for fine finishing qualities, ease of working, and good appearance. It varies somewhat in weight due to the range of its growth: the heavier, darker species is found in the vast area around the tributaries of the upper Amazon.

The heartwood varies from a pale to a dark reddish-brown. It glues very well and is much sought after as a boatbuilding lumber, being suitable for many uses, including planking and high-class joinerwork.

Because of its stability and ease of working, Honduras mahogany is a favorite choice for wood patterns in foundry work, but because of its popularity, this is generally an expensive lumber.

PHILIPPINE MAHOGANY
(Shorea, Parashorea, Pentacme)

Weight at 15 percent moisture content—37
  pounds per cubic foot
Durability—moderately resistant
Source—Philippines

As its botanical name shows, Philippine
mahogany is not a true mahogany at all,
although it often has a strong resemblance to the
genuine kinds. It is actually close to the cedar
family.

The term "lauan" or Philippine mahogany is
applied commercially to woods grown in the
islands; these woods usually are grouped by the
United States trade into "dark red" and "light
red" Philippine mahogany.

As a whole, these woods have a coarser
texture than the American or African mahoganies, but they have a similar interlocked
grain, and the darker varieties may be used in
much the same applications as the true
mahoganies. Much of the light red variety is soft,
with little strength and low durability; it is
unsuitable for boat construction due to its
tendency to absorb water in an extraordinary
manner. The dark red types, however, are good
lumbers: tanguile (*Shorea polysperma*) and red
lauan (*Shorea negrosensis*) are used extensively
in yacht construction for planking and interior
and exterior joinerwork.

These woods glue well and take paint and
varnish nicely, being easy to work with both
hand and power tools. Philippine mahogany
costs considerably less than true mahogany and
offers good value if used intelligently.

EASTERN HARD MAPLE
(Acer saccharum)

Weight at 15 percent moisture content—43
  pounds per cubic foot
Durability—not resistant
Source—North America

Eastern hard maple has many close cousins
that grow throughout much of the North
American continent, but the eastern hard
variety—also known as sugar maple and rock
maple—is confined to areas in eastern Canada
and the United States. The wood is light-
colored, white to pale brown, which sometimes
has a reddish tinge.

Large old-growth trees produce a brown
heartwood core that is not considered a high-
quality wood. Eastern hard maple is a dense,
tough timber; it is heavy, strong, and stiff, with
good resistance to shock but with large shrinkage. It is generally straight-grained but also
occurs with "birdseye," "curly," or "fiddle-
back" grain, which is not easy material to use
with hand tools.

It glues only moderately well due to its
density and tight grain, but it is generally used
for plywood and paneling. The wood is used for
furniture, cabinetwork, butcher blocks, shoe
lasts, and sports equipment. Its use in boatbuilding would be confined to interior finishing
work.

MERANTI
(Shorea)

Weight at 15 percent moisture content—25-44
  pounds per cubic foot
Durability—fairly resistant
Source—southeastern Asia

Meranti is the trade name that covers a
number of closely related species of *Shorea* from
which light or only moderately heavy timber is
produced. It grows on the Malay Peninsula and
in Indonesia, including North Borneo and
Sarawak, and it roughly corresponds to the
lauan from the Philippines that is generally
referred to as Philippine mahogany.

According to the species, Meranti varies
considerably in color, weight, texture, and
related properties. The grain tends to be slightly
interlocked, so that vertical-grain stock shows a
broad stripe figure. The texture is moderately
coarse but even. Resin ducts with or without
white contents occur in long, tangential lines on
the end surfaces of the wood, but it is not
resinous and can be glued relatively easily. Light
red meranti is classed as a lightweight utility
hardwood and comprises those species yielding a
red or reddish but not a dark red timber. The

actual color of the heartwood varies from a pale pink to a light reddish-brown, and the weight of the wood varies considerably, as indicated above.

Dark red Meranti is often used as a planking material, weighing an average of 43 pounds per cubic foot. It works easily with both hand and power tools and may be used for many purposes in boatbuilding. The wood is available in plywood and solid form and is used for much the same type of work as the Philippine lauans.

RED OAK
(Quercus ruba) northern
(Quercus falcata) southern

Weight at 15 percent moisture content—45 pounds
Durability—moderately resistant
Source—Europe, North America

Red oak varies in color from pinkish to light reddish-brown. It is a hard, strong wood that is shock resistant and bends well, but due to its open pores in the end grain, it needs protection from water. Because of its open-porous nature, it takes preservatives well and when thus treated can be considered as durable as white oak.

Red oak machines well and finishes smoothly, being relatively kind to cutting edges. It holds fastenings well and unless the wood is green and soft, all nail and screw holes must be pre-drilled. It is used as a substitute for white oak, being suitable for framing, flooring, and interior joinerwork. Like white oak, it has the unfortunate habit of staining black when wetted; when used with varnished finishes, it can soon have a neglected appearance.

WHITE OAK
(Quercus alba)

Weight at 15 percent moisture content—46 pounds per cubic foot
Durability—resistant
Source—Europe, North America

White oak has been used for centuries in the building of countless ships. Its excellent qualities of toughness, durability, and bending ability are well known, and the choice of this material for naval vessels in the days of sail shows the high regard for this wood. In yacht building, oak has an enviable record as a framing material for carvel construction. However, for steam bending it is essential that the wood be green and not seasoned by air- or kiln-drying.

The wood, although tough, works well when seasoned, gluing and painting easily. It has an unfortunate habit of staining black if allowed to weather or come in contact with steel. If it is to be finished clear, it is important that C-clamps be used with protective wooden pads. Steaming will cause the wood to stain badly, particularly if the steam box is made of iron pipe instead of wood. Galvanized fastenings are almost impossible to remove from oak once they have frozen into position.

White oak is more durable than red oak because its pores are plugged with a growth called tyloses, which restricts the amount of water the wood can absorb. Red oak does not have this benefit and will soak up considerably more water, which makes it softer, weaker, and more prone to rot. For all oak's fine qualities, many boatbuilders are prejudiced against its use in any part of a yacht—they claim that fastenings deteriorate in oak more quickly than in other woods and that it has the ability to rot easily. There may be some justification for this viewpoint if you consider that much oak is used quite unseasoned and subjected to torture when steamed and bent into position. When fully dried, it is a strong, handsome wood that makes excellent structural members and fine cabinetwork.

OBECHE
(Triplochiton scheroxylon)

Weight at 15 percent moisture content—24 pounds per cubic foot
Durability—not resistant
Source—West Africa

Obeche trees of West Central Africa reach heights of 150 feet or more and diameters of up to five feet. The trunk is usually free of branches for considerable heights, so that clear lumber of large size is obtainable.

The wood is creamy white to pale yellow, with little or no difference between the sapwood and heartwood. It is fairly soft, of a uniform texture, and the grain is usually straight, although it sometimes is interlocked. The wood is very light, being of a similar weight to western red cedar. It seasons readily with little splitting or excessive shrinking and warping, but it is not resistant to decay; it should be used with a suitable preservative, which it will take well.

Obeche is easy to work with machines and hand tools, it glues very well, and it is often used in the plywood industry as core stock for the inner laminates. It is fairly stable and may be used as a substitute for softwood. The species is also known as samba and wawa.

EASTERN WHITE PINE
(Pinus strobus)

Weight at 15 percent moisture content—25 pounds per cubic foot
Durability—not resistant
Source—eastern United States

Eastern white pine grows from Maine to northern Georgia and in the Great Lakes states. It is also known as white pine, Weymouth pine, and soft pine.

The heartwood of eastern white pine is a light brown, often with a reddish tinge. It turns considerably darker on exposure. The wood has a uniform texture and is straight-grained, being easily kiln-dried with little shrinkage and good stability. It is easy to work and glues well and is light in weight but firm.

Much of the production of this pine is second-growth knotty lumber, but prime stock is used for patternmaking in foundry work, for which use it is the best. Other important uses are for general millwork, paneling, furniture, coffins, and toys.

KAURI PINE
(Dammara australis)

Weight at 15 percent moisture content—30 pounds per cubic foot

Durability—moderately resistant
Source—New Zealand

Kauri pine is one of the great boatbuilding lumbers of the world, but unfortunately, due to its popularity, it is now very hard to obtain. A certain amount of closely related kauri pine is grown in the Pacific islands to the north of New Zealand, notably the Fiji Islands, and as a result is becoming more widely available.

Kauri pine is a honey-colored wood that has many desirable features. It comes from a large, very slow-growing tree, so the grain is tightly packed and even, without defects. The wood works easily, with both hand and machine tools. It glues well and takes paint and varnish readily. The most decorative feature of the planed wood is provided by the luster and the minute fleck caused by the resinous wood rays.

Kauri pine ranks among the strongest softwoods in the world and is the only native New Zealand timber that can be floated with ease in log form when freshly cut. Heart kauri is very durable under the most difficult conditions, but when in contact with the ground and unprotected, it is subject to decay.

MALAYAN KAURI PINE
(Agathis alba)

Weight at 15 percent moisture content—29 pounds per cubic foot
Durability—not resistant
Source—Malaysia

Malayan kauri pine is a coniferous softwood related to the kauri pine grown in New Zealand but lacking some of the excellent qualities of that species. The wood is a pale brown color with some darker streaks. It has a straight grain and fine texture, with only occasional faint growth rings visible. Unlike other conifers, Malayan kauri has no resin ducts.

Malayan kauri is easy to work with both hand and power tools, and it is used for general millwork and cabinetmaking. It lacks the strength and bending qualities of New Zealand kauri but is still a good material to use for boat construction, being suitable for planking. It glues well and finishes to a lustrous surface. Similar species of this tree are grown in the Fiji

Islands, and some of this wood is now being exported to North America.

PARANA PINE
(*Araucaria angustifolia*)

Weight at 15 percent moisture content—34 pounds per cubic foot
Durability—not resistant
Source—South America

Parana pine is the name given to a species that is not a true pine; its structure more closely resembles Alaska cedar or cypress. This excellent general-purpose wood is grown in southeastern Brazil and adjacent areas of Paraguay and Argentina.

Parana pine has many desirable features and is available in large sizes of clear boards with a uniform texture. The light brown or reddish-brown heartwood, which is frequently streaked with red, provides figured effects, which make good paneling and attractive interior finishes. The wood has a relatively straight grain, takes paint well, and glues easily. In strength it compares favorably with softwood species of similar density found in North America such as bald cypress and Douglas fir. It is especially good in shearing strength, hardness, and its ability to hold fastenings, but it is notably deficient in compression strength across the grain.

The principal uses of parana pine in the building industry are for shelving, interior trim, sash and door stock, etc. It can also be used successfully in a marine environment for similar requirements. Parana pine works easily with both hand and machine tools, and many European builders are familiar with this relatively inexpensive and versatile lumber.

SOUTHERN PINE
(*Pinus* spp.)

Weight at 15 percent moisture content—32-41 pounds per cubic foot
Durability—resistant
Source—southern United States

There are a number of species included in the lumber marketed as southern pine. Longleaf pine (*Pinus palustris*), shortleaf pine (*P. echinata*), loblolly pine (*P. taeda*), and slash pine (*P. elliottii*), and lumber from any one group or a mixture of two or more are all classified as southern pine by the grading standards of the industry. The lumber that is classified as longleaf in the domestic trade is known also as pitch pine in the export trade.

The wood of the various southern pines is quite similar in appearance, the sapwood being yellowish-white and the heartwood a reddish-brown. Heartwood of the longleaf and slash pines is classed as heavy, strong, stiff, hard, and moderately high in shock resistance. Shortleaf and loblolly pines are usually somewhat lighter in weight and, like the other types, have moderately large shrinkage during seasoning, becoming stable when this is completed.

The wood has a high resin content, making it a little difficult to work, but it holds fastenings well and is highly regarded in boatbuilding, being used for planking, decking, and structural beams. It takes glue moderately well and is used in the manufacture of structural-grade plywood.

WESTERN WHITE PINE
(*Pinus monticola*)

Weight at 15 percent moisture content—26 pounds per cubic foot
Durability—not resistant
Source—southern British Columbia, northwest United States

Western white pine—also known as silver pine and Idaho white pine—is a moderately soft, cream-colored wood that is used largely in the building industry for framing and finishwork. The wood works easily but usually bends poorly, due to its distinctive tight red knots. The better-quality wood is used mainly for paneling and cabinetwork. It glues well and does not split readily, but because of its softness does not hold fastenings well. Its main use as a boatbuilding material is for interior furnishings, due to its poor inherent resistance to conditions favoring decay.

RAMIN
(Gonystylus bancanus)

Weight at 15 percent moisture content—42 pounds per cubic foot
Durability—not resistant
Source—Malaysia, Indonesia

Ramin is a pale yellow to dark straw-colored wood that is native to Southeast Asia from the Malay Peninsula to Sumatra and Borneo. The grain is straight or shallowly interlocked, with a moderately fine texture similar to that of mahogany (*Swietenia*). Ramin is moderately hard and heavy, easy to work and finish, and glues well. Its principal use in North America is for high-class millwork, including hand rails, paneling, interior trim, and the plywood that is used on door faces. The natural durability of ramin is rated as perishable, but it takes preservative treatment well and is quite suitable for many applications in boatbuilding.

REDWOOD
(Sequoia sempervirens)

Weight at 15 percent moisture content—27 pounds per cubic foot
Durability—very resistant
Source—western United States

Redwoods are very large trees growing on the coast of California. The giant redwoods (*Sequoia gigantea*), the oldest living trees in the world, also grow in this area, but that lumber is very limited in supply due to the protection it receives from concerned authorities.

Production of redwood lumber is generally restricted to California, although it is a popular building material in Hawaii due to its remarkable resistance to termite and borer attack and its natural durability. The heartwood of redwood varies from a light cherry to a dark mahogany. The sapwood is almost white and usually quite narrow. The wood is light in weight, not unlike western red cedar, moderately strong, stiff, and moderately hard.

The wood works easily, is generally straight-grained, glues well, and is very stable. It would seem to be an ideal boatbuilding lumber, but although I have used it for interiors and exteriors, I have never heard of anyone using redwood as a planking material.

With cold-molded construction, redwood would appear to be a fine material, although it does not bend very well, and it is reported to be low in shock resistance. Redwood looks handsome when finished clear and is a good choice for interior cabinetwork and paneling.

SPOTTED GUM
(Eucalyptus maculata)

Weight at 15 percent moisture content—59 pounds per cubic foot
Durability—very resistant
Source—eastern Australia

Spotted gum is a boatbuilding wood popular with New Zealand and Australian builders. Used mainly as a framing material because of its good bending qualities, the wood is a light to dark brown color, with an interlocked grain that has a moderately coarse texture. Spotted gum has a somewhat greasy nature, so gluing needs care. The wood is worked relatively easily and because of the size of the trees—which often reach heights of over 150 feet with a five-foot diameter—the lumber is generally free from knots and is sometimes used for planking. Its considerable weight, however, is somewhat of a liability as care must be taken to avoid excessive weight in yacht construction.

Like other varieties of the *Eucalyptus* family, spotted gum seasons slowly and is rather prone to check. It is used extensively in general building construction for flooring and also for the manufacture of plywood.

EASTERN SPRUCE
(Picea rubens) red
(Picea glauca) white
(Picea mariana) black

Weight at 15 percent moisture content—27 pounds per cubic foot
Durability—not resistant
Source—northeastern United States

There are three species of eastern spruce

commercially available, all having about the same properties so that little distinction is made between them. White and black spruce grow mainly in the lake states and New England, and red spruce is found in New England and the Appalachian Mountains.

The wood is a silvery white in color, there being little difference in appearance between the heartwood and sapwood. It dries easily and is stable once seasoned. Like Sitka spruce it is light and strong, but its main problem is that it generally has many knots and is not available in the long, clear lengths that one is accustomed to getting Sitka spruce in.

Eastern spruce glues well and works easily, having a finer grain and texture than Sitka spruce, which is more stringy in nature. Used by shipbuilders in the Canadian maritime provinces and New England for several hundred years, it is popular for decking and sometimes planking in traditional construction. When combined with modern adhesives and preservatives, this wood has many uses if carefully selected.

SITKA SPRUCE
(Picea sitchensis)

Weight at 15 percent moisture content—27 pounds per cubic foot
Durability—not resistant
Source—North America

Sitka spruce grows along the entire coastal area of British Columbia and Alaska, seldom more than 50 miles from salt water or above an altitude exceeding 1,000 feet. It is most abundant in the northern area and the Queen Charlotte Islands. The heartwood is a light pinkish-yellow to very pale brown, with a creamy-white to pale yellow sapwood. The wood is straight-grained and even and works well with both hand and power tools, provided the cutting edges are sharp.

Sitka spruce has long, woolly fibers and thus demands sharp tools. It can be planed to a glossy luster that glues and varnishes beautifully. The wood has a fine strength-to-weight ratio and was once widely used in aircraft construction. It is still the best material for light wooden spars,

beams, and stringers in wooden boatbuilding, and it is a great pity that so much of it is used today in the manufacture of pulpwood for paper production.

Sitka spruce is one of the most important timbers of the Northwest; its large size and high proportion of defect-free stock make it a much-sought-after material. It is not considered durable and requires preservative treatment, which it takes well.

TEAK
(Tectona grandis)

Weight at 15 percent moisture content—44 pounds per cubic foot
Durability—very resistant
Source—Southeast Asia

Teak occurs in commercial quantities in India, Burma, Thailand, Laos, Cambodia, North and South Vietnam, and the East Indies. Numerous plantations have been developed within its natural range and in tropical areas of Latin America and Africa, and many of these are now producing timber.

The heartwood varies from a yellow brown to a rich brown, and freshly cut material is often streaked for a day or two before exposure to the air changes the color to the familiar rich brown. Teak works easily with both hand and machine tools, but because of its silica content, it soon blunts cutting edges. Carbide tips on saws and plane blades largely eliminate this problem. Teak has a natural oily texture that can clog sandpaper and cause problems in gluing. It glues moderately well with resorcinol and epoxy glues, but for reliable joints, it should be degreased with a solvent, such as acetone or MEK.

Teak has traditionally been the most-sought-after lumber for brightwork and high-quality furnishings aboard the world's most famous yachts and ships. Because of the tremendous demand for it, the quality of teak being marketed today often leaves much to be desired. At its best there is nothing to match it, but many other tropical hardwoods have qualitites that are a close match at a fraction of the price, and the cost-conscious builder would do well to consider one of these substitutes.

The great advantage of teak is its natural durability; it does not stain when weathered and requires little sanding to return its rich color.

PLYWOOD

One of the most important materials used for boatbuilding today is waterproof plywood. This excellent material has been available for many years, and the modern builder would be at a serious disadvantage without it.

Like many new products, plywood had its problems during the early stages of its development, and some of the more vocal traditional designers and boatbuilders were ever-ready to criticize its shortcomings. Those early problems were mainly due to delamination because of the nonwaterproof glues that were used in bonding the veneers together. Occasionally, one sees an older vessel in which some of this early plywood was used and the plies or laminates have separated into veneers—all of it looking very sad.

It seems incredible, but even today some manufacturers still bond plywood with these outdated glues and they are able to sell their products to an unsuspecting public. It is most important, therefore, to know if the plywood you intend to use is of good quality and suitable for marine use.

The Swiss were the first people to develop plywood on a commercial scale, and for many years Switzerland's exports supplied the world's needs. However, the potential of this product was realized in North America, and several huge factories were built to exploit the increasing demand for plywood.

Prior to World War II, the plywood industry in various parts of the world spent huge sums of money on research for better glues that would improve the durability of plywood. Casein glues were developed and had widespread use, thus considerably upgrading the quality of plywood.

With the outbreak of war, plywood became a vital commodity—aircraft, ships, and vehicles demanded huge quantities of this versatile material. With increased demand came new benefits, better waterproof glues, improved manufacturing methods, and radio-frequency heating to accelerate curing so that the panels could be bonded together permanently in just a few minutes.

Today there are hundreds of different plywoods being manufactured at various factories around the world, yet basically they are made up in much the same manner. Most plywood is built up from a number of single sheets of veneer, which are glued together so that each layer has its grain running at 90 degrees to the one next to it. The two outside laminates usually have the grain running in the same direction, and because of this, there is usually an odd number of laminations, such as 3-ply, 5-ply, or 7-ply, etc.

The inside laminate of a 3-ply sheet is termed the "core," and to make a more stable sheet when glued up, this core is often thicker than the two outside faces.

The manufacture of a sheet of plywood starts with the basic lumber in log form. These selected logs, sometimes called "peelers," are cut to length, immersed in huge vats of boiling water, and steam-cooked to make the wood supple. On removal from the vats, the bark of the log is removed either by a high-speed debarking lathe or high pressure jets of water that tear away the outer bark and expose the solid timber beneath.

The debarked log is transported by an overhead crane and positioned in a peeler lathe and rotated against a razor-sharp blade. As the log spins against the knife blade, a continuous ribbon of wood as wide as the length of the log is run off to a series of decks and then to the veneer wet table. As the thin veneer passes from the decks to the wet table, it is carefully inspected and defective portions are cut out.

The veneer is no longer a continuous ribbon but a series of varying-width sheets. These are carefully graded and sorted as they are conveyed along the veneer wet table. The poorer-quality veneer unsuitable for the exposed outside faces is used to form "cross bands," or the core material of the inside laminates. At this stage of the process, all the veneer is extremely wet due to the steam cooking, and the next operation is to dry this material to a low moisture content before further processing. This is done by feeding the veneer into a special dryer, which reduces the moisture content down to approximately 5 to 12 percent depending on the grade of plywood to be manufactured.

There is another method of producing the veneer that is generally done with hardwood facings; this method involves cutting thin slices from flitches of milled lumber. A square flitch of lumber is fastened securely to a stationary table, across which a knife slices off the thin veneers. It is in this manner that matched-grain pieces are cut to produce the attractive balanced appearance of high-quality hardwood-faced plywood.

The next operation is to bond the edges of the veneer together so that each lamination is a continuous sheet. This is done in a jointing machine, where they are glued before making a full-size face or back cover veneer, which is cut to size.

The veneers, having been dried and cut to size, are now ready to be made into plywood. The cores are run through glue rollers and carefully placed across the back sheet. Most of the glues used today in the manufacture of plywood are of the synthetic resin variety, but, as mentioned earlier, some misguided manufacturers persist in using nonwaterproof adhesives. The face sheet is then placed on top, and a metal sheet goes on top of this. The resulting sandwich of made-up sheets, together with the metal dividing sheet, is then sent to the hot press for pressing.

Pressure of up to 175 pounds per square inch (depending on the type of glue used) is maintained during the heat-curing process, with temperatures around 350°F for about six minutes with 1/4" 3-ply, to about 14 minutes for 3/4" 7-ply. After removal from the press, the sheets are flat-stacked for 24 to 48 hours prior to trimming to the finished sizes.

With the edges of the sheets trimmed to size, the sheets are fed through a drum sander, which surfaces the sheets to a smooth finish. Minor repair work is done at this stage and the sheets are finally graded and crated, ready for dispatch from the factory.

Plywood is manufactured in many different countries, and there is often some confusion as to the correct grading of foreign plywood. In North America, the American Plywood Association, which is composed of manufacturers of waterproof plywood, has a set of standards that their plywood must meet. However, all plywood manufactured by their members regardless of quality is glued with waterproof glue, with the grading of the finished product being based on the quality of the lumber and finish and not on the glue line.

In Britain and some of the other Commonwealth countries, there are various British Standards covering plywood; the best grades of plywood have stamped codes on the edges to identify them. Unless you are sure of the glue line, bargain-variety plywood has no place in a marine environment. Even treating the plywood with suitable wood preservatives is not the answer, as some of these plywoods are bonded with casein or urea resin adhesives, which cannot withstand the preservatives and may delaminate.

This does not mean that only the most expensive plywood should be used. There are many situations when cheaper grades of plywood are quite suitable, such as the facing of bulkheads and the covering of subdecks, etc., but when plywood is to be used as a planking material, it makes sense to get the best available. No plywood, whether cheap or expensive, is of any use unless the glue is 100 percent waterproof.

The modern builder uses plywood pretty extensively, and if the sheets are cut into narrow widths, they may be cold-molded into compound curves if necessary. Plywood makes a fine, stable base on which to fasten hardwood facings such as laid decks or cabin sides and roofs, but any exposed exterior plywood surfaces should be protected with a sheathing material rather than just paint or varnish. This is because most plywood is made from flat-grain material peeled from a rotated log. Any shrinkage or drying causes minute checking of the surface, which paint or varnish cannot prevent. However, modern sheathing materials can do this perfectly, and the use of these will be discussed next and in later chapters.

SHEATHING

The purpose of applying a sheathing to plywood or a cold-molded hull is to bar water absorption and protect the surface beneath from abrasion.

One of the first materials used for this purpose was fiberglass cloth impregnated with polyester resin. Once cured, this material will give good protection, but it has an unfortunate problem in that it cannot stretch. However, because plywood is stable and unable to swell significantly due to the glued laminates locking it together, fiberglass sheathing on plywood is generally quite successful. The problems arise where the cloth has to fold over the edge of the ply, for if moisture penetrates the cloth, it will swell the thickness of the laminates, causing a crack along the glass that will admit more water and ultimately may cause rot. The same applies to a cold-molded hull, for while the planking is stable, being locked up with glue, other areas of the hull where the grain runs parallel (such as the keel and deadwood) may have unstable laminations. A thin skin of unyielding glass is unable to contain the pressure of swelling lumber in this manner, and the glass may crack or peel off.

This problem is now understood, and a variety of remedies have been produced. Epoxy resins, more rubbery and flexible than the polyester resins, are used as the bonding agent, and flexible synthetic materials are used in place of the glass cloth. Now, even if the wood does swell slightly, the sheathing stays with it.

One of the best known sheathing materials is Dynel cloth, manufactured by Union Carbide. It is easy to use and folds around the inside corners considerably more easily than glass cloth, which also has the attendant problems of itching and skin rash caused by minute particles of glass becoming lodged in exposed skin. A material that looks similar to glass cloth but that will stretch is made from polypropylene, a synthetic that has been widely used in ropemaking and that also floats. Both this and Dynel materials are excellent for sheathing over plywood or cold-molded hulls, and there are several other products that will do a similar job. Anyone who doubts the quality of plywood-and-fiberglass should consider the durability of the Hawaiian catamarans designed by Woody Brown that have operated continuously off Waikiki Beach for over 20 years.

FASTENINGS

Fastenings for cold-molding are varied; it is possible to use nails, screws, and staples, with the latter probably being the best value today.

Several factors are required to glue wood together successfully. The wood should be of a satisfactory type and moisture content; the temperature must be within acceptable limits; and the application of glue demands that the material must be clamped or held together until curing has taken place. Whether the wood is held together during gluing by clamps or fastenings depends upon the nature of the job.

When laminating large members like keels and deadwood assemblies, it is common to use both clamps and fastenings. Planking, on the other hand, is secured in position with fastenings only, except for initial fitting of the first layer, when it is possible to clamp to the stringers or frames.

Nails and staples can be driven faster than screws if the thickness to which you are fastening is solid enough, such as with stringers, bulkheads, and keel members. There are many places between these members, though, that will also require fastenings to pull the planking together, and short screws are good for this. When planking with thin material less than 3/16 inch thick, a good hand staple gun does a fine job. Sometimes after the glue is cured the staples are removed, in which case it pays to use steel staples instead of bronze or stainless steel ones. For thicker planking, larger staples are available, but they usually have to be driven with an air-gun, which may be too much trouble or expense for the size of the job.

Having built several cold-molded dinghies in recent years, I have used a selection of hand-operated staple guns from various manufacturers. Some of these staple guns were tiring to use over an extended period of time, and my hands and fingers developed painful blisters. At present I use an Arrow stapler model T–50, which will drive a selection of staples up to 9/16 inch in length, which is adequate for thin veneer. For removing staples, the Bostitch people sell a handy tool that is very effective, although many builders prefer to make their own removers out of a small pinch bar or screwdriver.

Small electric staple guns are available from several manufacturers, although it is not always easy to find suitable staples to fit them, particularly if you require nonferrous fastenings. For thicker planking, it is essential to drive staples with a power gun, and the best method, in my opinion, is with compressed air. Again there are many manufacturers to choose from, and it is largely a matter of personal preference as to which is best. For boatbuilding where you often have to climb over an inverted skeleton framework, it is essential to have a lightweight, easily handled gun. I use an Atro model 5500, which will shoot up to 90/30 staples about 1-3/16 inches in length and 1/4 inch across the crown. This Italian gun requires an air pressure of between 65 to 75 pounds psi, depending on how deep the staple needs to be countersunk. I generally use bronze staples and leave them in the structure, but they can be removed easily after the glue has cured if shot through stout webbing or even old fire hose. A good, hard pull on the webbing will jerk them out and leave only tiny holes, which are easily filled later.

The modern boat nails with serrated shanks marketed under a variety of trade names are excellent fastenings. Available in bronze and Monel, they offer better value than screws of similar dimensions and require but a fraction of the time and effort to drive home. For the builder with minimum equipment, these fasteners are undoubtedly the best choice.

ADHESIVES

It is sometimes difficult to choose between the resorcinol-type glues and epoxy resin. Much will depend on the price, the material being glued, and the working conditions. Both types are excellent glues if used correctly, but they also have certain problems that often make one more favorable than the other, depending on the particular job.

Resorcinol glue, being a thinner formulation, requires good, tight joints, which means careful work and adequate pressure from clamps or fastenings during the curing period. A thin glue does allow good penetration of surface fibers, and even difficult hardwoods like teak are bonded successfully with resorcinol glues.

Resorcinol is an easy glue to mix and use. It is supplied in two containers, one containing a liquid and the other a powder hardener. The mixing ratio between liquid and hardener is usually given on the containers; it generally seems to be expressed on a weight basis. In practice it is usually mixed by volume, being approximately one part powder hardener to three parts liquid resin. When mixed, the resulting liquid has the consistency of thick cream and is a dark blackberry or blackcurrant purple color. (Many builders will not use resorcinol glue because the glue line is so clearly visible through a varnished surface.) The adhesive is easy to spread with brushes or paint rollers. Cleanup is also easy, as any drips or excess glue can be removed with a damp cloth and warm water.

The chief problem with resorcinol glue is that it requires adequate temperatures to enable it to cure effectively. Builders in colder climates often have difficulty in this respect, and air temperatures below 65°F will require artificial heat to effect a satisfactory bond. This is often done with various types of electric or oil heaters, and I have used hot water bottles and even an electric blanket when gluing relatively small areas.

Epoxy glue has been on the scene for several years—I first used it in the early 1960s. Being thicker than resorcinol, epoxy has better gap-filling properties, yet it can penetrate cracks and pinholes remarkably well. Some types, can fill even the smallest voids, penetrating to the extent that the wood is effectively sealed forever from moisture. This penetration should not be confused with saturation of the wood fibers, however, for it cannot be absorbed into the wood in the same manner that preservatives or oil will penetrate the wood over a long period.

Generally speaking, then, the degree that epoxy penetrates into the wood is relatively little. After mixing, epoxy glue will remain a liquid for a couple of hours at most, some types setting up in only a few minutes, so the epoxy has relatively little time to achieve any penetration. For this reason, many builders prefer to roughen the surfaces to be bonded either by sanding with coarse paper or by leaving a sawn surface instead of planing it. In practice, provided the wood is clean and free from grease or oil, epoxy (like resorcinol) will give such a secure bond that the wood will fail before the glue line does.

Epoxy glues are being used by an increasing number of amateur and professional builders who find they can use them more effectively than the resorcinol types. Besides its sealant properties, epoxy has a number of other advantages. The advantages of epoxy are these: it has the ability to cure at much lower temperatures than other glues; the honey-colored resin makes inconspicuous joints compared to the dark glue lines of resorcinol adhesives; open assembly time is not as critical, as the resin does not air-dry and evaporate in the same manner as other glues; and being a heavy, thick glue, it is often quite acceptable to coat only one surface when gluing two members together.

Epoxy glues are supplied in two separate containers, one the resin and the other a hardener; both are liquids. Depending on the type used, the proportions of the two components can vary considerably. I generally use a type that requires equal parts of hardener and resin, as there is little chance of making mistakes in mixing. Some epoxies require considerably more resin than hardener, and the proportions are sometimes difficult to mix accurately in small quantities without using special metering pumps. The storage of opened containers of epoxy requires care, as some types react to humidity, which often is the reason for prolonged and unsuccessful cures.

Some of the hardeners used with these resins have been responsible for allergies and skin rashes; this gave epoxy a bad name when it was first introduced. Fortunately, this problem has largely disappeared, thanks to improvements in the resins made by petrochemical engineers. Still, it is wise to take certain precautions when using epoxy resin, especially when using it in large quantities. The allergy effect from epoxy is said to be cumulative, and if your natural body resistance cannot tolerate much exposure to it, severe skin rashes can break out even though you have used it successfully in the past. To combat any possible allergic reaction, it is best to use the glue carefully, avoiding excessive skin contact or breathing the fumes for any length of time in poorly ventilated areas. As a professional builder who uses gallons of the stuff, I do not feel my health has been threatened, but I do carefully wash my hands in hot, soapy water immediately after using these resins. Obviously, for some people prone to allergic reactions, even this type of precaution will be inadequate.

Epoxy resin is a sticky material to use, and unless adequate care is taken, everything can soon get into a dreadful mess. Hot water and soap will remove wet resin from bare skin, but it takes acetone or lacquer thinner to effectively remove excess resin from around a glued joint or clothing; once set, nothing will dissolve it except high heat. When using adhesives continually, as when planking a boat, the constant contact of these resins will dry out the skin and, particularly with resorcinol, will discolor fingernails and calluses, making them look unsightly. I have noticed that when epoxy glue is not entirely removed from fingernails, it sometimes becomes bonded to the surrounding skin and can cause minor pain as the nails grow.

Having used many different types of glues and resins over the years on a variety of craft in various climates, I don't think it is easy to choose a clear favorite, as each type has certain advantages and drawbacks. Generally speaking, however, the epoxies are more versatile, being suitable for gluing, filling, and bonding a sheathing material such as fiberglass or Dynel cloth.

There are several other types of glues available that may be used successfully to bond wooden members together. Of these, the ureaformaldehyde glues and the so-called plastic resin adhesives, which are packaged as powders to be mixed with water, are probably the best known. Many professional builders obtain good results from these less-expensive glues, but I frankly question the wisdom of using them if the bond is important. These glues are not 100 percent waterproof indefinitely when the glued structure is subjected to tropical climates over an ex-

tended period. When gluing certain hardwoods used in joinerwork, there is much to be said for these glues, as they are clean to use and do not leave an unsightly stain.

The P.V.A. glues (polyvinyl acetate)—which are milky-white, ready-mixed, water-based adhesives—are also handy to use in certain applications, but few builders would seriously consider using these glues for important structural members such as hull planking, backbone, laminations, etc.

Sometimes a glue is required to bond metal to wood, as with a lead or iron keel or a stem band. Where there is a chance of movement between two different types of material, a flexible glue or adhesive is needed, and a product that does this is P.R.C. (polysulphide, rubber composition), also known as Thiokol. A few builders have used this material as a planking glue between skins, but it is extremely messy to use and is usually more expensive than the other glues discussed. It certainly is possible, however, to use it and obtain good results.

These, then, are some of the materials used by the modern wooden boatbuilder; they will be referred to constantly in the following pages.

5

Costing

Estimating building costs for a custom vessel is one of the chief headaches for any boatbuilder, particularly the professional who is often requested to quote a price for a finished job. With inflation now causing rapid cost increases, this is not an easy task, and most builders are reluctant to sign a contract for the complete job. Most prefer to quote on a portion of the work, such as a completed hull and deckworks, but without interior finishing work, which can cost almost anything, depending on the wishes of the owner.

Costing and estimating requires experience in purchasing materials and equipment, plus knowledge of how long it takes to assemble all those materials to produce a finished boat. Much of the work may be done by independent contractors—perhaps the wiring, sheetmetal work, foundry casting, spars, rigging, sails, etc.—and trying to pin down one of these contractors is sometimes impossible, for they may have problems similar to yours.

Few clients, however, are prepared to sign a blank check or open up an inexhaustible supply of funds. Materials and labor charges should be spelled out in some form of written contract. In order for the builder to obtain some idea of what the costs will be, it is necessary to carefully go over all the plans, drawings, and specifica-

tions, breaking down each job into a separate operation as to both material costs and calculated labor costs. This is where the builder's experience with former jobs of a similar nature is so valuable, yet the uncertainty of price changes for materials and equipment is often impossible to predict. For this reason, the builder will often make some separate provision in his contract regarding the purchase of necessary hardware and equipment.

The builder has to start somewhere in figuring his estimate, so it usually begins with the hull itself. He will note the type of construction and the area of the hull surface, the amount of displacement, and the type of ballast keel. The hull estimate will need to be broken down into material needs: the quantity of lumber required for the backbone, framing, planking, and any temporary framing such as molds or forms; then the fastenings, nails, screws, and bolts, plus the amount of adhesives if using cold-molded construction. Each and every aspect of the building procedures must be considered if the builder is not to err too far in his figuring. Some hulls with easy shapes are built more quickly and with less waste than other types, and he will have to keep this in mind. After the materials and labor for the hull are calculated, the same kind of scrutiny is given to needs for the closing in of the deck and the building of the superstructure or deckworks.

Every part of the job must be gone over to make sure that nothing has been omitted. For many builders who like working with their hands better than figuring costs, this can be tiresome work, which may prove financially disastrous if not done well.

The professional builder usually has some experience to fall back on in estimating costs. Perhaps he may recently have built a similar vessel. But the amateur builder is often hopelessly unaware of what is involved and may be attempting to build a vessel that is far beyond his financial capability. The days have gone when rules-of-thumb could be used to figure building costs; $1,000 a foot or £100 per ton were never accurate methods anyway.

When the estimate of all the materials and labor has been worked out, some relationship between the two can be ascertained, and it is this aspect that makes boatbuilding so attractive to the amateur builder, who generally is less conscious of his time value than the man who makes his living at the trade. By being able to shop around for bargain prices without considering the time spent in doing this, the amateur builder frequently can obtain good used equipment for a fraction of the cost that the professional has to pay. It must also be realized that when someone is paying a builder to construct his craft, he probably does not expect to have secondhand materials installed.

After going over the plans, gathering information from manufacturers' catalogs, and checking current costs for lumber, etc., it is possible to come up with a figure to cover the basic materials for building the vessel and putting her in the water. The interior cabinetwork materials will probably be included in that figure, although costs of upholstery and interior furnishings may be unknown.

A separate list of optional equipment can be added and the amount of time required to install these extras can be estimated so that a fairly accurate overall figure can be arrived at. As an example, let us consider what is involved in the building costs of a small vessel similar to the 37-foot motorsailer on page 26 of the plan section and see where all the money goes.

I would start by making several lists of all the materials required for the entire job and then break this down into three separate lists. First, the materials and expenses for construction of the basic hull, deck, and superstructure. Second, materials for the interior and exterior finishwork, such as cabin joinery and brightwork on deck. Third, fittings, hardware, and equipment required for the vessel. The third list is one that can cause the most problems, as costs for these items are constantly changing. After making up these three separate groups, I would then try to figure the labor costs of each one, the number of hours to build the hull, finish the interior, and install the equipment. We now have three more lists of figures to compute.

Another factor to take into account is the amount of expense generated by the job itself, usually termed "overhead." Overhead can vary considerably from builder to builder and boat to boat. It takes into account unpopular but necessary items like power, heat, rent, phone and mail charges, insurance, transportation costs for materials, and perhaps the running around one has to do in a car. The wear and tear on tools and machines is another item, for although the professional builder may be able to "write off" much of these expenses on taxes, he still has to find the money to pay for them, yet it is often difficult to see where the boat itself benefits from these charges.

Table 1:
BASIC MATERIALS

Plans, designer's fee
Temporary framing—molds, bracing, grid, hoops
    for turning hull
Plywood for bulkheads
Framing material, stringers, keel, deadwood
Planking
Glue

Fastenings—nails, bolts, screws, rod, etc.
Sheathing materials—cloth, resin
Lead keel

Table 2:
INTERIOR AND EXTERIOR FINISHWORK

Teak or hardwood for interior joinerwork, exterior brightwork, deck, and trim
Plywood for deck, superstructure, and interior joinerwork
Glue and fastenings
Sheathing materials—cloth and resin
Paint and varnish for entire job
Sandpaper, brushes, rollers, thinners, etc.

Table 3:
FITTINGS, HARDWARE, OTHER EQUIPMENT

Engine, controls, propeller shaft gear, exhaust and silencer
Steering system
Tanks—water and fuel
Winches for sail handling
Anchor winch and ground tackle
Castings—rudder gear, chainplates, stemhead fittings, etc.
Fabrications—pulpit and stanchions, mast fittings, deck hardware, etc.
Mast and spars
Rigging—wire and fittings
Running rigging, blocks, shackles, reefing gear
Sails
Electrics—wiring, switchboard, lamps, panel
Batteries
Plumbing—toilet, washbasins, galley sink, faucets, pressure pump, bilge pump, seacocks, skin fittings, and hoses or pipe
Galley stove cabin heating, stove with flue, deck ring
Upholstery and mattresses

The above items cover the main equipment required, but it may be good to make a list of optional equipment, which can add considerably to the overall cost of the vessel.

Table 4:
OPTIONAL EQUIPMENT

Refrigerator, freezer
Autopilot
Depth sounder
Radio
Instruments—knotmeter, wind direction and speed
Hot water heater

At this stage I would attempt to estimate how many hours or days would be required to finish each aspect of the job, from the moment of preparing the loft floor for laying down the lines to completion of the vessel. Next I would try to estimate how long it will take to install all the equipment listed in Table 3. The list of optional equipment may also be worked out, but it is usually best to keep these items separate.

When the total labor charges are added to the material costs and overhead charges, the resulting figure is usually hard to accept. Today's rising costs have caused many builders to go out of business. Still to be added to that figure are possible state sales taxes, plus moving charges for trucking and launching, with perhaps extra insurance costs.

This subject may sound depressing, but many amateur and professional builders are incurable optimists where costing is concerned and just do not realize how expensive boatbuilding can be. It is easy to be distracted by the blueprints of a dreamship, but the nuts-and-bolts practicality of building that vessel had better be estimated honestly or both builder and owner are going to be disillusioned. From past experience I have found that labor charges account for approximately 40 percent of the total cost of building a custom vessel similar to this motorsailer. The labor aspect might be ignored by the amateur builder, yet it is important that he realize that his time is worth something, for he possibly could be earning an income at another job during the construction period.

Obviously there are substantial savings to be made by doing much of the work yourself, but this must be balanced against the fact that the professional builder will probably be able to buy much of the materials and equipment at trade discount rates that will enable him to reduce his costs over those of amateurs. The true saving for the latter, therefore, is somewhat closer to 30 percent of the completed costs, assuming that he builds his boat to a similar standard and with identical equipment.

It is little wonder, then, that when the hard figuring is done, many amateur builders are far from their original estimates of what it takes financially to put a boat together. The assumption that professional boatbuilders earn high wages because of the high cost of their products, is a misconception. For the same hours and a lot less talent, there are many other jobs that pay far higher salaries. Those jobs, however, are seldom as rewarding emotionally as custom boatbuilding, and one of the chief benefits of this kind of work is a contented frame of mind.

6

Lofting

Few subjects concern the novice boatbuilder more than what is generally termed "lofting," which is the marking out of the many curved lines that represent the full-size shape of the vessel's hull.

For a beginner, lofting procedures seem very complicated and confusing, and because of this he is tempted to try shortcut methods, which can be demoralizing later and often disastrous to the finished boat. Put simply, lofting is a necessary operation to ensure that the boat is built with a "fair" set of lines; the enlarged lines will highlight bumps or hollows that would offend the eye. It is also a means of obtaining the full-size shape of various important parts of the structure that may be built separately yet must fit together to form the basic framework of the hull to which the planking is fastened.

The experienced builder knows the value of accurate lofting; it enables him to develop the necessary shapes with pencil lines far more easily than shaping large pieces of wood later with subsequent unnecessary waste of time and materials. Lofting is also a way for the builder to check the accuracy of the designer. When a designer draws up a set of boat plans, he is working to quite a small scale compared to the vessel's actual dimensions; sometimes an erroneous measurement of only a fraction of an inch in the drawings enlarges to a glaring error when the lines are marked full size on the loft floor, so one object of the operation is to correct any minor mistakes the designer may have made during the drawing of the plans.

Some designers send their lines plans and calculations to specialized computer service programs that allow many technical aspects of the design to be checked. Hull lines may be faired up in the computer and extremely complex formulas can be quickly worked out so that technically, a perfectly balanced design will result. The printout from the computer lists the corrected measurements or "offsets" for the various lines and enables the builder to loft the hull shape far more quickly than with an inaccurate set of offsets.

Some misguided builders have enlarged boat plans photographically without realizing that they are enlarging the errors as well. So don't be tempted to try shortcut methods; the time spent lofting is a good investment and will pay you a handsome dividend in savings of time and materials later.

Construction plywood can be used for the loft floor.

PREPARATION OF SPACE AND TOOLS

Laying out the lines of a vessel full size often requires the use of considerable floor space. The professional builder often uses a special area termed a "mold loft," which is traditionally a loft located above the workshop. But the amateur usually lofts in the area where the boat is to be built, setting up a temporary floor and possibly using material that will eventually be used in the construction of the vessel. Allow enough space at each end of your floor so that the long battens used for drawing the lines can extend about three feet beyond the bow and stern. By extending the batten past the ends of the vessel, it frequently is possible to obtain fairer lines. Above all, the important thing to strive for is a clean, level floor on which it is possible to lay a suitable covering to draw the many lines on.

The choice of material to loft onto will depend on what is available. I have frequently used plywood, which later was used to build the deck and superstructure. By the time this plywood is required, the need of the lofting is past. This solution also has the advantage that the sheets of plywood with the lofting information on them are available during much of the construction instead of being on the floor underneath a partly built hull. The plans, particularly the offset sheet, which receives much abuse during the lofting operation, should be protected as much as possible from getting torn or dirty. It's a good idea to mount them on a light plywood backing and cover them with a clear polyethylene sheet, which can be held in place with masking tape or staples.

Lofting requires the use of a few tools that you probably already have in your kit: a good steel measuring tape, steel square, adjustable bevel, hammer, and a selection of pencils or pens. You will also need several long battens, which usually are made up out of good, clear stock and scarf-jointed when the available material does not meet the required length.

Scarfing these battens together may be one of

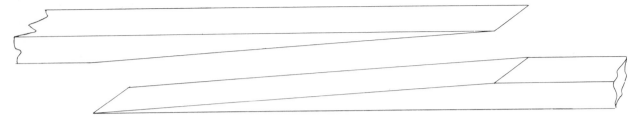

Figure 2. *A simple scarf joint cut to a 1-to-12 ratio.*

the first practical jobs you will tackle in the building of your vessel, so it seems like a good idea to say something here about these joints, which have a multitude of uses in glued laminated boat construction—from joining stringers and plywood sheets to produce greater lengths to the making of masts and spars. There are many different ways of cutting scarf joints, and at the risk of offending the "purist," I will state right now that in 99 cases out of 100, the simple plain scarf is the strongest, the easiest to make, and the most versatile joint you will use, provided it is made to the correct proportions and adequately glued. If this is done, the wood will fail before the joint does, and one can ask no more than that.

A plain scarf should have a proportion of 1:12; in other words, a 3/4-inch-thick batten requires a scarf not less than nine inches long. Why 1 to 12 and not 1 to 10 or 1 to 8? First, from long experience I recommend 1 to 12, although I cannot claim to have invented that formula. For many years the Douglas Fir Plywood Association (now the American Plywood Association) has used that ratio in scarfing sheets of plywood together. The huge laminated beams known as Glulam beams that you see in large grocery stores, auditoriums, and gymnasiums are also constructed of glued laminated material with the same proportions to their scarfed joints.

In recent years the plain scarf has been discontinued in some Glulam beam construction in favor of a finger joint, which is easier to make and wastes less material. Although the finger joint is more convenient, it cannot match the strength of the old plain scarf. I have no doubt

that someone, sometime did an engineering study to prove that this was the best shape for a scarf. However, if you are still not convinced, make them longer but not shorter!

When cutting these joints for your lofting battens, you will have to mark them with a plain taper from full thickness to a feather edge, and a good sharp plane is necessary to work the material down to its finished size. When you are planing it down, support the batten well with a solid backing under the joint. A work bench or sturdy sawhorse is usually best.

Gluing scarfs together is best done with a little preparation beforehand. The joints are fragile at the feather edge, so before gluing them together, see how they fit with a dry run. Then set the material out on sawhorses or blocks along the floor and provide yourself with a couple of straight pieces of lumber that will be used to sandwich the joint between them. You will also need some wax paper or polyethylene to prevent the glue from bonding the material to these cheek pieces when pressure is applied with clamps. After applying glue to the two halves of the joint, assemble them and drive a small finish nail through the joint to prevent it from sliding when clamped together. Instead of a finish nail you may prefer to use a small staple at each end of the feather; this has the advantage of being easily removable later and of "lining up" the joint so that the material is straight.

For lofting, you will require several battens of varying lengths and sizes, some quite small in section to be able to bend around the required shapes. Don't limit yourself on battens—you are bound to break some.

It is not generally realized that the hardest

lines to draw when lofting are the straight ones! To accomplish this requires care and concentration. Since the straight lines are the first to be laid down, let's begin by emphasizing that accuracy is the object of the exercise.

To draw straight lines up to about 14 or 16 feet long, you should make a straightedge out of a clear board, about 1 inch x 8 inches in section. Unless you have been extremely lucky in your selection, you will have to "shoot" the edges up straight with a plane. Look down the edge from each end of the plank to see where the bumps or hollows are. When you are satisfied that you have planed it straight enough, draw an experimental line down one edge and compare it by flopping the straightedge over on the other side. If your line stands this test, you are ready to proceed.

LAYING DOWN THE LINES

The set of plans that you have will be accompanied by a table of offsets that converts the lines drawings into horizontal and vertical measurements; these measurements will give you all the various dimensions required to loft your design. It must be remembered, however, that designers have various ways of drawing their

craft and setting up tables of offsets. In the case of the vertical heights, this can lead to confusion; some designers prefer to use the designed waterline as a standard and refer to it as a datum waterline. In this case, all vertical dimensions are expressed as heights above or below this datum waterline. Other designers prefer to measure all their heights above the baseline. All this may sound confusing; however, the offset sheet will tell you the correct procedure to follow. Here, I shall use the datum waterline approach.

Most all plans show a profile drawing of the hull, usually with the bow to the right. It is fairly standard practice to divide the hull into 12 stations, with station 0 at the datum waterline forward and station 12 at or slightly beyond the transom. Any stations ahead of station 0 are marked alphabetically, with the first being station A, which will of course be in the bow overhang.

The waterlines, which again are generally equally spaced apart, are usually marked with numbers below datum waterline and with letters above. These straight lines are long ones and will have to be marked carefully on the loft floor. The first line to be drawn will be the base waterline, which will also represent the centerline of the hull in the plan, or half-breadth, view.

Use a fine string stretched between two nails

Figure 3. *A sample table of offsets.*

OFFSET SHEET

HEIGHTS
(ABOVE AND BELOW DATUM W.L.)

HALF BREADTHS

			BUTTOCKS						WATERLINES						DIAGONALS		
STATION	UNDERSIDE RAIL CAP	TOP OF DECK	PROFILE	I	II	III	IV	STATION	B	A	DATUM	1	2		STATION	1	2
A	5-10-10	5-1-6	—	—	—	—		A	—	—	—	—			A	—	
O	5-1-8	4-3-8	1-2-12	2-2-8	—	—		O	1-7-5	1-0-11	0-8-0	—			O	1-7-0	
1	4-6-7	3-10-0	2-9-8	1-3-2	0-9-8	—		1	3-9-4	3-4-12	2-7-10	1-6-0			1	3-7-8	
2	3-11-0	3-2-1	3-7-2	2-0-2	1-1-8	0-7-5		2	5-0-8	4-7-11	4-4-13	2-9-8			2	4-11-0	
3	3-6-9	2-9-7	4-4-8	2-3-8	1-8-0	0-10-6		3	5-8-2	5-8-0	5-4-1	3-10-4			3	5-7-2	
4	3-4-0	2-7-1	4-10-2	2-4-0	1-10-2	1-2-0		4	6-1-2	6-2-1	5-11-2	4-4-3			4	5-10-4	
5	3-2-12	2-5-4	4-11-0	2-4-11	1-10-5	1-2-1		5	6-1-3	6-2-3	5-11-3	4-4-0			5	5-9-8	
6	3-3-0	2-6-0	4-11-8	2-1-8	1-6-4	0-9-7		6	5-10-11	5-9-1	5-4-6	3-6-0			6	5-5-0	
7	3-6-5	2-9-3	5-0-0	1-1-7	0-8-5	0-11-8		7	4-8-7	4-7-0	3-10-1	1-0-2			7	4-4-7	
8	4-0-8	3-4-1	0-0-0	1-3-2	0-7-5	—		8	1-10-12	1-5-12	—	—			8	1-11-9	
S	4-4-9	3-6-11	2-6-0	—	—	—		S	—	—	—	—			S		

OFFSETS INSIDE HEAVY LINE ARE
BELOW DATUM WATERLINE

ALL OFFSETS GIVEN IN FEET, INCHES AND SIXTEENTHS
TO OUTSIDE OF PLANKING

to line up your straightedge, or mark a series of points about three feet apart directly under the line and connect these to make your baseline. Use of the average cotton chalk line that builders and carpenters use is not accurate enough, and you will save yourself a lot of time and trouble by accepting that statement.

Waterlines and stations are permanent lines, so it's a good idea to mark them in with a black ballpoint pen; pencil marks tend to rub out when walked on. Incidentally, the loft floor and your markings will stay considerably cleaner if you wear slippers instead of boots, and keep a broom handy for sweeping the floor.

After getting your baseline down, the next step is to mark in the station positions. These lines must be exactly 90 degrees to the baseline; rather than use a steel square and straightedge, it's better to use the "3, 4, 5 method" of producing a right-angled triangle. You will recall from geometry lessons at school that Mr. Pythagoras figured that the hypotenuse of a right triangle squared equaled the sum of the other two sides squared.

It's good to mark the center station first, either station 4 or 5, rather than start at one end of the floor. This will reduce the chance of error creeping into the opposite end. When you have determined where the center station will intersect the baseline, put a mark three feet away from it along the baseline.

You will now need to draw a short parallel line four feet above the baseline where the station will pass through it. By measuring exactly five feet from the three-foot mark on the baseline, you will have an accurate right triangle with the station line exactly perpendicular. Obviously, these 3, 4, 5 proportions can be multiplied to mark out any size of right angle. At the back of this book are some other examples of right triangles with different proportions that may be more convenient. The station position can be marked in with a ballpoint pen. Then all the other stations are drawn in parallel to it.

Now the rest of the waterlines can be drawn in. Check the correct spacing from the table of offsets and mark this spacing at each station up

from the baseline. Draw in these lines with the straightedge or a long batten tacked down, and the foundation of your lofting is set.

These straight lines are most important, as the rest of the lofting will be built on them. Mark your stations and waterlines at each end with large bold letters so that you can easily identify them. A felt pen is good for this.

As an example of lofting practice, I am including some diagrams showing the various steps in this task, using the lines of the little Benford motorsailer (which have been simplified for clarity) to illustrate the correct procedure. Your foundation should look similar to what is shown in Figure 4, although your particular plans may show more or fewer stations.

Laying down the profile is the next step, and the sheerline is usually the first of the curved lines to be marked in. Consult your table of offsets and look for a column of figures that lists the height of the sheer at the various stations. These heights are usually given in feet, inches, and sixteenths, either above baseline or above datum waterline. A notation expressed as 2-11-9 would mean 2 feet 11 inches and 9 sixteenths. If you are lucky, you may have a metric table of offsets, in which cause the dimensions will be in meters and millimeters. This saves much confusion, and it will ultimately be the universal measure in any case. After the heights are marked at each station, a long batten is positioned and tacked down so that one edge lines up with these marks.

If you are lofting on a good floor or on sheets of plywood, you may be reluctant to spoil the surface with nail holes from holding the battens in position. It is possible to use heavy weights for this purpose instead, perhaps lead pigs that later may be used for ballast (*see* photo).

With the batten either tacked down or held along the marks, sight along the edge to see if it lies in a fair line. Sometimes one station may be a little high or low and the position will have to be changed slightly to give a fair line.

When you are satisfied that the sheerline is correct, mark it in in pen also, since this line will not be changed. There may be a bulwark rail

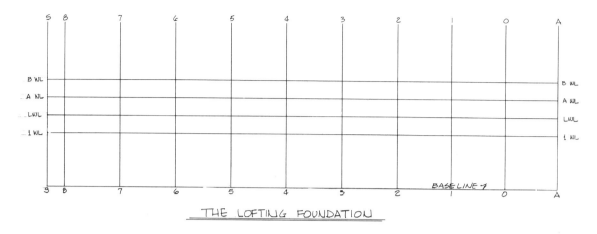

THE LOFTING FOUNDATION

Figure 4. *Drawing the foundation accurately is important as all the hull lines will be related to it.*

The author using weights to hold a batten during lofting.

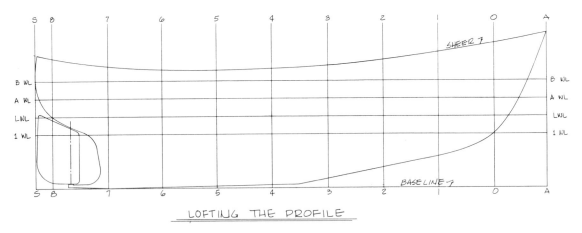

Figure 5. *The profile of the hull is the first part of the lines to be laid down.*

drawn on the plans, and if so, there will be another line to mark in below the sheerline; this will be the top of the deck at the side.

The other lines of the profile are likewise marked in from measurements in the table of offsets, and the whole of the profile can then be drawn in with a ballpoint pen, using the same method of nailing or holding a batten and sighting along it carefully before inking in the lines.

It will depend on the design of the vessel, but sometimes the lines as drawn are for a "runout" profile, which means that the shape drawn on the stem is projected out to a point or knife edge. Frequently steel boats are built to the runout profile, whereas wood vessels have "cut back" lines, which may be a radiused or rounded stem or even a shape with a small flat to it that is later protected with a metal band.

So far so good. By now you may be getting an idea of what it is all about. If the measurements on the offset sheet did not require much alteration, you are fortunate, having an accurate set of plans to work from. Some designers can produce drawings that require no corrections at all; lofting accurate plans is considerably easier and quicker than lofting poor ones.

Different builders have different procedures, but generally the next step after the profile has been drawn in is to mark in all the waterlines in plan view. Before marking in the waterlines, however, you should draw in the sheerline in plan view. This is drawn in by marking the

dimensions at each station as shown on the table of offsets. Again, a batten is bent around the various positions and adjusted until it lies in a pleasing line. (It should be mentioned at this point that although you should strive to make your batten conform to the measurements the designer has given you, it is pointless to do this if it means building an unfair hull.) At the bow, the batten will intersect the baseline/centerline directly below where the stem and sheer meet in the profile view. This will be measured from the first station in both profile and plan. Once you are satisfied that you have a fair sheerline, you should draw in the waterlines in the same manner.

You will be beginning to appreciate the object of all the lines now, but in order not to confuse yourself, you might consider marking some of the lines in different colors—waterlines blue, buttocks red, diagonals green, etc. If you find that you are having to change the batten positions, from the designer's measurements in order to obtain true curves, it is advisable to mark the waterlines with a pencil, as they may have to be changed during the fairing up of the body plan later.

After drawing in all the waterlines, the buttocks are next run in the profile. Some designers space the buttocks the same distance apart as the waterlines; this has the advantage that the straight buttock lines in plan view do not have to be drawn, for they are already marked in as waterlines in the profile view. If not, you will

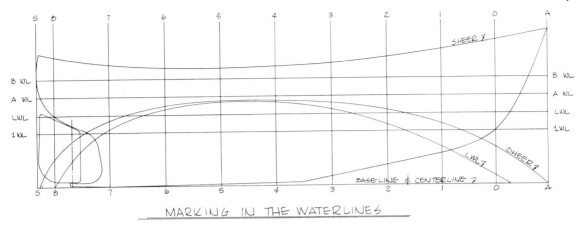

MARKING IN THE WATERLINES

Figure 6. *The baseline is used as a centerline in marking in the half-breadth waterlines.*

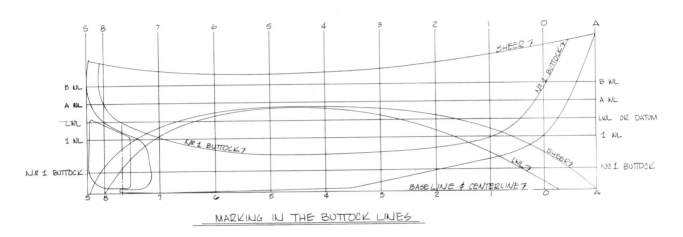

MARKING IN THE BUTTOCK LINES

Figure 7. *Curved buttock lines are drawn in on the profile view.*

have to run these straight lines in at the correct spacing out from the baseline.

To mark in the buttock lines in profile view, begin by using the offset heights above or below datum waterline at each station. When plotted, these marks will give a curved line somewhat smaller than the hull profile. But before you lay down a batten, there are some additional points to mark in. Take a look at the half-breadth waterlines in plan view; they are intersected by the straight buttock lines. Each of those points of intersection must be marked in on the profile. To do this, proceed as follows: Measure the distance between the buttock/waterline intersection and the nearest station. Then on the corresponding straight waterline in the profile plan, mark a point the same distance away from

the station that you used as a benchmark in taking the measurement. This procedure should be followed in transferring all such points of intersection. When you mark in these points on the profile, they should lie on, or nearly on, a smoothly curved line with the points previously marked out. However, don't be discouraged if you find the buttock lines in the ends difficult to line up with your marks. The hull shape is almost vertical in the ends, and the buttock lines can easily be changed later on in these areas. However, if you have been careful, they will not be far off.

The other buttock lines are run in the same manner, and you will note some strange shapes in the topsides, particularly if there is any tumblehome. Again, don't be concerned if the

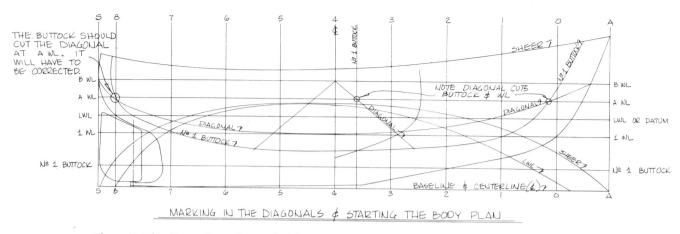

THE BUTTOCK SHOULD CUT THE DIAGONAL AT A WL. IT WILL HAVE TO BE CORRECTED.

NOTE DIAGONAL CUTS BUTTOCK & WL

MARKING IN THE DIAGONALS & STARTING THE BODY PLAN

Figure 8. *The diagonals can be marked in so that they tie into the waterlines and the buttocks.*

outside buttock at the ends is difficult to fair up; the hull shape is almost vertical here, too.

With waterlines and buttocks laid down, some builders start to lay off the body plan, which shows the hull's cross-sections at each station. Others prefer to loft the diagonals and use all three sets of lines before drawing the body sections. The latter method certainly does give one the maximum information to work from, and it will be the method described here.

Designers vary in how they draw in the diagonals on a set of plans. Some cut several diagonals at random angles and positions through the hull, while others cleverly tie the diagonals into the waterlines and buttocks by having them intersect at key points in the drawing. To do this, the diagonals are usually drawn at an angle of 45 degrees in the body plan and intersect the buttocks and waterlines at this angle. I prefer this latter method, as it is an excellent check and will produce a very fair set of lines.

For lofting the diagonals in on the profile view, the measurements are usually given in the table of offsets as "heights above or below datum waterline." Begin by marking these measurements at each station; the position of the diagonal at the stem will be on a waterline. Because the diagonals cross the waterlines and buttocks at the same point in the body plan, they will or should also do so in the profile. For example, if the highest diagonal passes through

No. 1 buttock at A waterline in the body plan, then it will also do so in profile, so check where the curved No. 1 buttock line crosses the straight A waterline in the profile view. This point should be on the curved line of the diagonal that your batten will follow when laid along the offset marks at the stations. The same diagonal will also cross the next buttock at a waterline, and you should begin to see how all the lines are starting to knit together.

The diagonals can also be lofted in on the plan view. For this, the offset table gives measurements from the centerline to the outside of the hull at each station along the diagonal. The method for laying off these measurements is similar to that used for the curved waterlines, and the batten is trued up accordingly.

Having reached this stage in the lofting, you will begin to see why colored lines are an advantage in identifying the various curves.

With all the information from these lines, you can now set about drawing in the body plan. This view is perhaps the most important view of all, for it is from the full-sized cross-sections that the shapes for the molds and bulkheads are obtained. Obtaining these shapes is one of the principal reasons for lofting.

When lofting the body plan, the center station is generally used as the centerline. Having established this, you must now mark in the vertical straight lines that will represent the various buttocks. This should be done on both

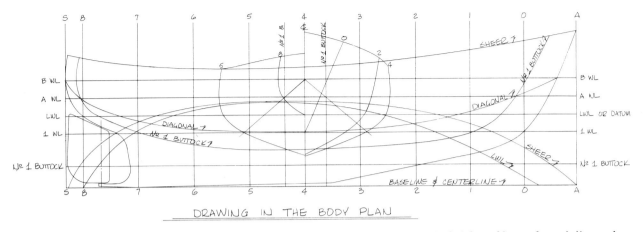

Figure 9. *The body plan is developed from the half-breadths of waterlines and the heights of buttocks and diagonals.*

sides of the center station, for the bow stations will be drawn in on the bow side of the center-line, and the aft ones on the stern side. Draw in the diagonal lines also.

Now you are ready to start picking up dimensions off the floor for each station. This can be done with a tape measure, of course, but to save time and eliminate mistakes, an aid named a "marking staff" is used. This is simply a straight wood batten, usually about 3/4-inch square, which is placed along a station line with an end butted against a batten nailed along the lower edge of the baseline. All the dimensions that belong to this particular station are marked onto one edge of the batten with a simple code beside them, so that you know which marks are which: the various half-breadths of the water-lines, the heights of the buttocks and diagonals, the height of the sheer, and the base of the keel. The marking staff is then butted against the centerline in body view, and the half-breadth measurement of each waterline is marked in from the ticks on the staff.

The same procedure is used for marking the buttock heights, but of course the staff must be butted against the baseline at the appropriate buttock in body view. When all the marks have been transferred to their respective positions, you should be able to connect them with a thin batten and draw in the shape of the station.

It's possible that some of these marks do not coincide, and if not, you will have to fair up the

body section, noting which particular line did not conform. A buttock may be out and you will have to see what the changed dimension does when altered in the profile view. This process is known as "fairing up." When all the other stations have been marked in and you are satisfied that the lines are fair, you have got it made, because it is now possible to find out the shape of any part of the hull, not only at a vertical position between stations but at an angle, too, if necessary.

LOFTING THE TRANSOM

The accompanying diagrams show the hull lines for a canoe-sterned motorsailer, so until now there has been no mention of how to loft a transom stern. The laying out of a plumb or raked flat transom is quite easy, but one of the most difficult jobs for the amateur or professional builder is to lay out and construct a raked curved transom. It is difficult enough to mark it out and even worse to lift the lines off the floor, transfer them to suitable lumber, and cut out the shapes.

A simple method of building this type of transom will be described and shown in later pages—this will eliminate all the pages of confusing instructions normally given for this complex operation. The only lofting require-ment for this simple method is that there be a vertical station aft of the transom, as it is necessary to construct a mold to support the stringers.

Usually lines plans showing curved transoms have station 12 just aft of the transom, but if not, you will have to extend the lines aft a distance of about nine inches. The profile of the hull will already show the transom rake, and the desired curve is usually expressed as a radius to be drawn in on the plan view. If you wish, you can draw in the radius to complete the sheerline, which still must extend past to station 12. Don't bother drawing any more lines at this stage if you are going to build a curved transom.

The method of drawing a flat raked transom is simple. It is drawn as a half-section, with the centerline parallel to the rake of the transom. After drawing in the centerline, extend the waterlines square off the face of the transom in the profile, using a steel square lined up to the rake. You then need to find out the half-breadths of the curved waterlines where they intersect the transom face. These are obtained

from the plan view, measuring the distance out from the baseline to the curved waterlines at the point where the raked face crosses the straight waterline in the profile. You will then have to draw in straight buttock lines parallel to the rake and also mark the straight diagonals. The method of obtaining the measurements for these lines is the same as mentioned earlier. Measure the heights above datum waterline where the curved buttocks and diagonals intersect the transom rake and transfer them to the transom section.

Because the transom should be framed to provide good fastening for the planking, it is necessary to obtain the transom framing shape. To determine this, the thickness of both transom planking and framing must be allowed for. This is because the transom shape on the lofting is drawn to the outside of the planking, or the *outside face* of the transom. As we move forward, deducting the thickness of transom planking and transom framing, the transom shape becomes somewhat enlarged due to the

Figure 10. *The raked transom is developed from dimensions taken from the loft floor. The arrows show how the positions for taking the half-breadth measurements are found.*

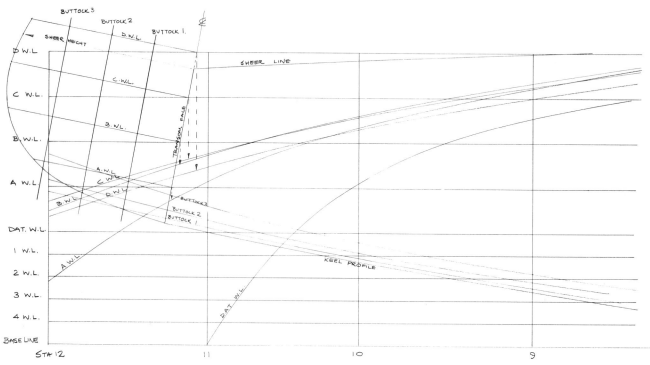

increasing girth of the hull. It is this enlarging shape that causes the complications: we need the shape of the *forward* face of the transom framing so that the frame will be cut large enough to allow for beveling the edges.

DRAWING IN BULKHEADS AND MOLDS

The procedures outlined in this chapter will be a good foundation for any kind of construction method, but the type of construction dictates how the remainder of the marking out is completed. For instance, if you were building a steel vessel, the body sections would probably represent bulkhead or frame shapes to the inside of plating. Obviously a wooden vessel has thicker planking so the offsets are usually drawn to the outside of the hull, which means that the planking thickness will have to be deducted before molds and bulkheads can be constructed.

For cold-molded construction, it is necessary to have molds and bulkheads made before the vessel is set up, so you should consult your plans and check where the bulkheads and other transverse partitions are located. Some of these partitions may be on one side of the vessel only, so it may be necessary to complement this with a mold on the other side. Also, sometimes these bulkheads and partitions are not on a station, but it is easy to determine their shape. Draw in the position of the desired bulkhead by erecting a new vertical line, which will be between two of the stations. Mark it clearly as a bulkhead and then pick up the half-breadths of the waterlines from the plan view with the marking staff and the heights of buttocks and diagonals in profile. With these new dimensions you can draw out the shape of the new bulkhead on the body plan.

The most usual method of deducting planking thickness from bulkheads is to cut a pattern out of a short scrap of planking stock to represent the finished planking thickness; then use this pattern to check the various lines where they cross the bulkhead positions. The midship bulkheads are easily reduced, as the planking lies at about 90 degrees to the edge of the bulkhead. Thus only the given thickness of the planking need be deducted. However, toward the ends of the vessel, the planking lies at an acute angle to the bulkheads, which increases the apparent planking thickness in the plane of the bulkhead. Therefore, it is necessary to deduct more than the given thickness of the planking. This is done by lining up the planking pattern on the curved waterlines at a bulkhead position in the plan view and noting how much must be deducted. The waterlines may not be suitable for all these deductions, so you may also have to have to check buttock lines and diagonals to be accurate. However, in practice these bulkheads toward the ends seldom have to be reduced much more than 1/8 inch over the pattern.

In determining how much to deduct from the bulkheads, only the thickness of the planking is considered, as the stringers are notched into the bulkheads, allowing the planking to be fastened diagonally across both. The molds, on the other hand, should not have the stringers notched into them. In this case, you must deduct the thickness of the planking and the stringer wherever you intend to position a mold. This is done the same way as in reducing the bulkheads by using a pattern, only including the thickness of the stringer in this instance.

When the bulkhead and mold shapes have been marked in, the lofting can be considered completed. It will be necessary to use this information to develop shapes and templates and to check all manner of sections and sizes, but it's all there on the floor if you know where to look. The time spent during the lofting operation will be saved many times over during the actual construction, which you are now ready to commence.

7

Constructing the Framework

Upon completion of the full-scale lines drawings, you are now ready to proceed with the actual construction of the vessel. As with the lofting, it is essential that you approach the steps involved in setting up the boat with great care. This is where the boat actually takes shape, and mistakes made here will be carried throughout the construction of the vessel. Chances are that short-cuts may catch up with you in the future and cost you a lot of time in the long run.

MOLDS AND BULKHEADS

The positions of the bulkheads and permanent transverse framing are shown on the construction plans, but it is up to the builder to decide where to site the molds. The span between molds and bulkheads depends on the size of the stringers, for too great a span will allow the stringers to flatten out during the fastening of the planking, allowing an unfair shape. For the average 40-foot vessel with 2-inch x 2-inch stringers, a span of between 30 and 36 inches would be about right.

With the final shape of the bulkheads and molds drawn in on the body plan, it is now possible to make molds and bulkheads. Al-though it is possible to make them directly from the loft floor, when the mold stock is to be of considerable thickness, it is generally much easier and more accurate to take the inter-mediate step of constructing templates.

Templates are built in segments and can be made out of any stable material, but 1/4-inch second-grade plywood is probably the most convenient. The ply should be sawed into about 8-inch widths so that the lines on the loft floor can be seen easily to be transferred. The lines can be transferred in several ways, one of which involves laying down round-headed nails with the heads along the desired line and pressing the plywood on top of them, which leaves marks on the underside that can be joined up with a thin, flexible batten. Possibly the easiest method uses wooden pointers, which are tacked or weighted down so that the points are above the line. The template material is then slid in under the pointers and tacked temporarily to the floor. A thin batten is sprung around the points and the shape is drawn in. After cutting, the plywood is returned to the loft floor and tacked down. The final shaping of the edge is done with a bullnose plane or compass plane. When the edge conforms exactly with the lofting, the positions of the various waterlines are marked in. The

Pointers can be used to lift lines from the loft floor.

a distance off the ground if the boat is set up level. The hull will be much easier to work on if each end is approximately the same height off the grid, which will mean canting the molds and bulkheads slightly to the desired angle or declivity. To do this, a straight line will have to be drawn in above the sheerline on the profile to represent the face of the grid when the boat is set up. A line drawn at 90 degrees to this grid will show how far from the vertical that the molds and bulkheads will be set up. A tapered pattern called a declivity board is made to be used between bulkheads and a spirit level or plumb-bob to show this angle when setting up the boat.

The grid line is usually determined so that it is above the top of the bulkheads. It is then unnecessary to cut slots into them to rest on the grid. Each mold cross spall can now be set at its correct height, which will vary, of course, due to the declivity.

Bulkheads are normally made of plywood, although they can be made of solid wood—either single thickness with vertical vee joints (sometimes machined with tongue-and-groove edges) or double-diagonal construction. Plywood is certainly the most convenient material to use, since it is available in a variety of sizes and thicknesses. Small plywood bulkheads are usually made single thickness, with some solid frame glued on one face around the outside to stiffen it and provide good fastening for planking or stringers.

Bulkheads often require several sheets of plywood to make up the required width, so some method of joining the edges is required. Undoubtedly the best arrangement is to scarf-joint the edges to the 1:12 ratio previously mentioned, but it is seldom necessary to go to this amount of work, as satisfactory joints can be made in other ways that are quite adequate. Among these are a rabbeted half-lap joint or a tongue-and-groove joint. In the latter case, a groove is cut with either a power saw or a router to fit a loose plywood tongue, which can be glued into position when the bulkhead is assembled.

Sometimes bulkheads are made from more

remaining segments of the template are then cut out and fastened together securely, to produce a completed half-template that, when flopped over, will give the full section, so that each side is the same.

Molds are usually built by marking the shapes of the various segments of the templates onto the mold material. If a band saw is available, the pieces doubled up so that both sides are sawn as one. If not, they can be cut out separately with a jigsaw. Make them of ample strength, because they will have to support all the bent stringers plus the builder's weight. When assembling, it's best to mark in the missing side on the body plan with the flopped template, so that the framework is symmetrical. Mark in all waterlines while on the loft floor; this will be useful later when the boat is set up.

These molds are to be set upside down onto a level bed termed the "grid." Since some vessels have a considerable sheer, the stern may be quite

Building a sandwich bulkhead for Treasure.

than one thickness of plywood. In order to stagger joints made in this manner, it is usually best to have one face thicker than the other, such as a 3/8-inch face glued to a 1/2-inch face. This arrangement allows 3/4-inch screws to be used to fasten the thinner ply to the thicker without the points projecting through. This technique of building up the plywood thickness will be mentioned in future chapters, as it is an excellent way of constructing decks, cabin sides, and coach roofs. The screw holes should be marked and drilled before the bulkhead is glued together. The spacing of fastenings and plywood thickness are referred to in Chapter 13 in the discussion of decks.

Where a light, strong bulkhead is required, perhaps the best arrangement is sandwich construction. Two light skins of plywood are glued and fastened to solid framing, which is concealed inside. This allows flush surfaces on both sides and makes a very neat job. When building this type of bulkhead, it is good to remember

not to place fastenings too close to the outside edges, which may cause problems later when the edges are beveled to receive the planking.

By filling the voids between the framing with rigid foam planks before the final face is glued down, a really strong, light bulkhead can be produced. The chief disadvantage of this type of construction is that it is often difficult to fasten bearers or cabin joinery to the thin faces unless provision was made beforehand to position solid framing in the correct locations. Whatever method is used to construct the bulkheads, be sure to mark in the centerline and waterlines accurately, as these reference marks will be used during the setting up of the boat and during the fitting out of the interior accommodations.

DECK BEAM PATTERN

It will be necessary to develop a template of the deck beam camber. The deck beams will inter-

90

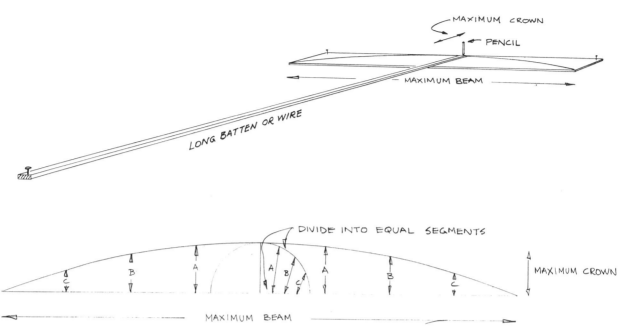

Figure 11. *Methods of marking deck camber.*

sect and be fastened to the clamp, so the top edge of the clamp must have the same bevel as the deck camber if that structure is to fit the underside of the deck. An accurate deck camber pattern is also required to mark the crown at the top of the bulkheads.

If laminated beams are to be made, a form must be built to the shape of the underside of the beam so that the laminations can be clamped to it. The usual method of marking this camber is shown in Figure 11. Some builders prefer to mark the deck crown by using a radius marked with a long batten. This means that the arc is constant, but in practice, when a beam has been glued up on a form marked out in either manner, the beam will straighten out slightly in the ends so that a tighter radius is required on the form to produce the desired shape.

It will save problems later if a sample deck beam is glued up on the form and used as a

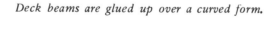

Deck beams are glued up over a curved form.

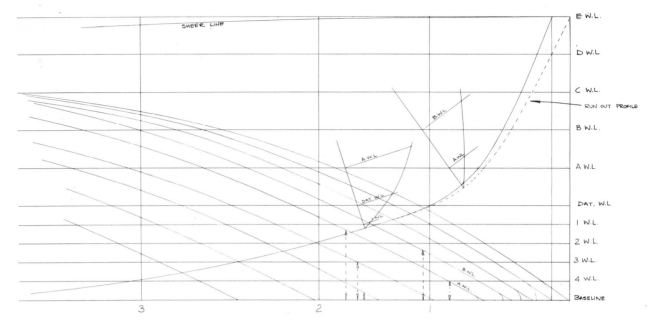

Above: Figure 12. Trekka's *bow sections lofted square off the stem and keel.*

Right: Figure 13. *A lofted bow section showing keel and stem shapes.*

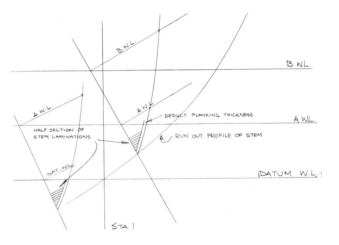

pattern for all the marking out. All the other deck beams can be glued up later on the same form so that the shape will remain constant.

DEVELOPING THE BACKBONE TIMBERS

After construction of the bulkheads and molds, it is good to develop the shape of some of the other hull components, such as the keel and stem, horn timber, and deadwood assembly.

To tie planking to keel and stem solidly, it is desirable to have plenty of landing room for the strakes; a rabbet considerably reduces this landing and also makes for a lot of unnecessary work. With this in mind, the keel and stem should be designed so that there is no apparent rabbet; the strakes should be allowed to extend past the keel and, at the bow, to terminate along the edge of the stem, which will later receive a capping and thus form a rabbet.

This same technique can be adopted along the horn timber, except that the planking from each side of the hull normally butts together along the centerline. Because of a normally thin trailing edge along the sternpost deadwood, it will be necessary to cut a rabbet for a short section if the hull has a reverse curve in the bilge aft.

To develop the stem shape, draw straight lines at 90 degrees to the stem on the profile plan. On these lines, develop the section in a similar manner to that used in determining the shape of a raked flat transom. In this manner, it is possible to obtain a series of reference points that will show the shape of the stem and forefoot. Since there is not going to be a rabbet cut in, don't forget to deduct for plank thickness, as you are only interested in the shape from the "knife-edge." The keel and stem may

Laminating a deadwood using 2-inch stock. This lamination was preassembled in order to check its fit and label the laminates with positioning marks. Nails were used to hold the laminates in position until clamps could be applied.

have several laminations to them; and remember that these will be parallel in a profile view. The techniques used to produce these laminations, which save a lot of heavy and difficult work, will be covered later.

While the loft floor is intact, another task is to draw in the shaft line if the vessel is to have an engine. The position of the shaft and the type of vessel will determine how the deadwood structure will be built. Much of this will be more stable if it is laminated up out of 2- or 3-inch-thick material rather than built up out of heavy balks, which are difficult to cut out unless large saws are available. With thin stock, a Skilsaw can be used to cut much of this to size. The maximum width or sided measurement of the deadwood (and the horn timber as well) is dictated by either plans or available material. It is helpful to make templates of the proposed members and mark all waterlines and other reference points so that the half-breadth sizes can be marked at the appropriate positions.

Mark centerlines and stations so that these half-breadth dimensions can be marked on the plan or body view of the deadwood material from the profile view of the templates.

Sometimes the deadwood is arranged vertically so that a hole will have to be bored for the shaft. If the hole is to be long, it is best to bore a pilot hole before too many laminations are glued up, so that a boring bar can later be used to enlarge the hole to its correct size and position. (This will be discussed in greater detail in Chapter 15.) When the deadwood is horizontal, the shaft is usually arranged to be in line with one of the joints, so that each side can be shaped out. This was often done by hand with a round plane and gouge in the past, but it can now be done with a Skilsaw or a router.

When the design of the assembly calls for vertical laminations, it is usual to cut tenons in the ends of them to fit into mortises, or slots, in both horn and keel timbers. The addition of glue and bolts makes for a very strong structure. One advantage of vertical deadwood laminations is that it is not necessary to drill holes for the bolts that tie the structure together, for it is possible to cut slots inside the laminations before gluing up. This avoids such possibilities as the bolt hole wandering off course or the drill hitting the stern tube.

Once the deadwood is glued together, it is possible to cut out the short section of rabbet that will end at the horn timber. The rabbet line is located where the *outside* of the planking meets the deadwood or keel, while the bearding line is where the *inside* of the planking meets these members. The positions of these lines can be obtained from the loft floor and should be marked in on the profile view after measurements are obtained from both body and plan view.

In determining the rabbet position, draw in the half-breadth dimension of the deadwood in plan view; this line will intersect the curved waterlines in much the same way that a straight buttock line does. These points of intersection have to be transferred to the straight waterlines in profile view and will be the same distance ahead or aft of the stations in profile as they are in plan view. If these points are connected with a batten in profile view, they should show a fair curved line, which is the outside of the rabbet (where the *outside* edge of the planking will meet the deadwood). Sometimes additional points can be marked in by drawing the half-breadth deadwood dimension on the body plan and noting where this line cuts the body shape to the outside of planking. This measurement, taken as a height above the baseline, is marked at the same station in profile view.

Marking in the bearding line entails much the same procedure. It helps to use a short piece of wood as a pattern to represent the planking thickness. The pattern is placed along the curved waterlines in plan view in the area of the rabbet line. Note where the *inside* of the pattern cuts the half-breadth deadwood line and transfer these points to the appropriate waterlines in profile view. Again, some information can be obtained in the body plan by placing the pattern

Rough-shaping a vertically laminated deadwood. Note that a pilot hole has been bored for the shaft.

on the body sections and noting where the *inside* of planking cuts the half-breadth deadwood line; these heights should be marked at the correct stations in profile view.

Sometimes there just are not enough points marked in to draw either the rabbet or bearding lines with any certainty. If this is the case, it is best to draw in a couple of extra stations in that area to give you more information to go on. By marking in these new stations in the body plan, or even extra waterlines if need be, you will have less chance of making an error. Remember, it is much easier to change a few lines than alter the material later.

The rabbet is usually cut out with a large chisel and mallet, but much of it can be removed in the initial stages with the use of a Skilsaw. Final shaping is best left until the boat is set up and stringers installed.

SETTING UP

With the molds, bulkheads, and deadwood assembly ready, the next job will be to set up the boat, which probably will mean removal of the loft floor. Make sure that each mold or

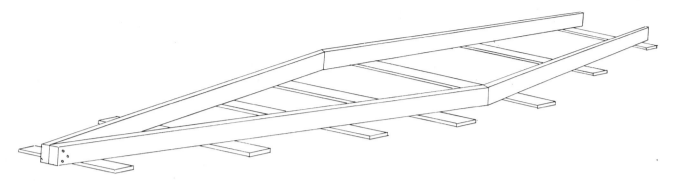

Figure 14. *The building grid.*

bulkhead has the waterlines marked on it, as these reference points will be needed during the setting up and for installation of structural members and the interior later.

The molds and bulkheads are set up upside down on a grid. The grid needs to be made of substantial material for eventually it will have to support the full weight of the planked hull. In addition, it must be strong and rigid enough to remain stable and level during the initial setting-up operation while the molds and bulkheads are secured and braced to it.

In order to keep the grid under the boat and out of the way of feet, it's a good idea to set the longitudinal timbers so that they approximate the shape of the deck edge, with maximum width at the midpoint and tapering toward the ends. Stretch a line between the timbers of the grid to use as a guideline (it will also be used to align the bulkheads and molds). Measured from this centerline, the grid timbers can be set equally apart and as wide as possible, but inside the deck edge enough to allow room for the clamp to be installed. These timbers can be bolted together at the bow where the two sides meet. The midpoint, where the two rear timbers join the forward ones, should also be secured firmly. Place a straightedge across the timbers at various points and check with a spirit level to make sure that the grid is level. Provide plenty of support under the timbers to make sure there is no danger of the grid bending due to settling or applied weight.

With this level foundation to support the boat in place, it is now necessary to mark in the positions of the molds and bulkheads. A straightedge placed across the grid timbers at 90 degrees to the stretched-string centerline can be used to do this. Small cleats nailed to the grid at those positions will allow for the cross spalls to be butted against them and skew-nailed into the grid.

When setting up the molds, keep the forward ones aft of their stations and the aft ones forward, so that it will be unnecessary to bevel their edges when installing the stringers. As for the bulkheads, they are placed on station with the edges beveled after all stringers are permanently fastened.

The molds and bulkheads should be well fastened to the grid and braced either vertically or to the correct declivity as decided on the loft floor. A stout batten or plank nailed along the center of the keel line will allow you to check if the molds or bulkheads are correctly aligned. Standing well back and lining up the waterlines by eye is also a good method of checking, and it will probably be necessary to place an odd wedge to raise one side or trim some off a cross spall before everything is correctly spaced and trued up.

It may be necessary to make a temporary form of the inside of the stem and forefoot so that the stem can be laminated to the desired shape. This form can be secured to the building grid and to the first bulkhead or mold to provide

Above: *Setting up molds and bulkheads on a grid. A string stretched down the middle of the grid represents the vessel's centerline.* Right: *Forward molds and bulkheads set up and braced. The structure at the bow is a form for laminating the stem in place.*

96

a strong base to clamp the laminations to. Then the horn timber and deadwood are fitted into notches on top of the molds and bulkheads. When all marks are correct, glue and fasten, making sure that the centerline coincides with the keel line center. The horn timber should be long enough to extend to the last mold if the transom is to be a curved one.

INSTALLING THE CLAMP AND BACKBONE

The installation of the clamp or beam shelf is usually the next operation, and the bulkheads and molds will need notches cut at the deck edge to receive this member, which, because of its size, is normally laminated rather than steam-bent to avoid placing too much strain on the alignment of the boat.

The clamp needs to be fairly substantial. Aside from providing a solid member to fasten the ends of the planking to, it must also provide enough area to tie the edge of the deck to. Deck beams will also be secured to it, and possibly chainplates.

When marking out the notches for the clamp, it will help to nail a full-length batten to the bulkheads; this will show the required angles at each station. Since the maximum strength of the clamp needs to be near the greatest beam, it makes sense to taper the molded dimension of the laminations at each end, the sided thickness remaining constant. This shaping will reduce the section and allow it to be sprung into place more easily. In order to have a reference point later when planing off the planking for the deck, it's a good idea to try to cut the notches so that the top inside edge of the clamp will fit snugly up against the underside of the deck. The position of this edge can be calculated at each station with a deck camber mold and by measuring inward the thickness of the clamp.

If the clamp is to be laminated to finished thickness, it is essential to cut the notches the correct depth, as the object is to be sure the outside of the final lamination is at the correct position and angle to fasten the planking to. A

wood block representing the clamp's sided dimension, which will be constant throughout its length, should be used as a check to make sure the notches are cut out correctly.

Unless a small vessel is being built, it is unlikely that lumber long enough for a full length will be available, so it will be necessary to scarf material together before installation. The scarfs should be cut to not less than the 1:12 ratio mentioned previously and positioned so that they are staggered away from joints in other laminations.

When installing the first lamination, it is best to secure the bow first and work toward the stern, using C-clamps to hold the material at the various stations. The clamp for a double-ended hull with a severe curve in the after section may have to be built up of thinner material and scarf-jointed later into heavier material. Once the first lamination is secured on both sides, the remaining ones are easy, as there is something to clamp to. The whole framework will now feel considerably more rigid.

The next job will be to glue up the stem and keel laminations. The feasibility of making the keel one continuous lamination will depend largely on the amount of shape to its profile. Curved sections should be laminated in place, while straight ones are more easily glued together on the ground and installed later. The stem, being curved, is best glued into place in the same manner as the clamp, using the form described earlier. Before the first stem lamination can be secured to the molds and bulkheads, the forward end of the clamp will have to be trimmed to the correct angle to fit the inside of the stem. Don't try to glue all the remaining laminations in one operation; this places considerable strain on the framework and may change its shape.

When gluing large surfaces, as in this type of job, it is considerably more convenient to use paint rollers to spread the glue evenly rather than brushes, which are slower and tend to make more mess on the floor. When gluing curved members, which sometimes want to slide as pressure is applied, try temporary nailing with double-headed nails. These nails are often ex-

Laminating the stem in place.

give best support if installed "on edge," so that the planking is nailed to the section having the greatest thickness. This does take up more interior space, though, and a compromise is normally reached by having stringers almost square in section.

Whereas bent frames are normally made of heavy hardwoods, long-grained softwoods such as pine, Douglas fir, and spruce are used to make excellent stringers, being lighter and having excellent qualities for gluing techniques. Stringers are installed in full-length runs and are sometimes laminated if the bends are excessive.

Where scarfs are employed, it is frequently possible to shorten the scarf-jointing operation by making a "jig" into which stringer stock is clamped. A Skilsaw can be guided along a fence so that scarfs can be cut accurately and quickly without the need of planing. A type of saw blade that is hollow-ground and sometimes called a "planer blade" can be used—it leaves an excellent surface for gluing. If the stringers are made in pairs so that scarf joints are equally spaced, they can be clamped together with the same number of clamps it takes to glue one stringer.

As mentioned previously, the use of waxed paper or a polyethylene sheet between cheek supports or pairs of stringers will prevent "embarrassing" glue joints.

At what point on the hull a builder starts to fasten the stringers is usually left to his discretion. However, it it advisable to start around the turn of the bilge to see how a batten will lie without any edge set.

The diagonals in the body plan are sometimes a good indication of where to start, but the best guide is a full-length batten that will conform to the changing angles at each station. To avoid extra material in the ends of the vessel where the stringers are more closely spaced, it is common to run the stringer nearest to the clamp so that it does not reach the stem or stern. Sometimes this stringer terminates at a bulkhead at each end, but this can make the shape unfair. It is better to extend the ends and secure them to the clamp. When building a light-displacement boat

cellent for holding down edges until glue is cured, at which point they can be withdrawn easily and used again. If any permanent fastenings are used during gluing, make sure they won't be hit with a plane when the stem is shaped up.

The keel and stem can also be joined with a long scarf. It's good to plan some through-bolts in this area also. The bases of the bulkheads need a good hardwood "floor" bolted on each side of them so that the keel can be through-bolted to these floors and tie the backbone together.

Before attempting to shape the sides of the keel and stem, it is best to fit all the stringers, which will allow you to check the shape of the keel with flexible battens.

INSTALLING THE STRINGERS

The spacing of the stringers is not unlike the frame spacing in carvel construction. Stringers

Above and below: *Installing the stringers.*

where weight-saving is desirable, stringers can be tapered at each end, which will have little adverse effect on the hull's strength. *Be sure to install enough stringers.* Many builders make the mistake of spacing them too far apart, which results in flat spots that develop in the first layer of planking and can never be removed.

The use of a long batten tacked to the bulkheads is the easiest way of marking the position and angles at which the stringers are notched into the bulkheads. The spacing between stringers is determined at the largest bulkhead and is divided up equally at the other stations. With care and some edge-setting, it is possible to avoid having the stringers converge too much at each end of the hull.

After the bilge stringer is fitted, the remaining space between it and the clamp is divided up for the other stringers. The notches can be cut with a Skilsaw using a fine crosscut blade, but care needs to be taken to avoid placing any fastenings in the framing around the bulkheads. Before installing a stringer permanently, it makes a neat job if the inside edges are rounded off between bulkheads. A router does this quickly and well.

Stringers are glued into the notches. Sometimes thin wedges will have to be inserted to make a tight joint. It is usual to fasten the stringers at the bulkheads with a nail, screw, or bolt, depending on size. At the stem the stringers are fitted to butt up against the inside laminations after removal of the stem mold. Sometimes breasthooks are fitted to the stringers and bolted through the stem. However, the planking ties this joint together later, and the ends are normally nailed or screwed to hold them in position until the first skin of planking is secured.

Some designers and builders prefer not to notch the stringers into the bulkheads or frames, claiming that these latter members create a stress point in the planking. This opinion has some merit, particularly in light-displacement construction, where the skin is of minimum thickness. However, such construction does not suit every vessel, and in general, I feel that provided the planking is of adequate thickness,

having the stringers notched into the bulkheads is superior, for it makes for a stiffer and stronger structure.

Before fastening the remainder of the stringers, it may be a good idea to install the engine beds. These can be notched into a bulkhead and held at the required position and spacing with a cross spall at a mold. Stringers can be notched into the beds until they assume a fair line, and surplus material can be shaped away far more easily than if this job were left until completion of the planking. Since some stringers are installed near the keel, some will need to be fastened to the deadwood. The outsides of the stringers meet the deadwood at the bearding line, and once all these are in, the final shaping of the rabbet can be done.

A small bullnose plane and a thin, flexible batten are useful aids in the final shaping of the rabbet. Sometimes a disc sander with coarse paper can also be used, as there is often a certain amount of hollowing required for the planking to fit fairly.

The shaping of the edges of the keel and stem are best done with a power plane and checked with a flexible batten to make sure the correct shape is attained. With this work completed, the hull is about ready to be planked, unless the design calls for the building of a curved transom.

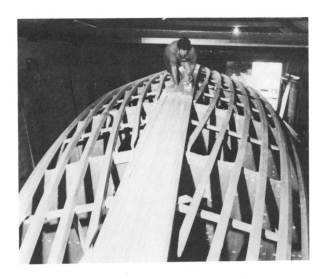

Fairing stringers and keel on Buccaneer. *(Sea Spray)*

BUILDING A CURVED TRANSOM

Building a curved transom is a task that defeats many builders and has been the subject of endless headaches for others. The method described here is one I have used on several boats and requires little explanation.

Two identical templates are cut out to the desired radius to the inside of planking. These are set up athwartship and braced square to the rake, one above the horn timber and one below the clamp. A straight line stretched vertically between these templates will give the correct position at each stringer of the inside of transom planking. (It should be remembered that the stringers have been extended to a mold aft of the transom position.) It's usually easiest to use a straightedge for marking the point where the plane of the transom intersects the stringers. When several stringers have been marked, it is easy to clamp a small batten across them to join up the marks. The width of the transom frame can be marked in, using the same straightedge but with a block of wood to represent the desired frame width. Once again, the marks are joined with the light batten.

Notches are then cut into the stringers for the transom frame to a depth of a little more than half the stringer thickness. It is advisable to extend this notch about 1/2 inch aft of the line representing the inside of transom planking, so that a slightly wider frame is made to allow for fitting later. It will also be necessary to cut a notch on each side of the horn timber to receive the two inboard ends of the frame. The clamps also need notching so that the framework can extend past and provide support for the bulwark if required. A cardboard or thin plywood template of the frame shape is then made by bending the template material around the stringer notches. Reverse it to check the other side. If it is too far out, you will have to cut another pattern.

The frame material can be made of thin stock that will bend around the stringers. However, it is generally a shape that requires wide material. Good-quality waterproof plywood is an excellent choice. The thickness of the plywood will depend on the size and shape of the transome; five 1/4-inch laminations were used for the framing on *Sunrise*, shown in the accompanying photographs.

It will be necessary to mask off the stringer notches with tape to prevent the laminated plywood frame from sticking to the stringers during the gluing-up operation. A roll of wide masking tape is a good investment for this job. Because of the greater radius, the outside laminations should be slightly longer than the inside. Before any glue is mixed, it is best to have a "dry run" and clamp the required number of laminations into position without glue. If the framework can be bent dry, it will bend much more easily with the application of wet glue, which allows the laminations to slide and moistens the wood fibers.

With this and any similar operation, it is essential that the material be clamped and fastened before the glue has dried. Since it may take some time before all the clamps are set up, choose a good time of day so that the weather is not against you. Gluing in full sunlight with a breeze blowing can drastically reduce the amount of "open assembly" time and result in poor glue joints.

Each framework lamination can be glued slightly ahead of the previous one to allow for the transom radius. This will, however, leave a series of steps along the forward edge that will need to be planed off once the glue is dry and the frame is removed from the stringers. The aft edge is shaped later. When the frame has been fitted, it can be glued into the notches and secured with screws and nails.

The next operation is to cut off the stringers and remove the mold aft of the transom. Once this is done, the aft edge of the framing can be planed to the correct angle and radius, using a straightedge over the curved transom molds. A power plane is the tool for this job, because the wood grain goes in every direction.

At this point you will need to decide on the transom knee arrangement. A transom knee is usually fastened to the top of the horn timber and to a vertical transom framing member. On

Left: *The transom frame is laminated out of plywood and set into notches in the stringers and horn timber.* Right: *After the stringers have been cut off, the transom frame is shaped and the vertical members installed. The radiused templates have been set up to aid in the installation of the vertical members.*

some sailing vessels where it may be necessary later to fit some form of wind vane steering system, a knee on the centerline may be an inconvenience. An alternative is to fasten two knees at the outside edges of the horn timber, which will leave the center clear so that a rudder stock for a self-steering rudder can be positioned well aft but inside the hull.

Knees are usually laminated over a simple wooden form, after making a plywood template to determine the desired shape. The form or mold is sawn to the inside shape of the template, allowing extra length for the arms. It is usually necessary to saw the back of the form parallel to the front, so that C-clamps can be used to hold the laminations in position until the glue cures. Cover the form surface with polyethylene or waxed paper so that the glue does not make the laminations stick to the form. When gluing, make sure each glued surface is well wetted

before clamping is begun. It is advisable to use a strip of wood or metal (the same width and length as the laminations) under the feet of the clamps, which might otherwise leave marks on the laminations.

Start clamping in the center and work toward the ends, constantly returning to check the torque on the clamp handles as the ends are pulled into position. If the laminations start to slide sideways, it will be necessary to place a block of wood on each side and, with another clamp, pull the edges of the laminations back into position. To save extra material and added work, a small block is usually cut to shape and glued to the throat of the knee when the laminations are removed from the form. This block is a filler piece and replaces what would only be a lot of short laminations.

The sides of the knee are planed up and sanded at this stage, and the template is laid on top to mark out the desired shape. Remember that whenever material is cut from the outside edges of a laminated knee, it has a tendency to straighten out, so leave on a little extra material in the throat area when cutting to shape.

Aside from the knee assembly, some other vertical members are needed for the transom framework. Make them deep enough so that they can be notched for a transverse deck beam, which will provide material to fasten the deck to later. The crown can be marked by fixing a couple of short battens to extend the inside bottom edges of the clamps. (This, you will recall, is the underside of the deck.) The deck camber mold is supported on these two battens and the camber is marked onto the upright framing. This transverse deck beam also has a lot of shape to it and can be sawn to shape and bent into position in a similar manner to that used for the plywood frame.

Some sailing vessel transoms require metal chainplates for the attachment of backstays or preventers. It is best to decide on their arrangement before planking the transom so that the metal plates can be fitted to the framing. Sometimes bronze or stainless steel strapping is bolted to the inside of the transom planking, which means that notches will have to be cut through the curved deck beam. Obviously, this is done

more easily before the planking is secured. This also applies to the shroud chainplates, which may have to be notched through the clamp and adjacent stringers.

At this stage the transom is ready for planking. Some builders prefer to fasten a sheet of plywood over the framing and then apply horizontal planking, such as teak or mahogany. Others prefer to plank the transom double-diagonally and then fasten the final layer horizontally.

Whatever method is used, it is well to leave the final horizontal skin until just before the final skin is fastened to the hull, as this allows the end grain of the inside transom planking to be covered by the inside layers of hull planking, which in turn can have its ends covered by the final horizontal transom planking. The end result is a rabbeted lock joint around the edge of the transom. This is much stronger than the usual method of allowing all the hood ends of the hull planking to be exposed.

This method of building a transom can also be used with carvel construction by extending ribbands to a mold aft of the transom position and gluing the laminated plywood framework inside the ribbands. This practice guarantees that the hull shape will not be distorted, which is often the case with transoms that are built separately.

8

Making the Ballast Keel

If the design to be built is a sailing vessel, consideration must be given to building a ballast keel. It is best not to delay this project for too long, since measurements from the loft floor are needed to build a "plug" or template for it.

The ease of building the keel plug varies with the design. On some older designs, the plug is relatively simple to build as the keels on these vessels are little more than slightly rounded sections forward. Some of the modern keels, however, require a complicated plug that needs to be made carefully and accurately if it is to fit without a great deal of shaping or filling.

Lead is superior to cast iron for a ballast keel because of its greater density. It is also a more forgiving material, for if the resulting casting is too large, it is possible to work lead in much the same manner as some of the tougher hardwoods; it can be bored, sawed, and planed, which is more than can be said for cast iron.

Many amateur builders are quite capable of casting their own lead keels, which will save considerable expense, but it is not a project to be taken lightly, and a great deal of care and thought are required to produce a good keel.

Whichever material is used, accurate dimensions are required to build the plug, which should be enlarged slightly to allow for con-traction of the metal as it cools during the casting operation. The recommended allowance is 1/8 inch per foot for both cast iron and lead. It should be explained that the lead shrinkage rate does vary somewhat from keel to keel, depending on the shape and weight involved and the technique used during the casting operation. Some builders stir the molten lead with a green branch of a hardwood tree, maintaining that this allows the lead to cool more evenly, thus avoiding excessive shrinkage. Another way of reducing shrinkage is to add more lead as the molten metal cools. The shrinkage allowance that I recommend is an average of 1/8 inch to the foot based on personal experience.

Keel plugs are usually made of wood but can also be made of P.V.C. rigid foam, which is easily cut and shaped. A simple keel shape can often be made up with sheets of plywood, but if there is any reverse curve to the sections, it will have to be built of solid material, bread and butter style, planked, or of cold-molded construction.

The lines for the plug should be marked out on a suitable material, such as plywood, that is long enough to extend a short distance past the ends of the ballast keel. Begin by drawing in a baseline and spacing the waterlines

Left: *Lead can be worked almost as well as wood.* Right: *Planking a ballast keel plug.*

and stations the extra 1/8 inch to the foot apart. Use of a patternmaker's rule, which has expanded scales on it, makes the task easier. The waterlines are lofted in the plan view, and the shape of the various sections in the body plan are determined.

Molds are made from these shapes after deducting the planking or covering thickness. They are set up on the top or bottom, which is best cut from plywood. The leading edge of the plug may have to be cut from solid material to receive the ends of the stringers, which should be closely spaced. The planking can be 1/8-inch to 1/4-inch plywood ripped into suitable widths, glued, and nailed or stapled diagonally across the stringers. Two or three skins are usually required.

It is also possible to plank the plug with strips of lumber, edge-glued and nailed directly to the molds. The material used, however, should be dry and of good quality or considerable splitting will result—any defects will be visible in the finished casting.

With the plug built, the expanded positions of the stations should be marked in so that core prints can be positioned on the plug for marking the location of keel bolt holes in the mold. Core prints make indentations into which cores can be inserted. In this case, the core print patterns should be round, because round sand cores will be used to make holes in the final casting for the keel bolts. By "coring" the mold, the builder saves the labor of drilling holes through the lead or iron later. Since an iron keel is always cast in a foundry, you should check with the foundry as to how the keel bolt hole positions should be marked.

The plug is only used to produce the shape of the ballast casting; it must be built so that it can be removed from the mold. Sometimes the rear portion of the plug has to be separate so that this part can be removed after the main part has been withdrawn. Modern keel shapes are sometimes so complex that it is very difficult to remove the plug from the cement mold. In this case, some builders prefer to make the plug from P.V.C. rigid foam, which they break out or burn out after the cement has hardened. The molten lead will burn out any foam not removed, but beware of the fumes from these plastics; many of them are highly toxic.

Some builders prefer to cast keels in a strong box above ground, but it is generally easier and safer to dig a hole and make a mold of a weak cement mixture by pouring it around the plug and allowing it to set. Before the cement is poured, it is worthwhile to consider how the lead will be lifted from the ground. This can be done by placing wire or chain slings under the mold so that a crane or derrick can be used for lifting. The plug must be securely anchored to the ground with its top level before pouring the cement mixture. Some plugs are very buoyant and require considerable weight to prevent them from floating out of the hole when the cement is poured. While the cement is being poured, plenty of agitation with long sticks will prevent voids from forming. The most troublesome area usually is immediately under the plug and close to the core prints.

Pouring molten lead into a wet or damp mold generates steam, which escapes through the liquid metal with considerable popping and splattering, which can result in serious burns. It is essential to make every effort to dry the mold thoroughly after the form is removed; this usually takes several days.

Some builders use wood dowels or steel rod for cores, but sometimes it is difficult to remove these. It is possible to use copper tubing and leave it in the lead. This tubing will have to be filled with cement or sand and tightly capped or crimped at the top to prevent the molten lead from forcing its way up the tubing. Recesses for the heads of bolts or nuts are made by attaching hardwood blocks to the tubing before the tubing is positioned in the holes left by the core prints in the bottom of the mold. The tubing should be held securely at the correct angle at the top with fireproof material, such as steel rod or wire. The tubing can extend well above the top of the lead and easily be cut off later. You may wish to cast copper tubing into the lead and use it as a heat exchanger for a small engine or for refrigeration equipment. If so, the tubing will have to be

A cement mold for a lead keel, with copper tubing used for cores. The copper tubing is securely held in place to prevent the lead from displacing it.

fastened securely to the keel bolt cores to prevent it from floating to the surface of the molten lead.

A melting pot for the lead should be set up securely a few feet from the mold; sometimes old boilers or cast iron baths are used for this. A good method of arranging a pipe drain is to use a 90-degree elbow in it so that the pipe can be raised or lowered to control the flow of molten metal. To develop added heat when melting down the lead, use some sheet iron to contain the flames around the melting pot and some forced draft from the rear of a vacuum cleaner. Much time and effort will be saved if the pot is large enough to load the entire amount of lead beforehand, so as to make a continuous pour, avoiding laminations and the need to reload the pot. Lead casting is hot and thirsty work, however, and many keel pourings turn into a bit of a "bust" as the relief of completing the job is felt by those concerned.

A good method of removing the keel from its mold is to insert two strong eyebolts with nuts into the lead while it is still molten. These eyebolts should be positioned so that the center of gravity is midway between them, which is usually a bit of guesswork, but the eyebolts allow for a wire strop to be attached to the lead so that a crane or tripod arrangement can be used to lift the lead out of the mold. These eyebolts can be unscrewed easily from the lead with a crowbar when desired.

To prevent the mold from being damaged during the first moments when the molten lead contacts the cool surface, it is good practice to place a couple of pigs of lead in the mold beforehand. They will melt down in the mold and will dissipate much of the initial heat.

Finally, do take care. There have been some horrible accidents with molten lead. The pressure due to its density is surprising, which is why I recommend digging a hole for the mold rather than constructing a box. It is not uncommon to hear of accidents that occur when the box sides have collapsed and spilled molten lead over bystanders' feet. If too hot, molten lead will run through the tiniest crack and pop and spit dangerously if there is any moisture present in the mold.

Wear protective clothing and stout boots; a swimsuit is no garment to wear at a keel pouring. A pair of goggles will keep a stray splatter of lead from hitting you in the eye, as it did to a friend of mine some years ago. Plan your operation carefully and respect the weights involved. It's easy to smash the bones in your foot with a dry pig of lead or step on a nail from a load of old lumber used to fire the pot, so do yourself a favor and be careful!

9

Cold-Molded Planking

Before starting to plank the vessel, it is best to check the entire framework for fairness. Look along the stringers to see if there are any hollows or bumps, which can sometimes be corrected at the molds with a wedge or clamp. Try bending light battens over the stringers close to bulkheads, keel, and deadwood to make sure that the framework is fair. This is important because the diagonal planking is quite thin and cannot pull the framework to shape.

Another job at this time is to cut limber holes to allow water to collect at the lowest point of the bilge. This is done by cutting a groove on the outside edge of the bulkheads where they meet the keel. It is also advisable to cut some slots across the stringers to allow drainage to the bilge. These slots are best placed at the lowest sweep of the stringer around the midship area and close to the bulkheads, where water could lie. The stringer slots can be cut with a semicircular router bit to a width of about 1/2 inch and a depth of 1/4 inch. The limber holes should be larger so that there is little chance of their becoming clogged. Although a cold-molded hull is usually completely waterproof, water can get below via anchor chain or the propeller shaft stuffing box, so it is best to assume that at some stage water will have to be pumped out of the bilge.

The material for the diagonal planking should be surfaced on four sides. This will save a lot of unnecessary work and handling. It is generally better to apply an extra skin of thin stock than to attempt to bend heavier planking to a hull with severe bends. I use 5/16-inch-thick strakes that have been milled in pairs from 1-inch stock. This thickness minimizes waste while still being thin enough to bend easily around most any shape. The average 40-foot sailboat hull will require planking about one-inch thick, so three skins of 5/16-inch thickness would be about right. Sometimes the final skin is laid fore and aft and is a little heavier so that fastenings can be countersunk below the surface and covered with wooden plugs. The width of the diagonal planking is usually decided by what is available at the sawmill; around four to six inches is normal.

The skins will cross one another at about 90 degrees, with one direction being more difficult to bend than the other. Because it is possible to use C-clamps for the first skin, it is best to begin with the most difficult diagonal—on a sailing hull, this is usually the diagonal that runs forward from the base of the keel to the sheer clamp, following the same direction as the bow overhang. On a powerboat with a lot of flare to

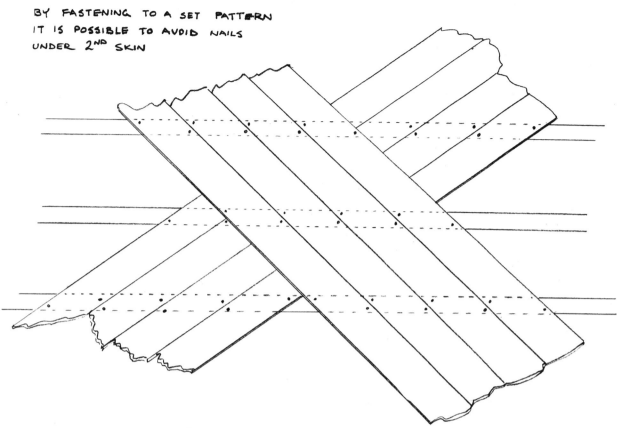

BY FASTENING TO A SET PATTERN
IT IS POSSIBLE TO AVOID NAILS
UNDER 2ND SKIN

Figure 15. *Nail pattern for fastening planking.*

the hull, it is often better to start with the other diagonal.

There is no set angle to begin with. This will depend on the length of material available, but the steeper the diagonals (and shorter), the harder the bends will be. Start by clamping a straight strake at the sheer clamp a little forward of the midsection of the hull, and allow the strake to be clamped to the stringers without any edge-setting or twisting.

The top end of the strake should be clear of the rabbet line in the deadwood; if not, move the strake ahead more. When satisfied with the lay of the strake, mark the position of the strake down each edge across the stringers and bulkheads. Some reference points from this strake can be marked on the other side of the hull—the distance ahead of a bulkhead at sheer clamp and keel, and perhaps a stringer midway between so that an identical strake can be positioned to match the one already clamped down. When selecting strakes, you will find that few are very straight, but if they are selected in pairs, it is possible to cut both at once, fitting one at a time.

The first strake is temporarily fastened into position using ordinary bright steel common nails, which are first driven through a small 1/4-inch plywood pad. This allows adequate pressure and easy removal later. When nailing the strake to the stringers, use a set pattern for your nail spacing. This will help to avoid striking the heads when the next skin is fastened. On a 4-inch strake, it is usually enough to place two nails at each stringer. Position one toward the top edge of the stringer and the other at the bottom. If this pattern is followed throughout the first skin, the nail positions will be known when fastening the next.

Cost and weight are two other important reasons for establishing a definite fastening pattern at an early stage of construction. With the current price of good-quality fastenings, such as silicon bronze and Monel nails and screws, most builders simply cannot afford to waste these items by hit-and-miss positioning. The main object should be to obtain maximum holding power for the least possible number of fastenings.

Staples can be used to fasten planking. Here an air-operated gun is being used to ensure that the staples penetrate the relatively thick planking.

On super-light construction, particularly of small yachts and multihulls, excess fastening means needless weight—unless, of course, the fastenings are to be withdrawn later. (Staple fasteners and double-headed construction nails allow this to be done relatively easily.) It must also be realized that while the function of any fastening is to hold two or more pieces of material together, each fastening robs strength from these individual pieces, because the holes force the wood fibers apart. While this strength loss is insignificant generally, it is obvious that excess fastening will destroy the basic objective of intelligent construction.

With the first strake temporarily fastened on each side of the hull, the adjoining strake can be fitted. It is advisable for the beginner to work toward the bow, as these strakes are fitted more easily.

Start by clamping the next strake so that it is almost touching the first at the sheer clamp, but angle it slightly away so that a gap of about 1/2 inch to 3/4-inch develops around the turn of the bilge. Continue placing clamps at each stringer, allowing the strake to lie flat without edge-setting; the gap will probably narrow down again toward the end of the strake. It may be necessary to shift the strake slightly, but the object is to have a similar gap at each end of the strake with the maximum around the turn of the bilge. Use a pencil compass or scriber set to the maximum gap to mark a parallel line off the edge of the first strake onto the second strake—this will show how much material has to be removed from the second strake to allow it to butt up against the first.

Remove the clamps and pick out another matching strake from the pile for the other side of the hull. Both can be tacked or clamped together while the edges are shaped with a saw or a power plane. While these two strakes are together, check the other edge to make sure they are flush with each other, then clamp them into position on the hull and temporarily fasten with nails.

Once again, mark the stringers, bulkheads, keel, and sheer clamp where the strake crosses them. As the planking continues, the stringers will be covered up, so be sure also to mark the outside of the strakes wherever there is something solid to nail into—keel, engine beds, bulkheads, etc.—so that when the next diagonal skin is fastened, you will know where to place the fastenings. Mark the positions of the stringers, etc., on the inside of the strakes, so that you will know where to apply glue. Each strake should also be marked with a number before removing it for gluing so that it can be returned to its allotted position.

A small paint roller about 2 inches wide is the cleanest way of applying the glue, which must be on both surfaces, the strakes, and the hull framing. Be sure to mark the positions of the stringers, etc., so that you will know where to apply glue. *Don't* glue the edges of the strakes. This is important, because the edges will be pulled flush when the second skin is fastened.

Nail the strakes permanently into position in the same holes left by the temporary fastenings, taking care not to nail into any limber holes. It will save problems later if you use temporary fastenings through plywood blocks to secure the ends of the strakes to the sheer clamp, as this will have to be planed off later when the deck is built.

Continue fitting and fastening strakes in the same manner until six have been fastened on each side. By alternating sides, it's possible to average out the slight error that tends to creep into the shapes due to slight differences in the pairs of strakes. As you work toward the bow,

however, it will probably be faster to fit each side separately, as the amount of material to be removed from each strake can often be anticipated and cut off before clamping into position.

Working aft from the center of the hull does get more difficult, although the procedure is much the same. As the planking advances along the rabbet line, the bend moves farther and farther toward the ends of the strakes, and it takes care to fit them without breaking them. Sometimes soaking the end of the strake in a bucket of hot water is the easiest way out, and strakes thus treated should be left temporarily fastened for a day or so until they are dry enough for gluing.

Applying the first skin to the framework.

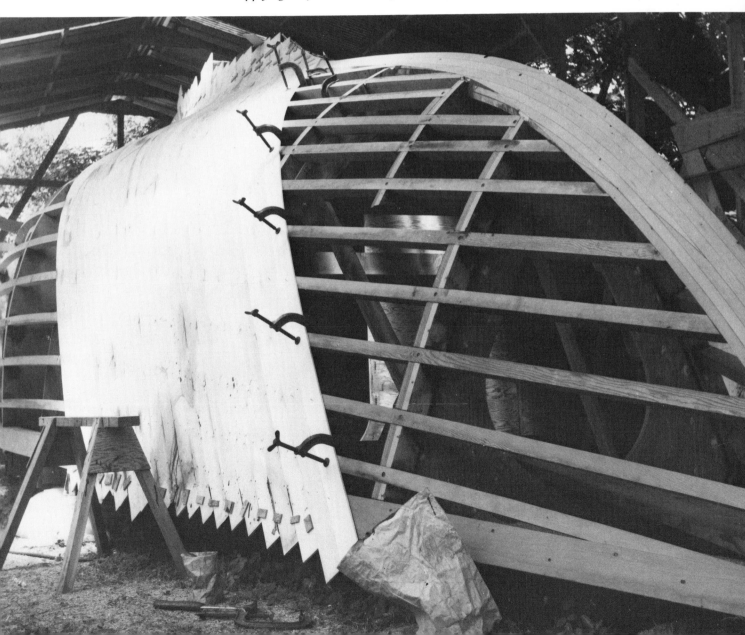

First skin planking being fit into the deadwood rabbet. Note that limber holes have been cut in the stringers at the after face of the bulkhead.

Once past the deadwood section, progress is usually straightforward all the way to the transom. Use plywood blocks and common nails to secure the strakes at the edge of the transom. By spreading the load in this manner, the splitting that would surely occur due to twist is avoided. Once the glue has cured, permanent fastenings can be substituted.

There should be little cleanup required before commencing the second diagonal skin. It is quite possible that the first skin may shrink somewhat after being fastened to the hull. Also, some of the edges of the strakes may not align with those adjacent, but these matters will be corrected when the second skin is fastened. Do not attempt to sand or plane these edges; they will be pulled flush with the second skin fastenings, which is the reason the edges were not glued.

The temporary fastenings along the sheer will have to be removed, and a quick pass with a disc sander will remove any blocks that are stuck down.

Start the second skin at about 90 degrees to the first at the center of the hull again. This time you do not have the use of C-clamps except at the sheer, so it will be necessary to hold the strakes down by nailing through a plywood block alongside the strake. This will allow it to be moved slightly until it lies flat. Although clamps cannot be used, the strakes will be considerably easier to bend and fit. Once again, be sure to mark the edges onto the first skin, so you know where to glue, and also transfer the stringer and framing positions to the outside surface of the second skin. It is easy to estimate the location of the first skin fastenings from the

Chine hulls can also be constructed in this manner. The author cold-molded this high-speed powerboat in New Zealand. (Malitte)

The second skin is laid 90 degrees to the first. The blocks shown are used to prevent the ends of the planking from splitting.

stringer positions, even though they are being covered by the new strakes.

Adopt the same pattern with the fastenings on the stringers, keeping one up and one down to avoid the nails underneath. Additional fastenings are required between the stringers to pull the two diagonals together, or else voids will result. Nails are a poor fastening for this, as there is nothing solid to fasten into. Small screws offer the best means of drawing the two skins together; they are driven in wherever needed after the strake has been glued and nailed down. When screwing two thin skins together, fastenings that are longer than the total thickness must be used or the threads will not get a good grip. This means, of course, that when the skins are pulled together, the points of the screws will be exposed inside.

A specially ground countersink drill bit should be used to drill pilot holes for the screws. A power screwdriver also speeds up the operation. When these screws are driven in, the pressure causes the glue to be forced through the edges of the first skin. The wet glue also swells these strakes slightly and glues the edges together completely flush. This is where the excel-

lence of cold-molded construction is apparent.

When gluing down these second-skin strakes, use a tray and a paint roller about the same width as the strakes for quick and neat glue spreading. This time the edges can be glued. As more of the second skin is fastened, the hull will start to sound more solid when driving in nails.

The technique of planking is largely repetitious, and because of this, it is possible to do the job considerably faster with experience.

After completion of the second skin, it is usual to sand the hull lightly to remove beads of glue or any edges that should have been pulled flush, but were not. Take care not to remove the markings for the positions of the stringers and other solid framing.

Before working on the final skin of planking, you will need to finish the transom. The hood ends of the diagonal planking must be cut off and planed to conform to the transom face. Then the last skin is fastened and glued to the diagonal or plywood face. This is frequently done with teak, which makes a fine job and also allows the name of the vessel and homeport to be carved into it.

When fastening a thin facing to a transom

114

with a good bit of curvature to it, there is less danger of splitting the ends of the strips if plywood blocks are placed on top of the strip and nails or screws are fastened through them to spread the pressure over a wider area. If the transom is to be finished clear, line up the fastenings so that they are spaced equally and not driven at random. There is nothing unsightly about plugs if they are positioned neatly.

Succeeding skins of diagonal planking can be applied in much the same manner as the second skin, except that it probably won't be necessary to use screws between the stringers, because there may be sufficient thickness to use serrated nails without having them break through on the inside.

Some builders prefer to run the final skin of planking in a fore and aft line, as with carvel construction. Whether this is done will depend on how the final skin is to be finished. If you apply one of the modern synthetic sheathing materials, like fiberglass, Dynel and polypropylene cloth, which add a tough waterproof skin to the wood, it does not matter if the last skin of planking is diagonal, provided the hull is to be painted. However, a clear varnished hull certainly looks best with the planking running in a fore and aft line, with perhaps the underwater areas sheathed.

Applying an outer fore and aft skin is not difficult, but it is considerably slower than diagonal planking and also uses a lot more material because of waste due to tapering the strakes at each end of the hull. Each strake will also have to be scarf-jointed to make it long enough, whereas the diagonal strakes are all full length. Some beautiful effects can be obtained, however, with longitudinal planking, and for those who wish to finish their hulls in this manner, the following advice is offered.

The longitudinal planking for cold-molded hulls differs from normal carvel construction in several important ways. It is probably less than half the thickness than it would be if it were carvel. It has a supported backing and is glued along its entire length, as against only the frame position in carvel, with no glue, of course. Also

the strakes are small enough in section that they can be edge-set into position, which has a big advantage. It means that a "master" pattern strake can be marked out and used to produce a series of identically shaped strakes that will give a uniform appearance to the topsides and eliminate a lot of tedious measuring and spiling.

To develop the master strake it is first necessary to decide how many strakes you will use. You must have a full-length run of planking material scarfed up to be as straight as possible. Tack this to the hull at the turn of the bilge and allow it to lie flat without any edge-setting. Position this plank on the hull so that it runs in a pleasing line toward the bow and stern. The ends should sweep toward the sheer, but not excessively.

Tack a full-length batten with its lower edge (the boat is still upside down) along the sheerline to represent the edge of the last strake. Measure from this lower edge to determine the point of greatest distance to the bilge plank. With this dimension, calculate the number of strakes it will take to fill up this space. For example, a 35-1/2-inch gap will use nine strakes just under four inches wide, or 10 strakes a shade over 3-1/2 inches. The decision on the number of strakes and width will probably depend on the material you have. Often it is better to cut two narrow strakes than one wider one.

Having decided on the number of strakes, you can now proceed to determine the shape of the master strake. First, measure the gap between the batten and the plank at various positions along the entire length. A quick and easy method is to find the places where the measurement can be divided easily by the number of strakes you have decided to use. As an example, let us suppose you decided to use 10 strakes. By moving along the hull until you find a measurement of 35 inches, you know the strakes will be 3-1/2 inches wide at this point. Mark the position on the bilge plank and the width, and then move along until the rule reads 32-1/2 inches (32-1/2" ÷ 10 = 3-1/4). This method is easier to mark out than trying to figure out uneven measurements.

From these dimensions taken at various points along the entire length of the hull, you can develop the shape of the master strake. The bilge plank can now be removed from the hull and laid out flat on sawhorses or a long bench. Stretch a line down the center of the plank from each end and mark the widths of the master strake, using the line as the center of the strake. A long batten tacked along the marks should give you a fair line so you can draw in the edges of the strake. Carefully cut out the shape and plane the edges square. A portable electric saw is an excellent tool for this and will save much time.

This master pattern could be used to mark out all the other strakes—in this instance, another 19 of them—but I use a shortcut method that eliminates this. It is still necessary, of course, to scarf up full-length stock, but with this at hand, the master pattern is tacked down to the stock with small finish nails, the heads flush with the surface. A nail will be required about every three feet to hold the pattern firmly in position.

The strakes are then cut out with a portable electric saw that has been slightly modified by securing a 1/2-inch plywood shoe to the base, with the blade projecting through a slot slightly more than the thickness of the master strake and stock combined. Now comes the sneaky part. Select two one-inch screws that have shanks slightly thicker than the slot cut in the plywood shoe. Screw them into the plywood directly in line with the slot, one ahead of the blade and one behind, and as close to the blade as possible. The screws should be well secured so that the heads are about 1/2 inch from the surface. Cut off the heads with a hacksaw so that the remaining shank is shorter than the thickness of the master pattern. With a file, round off the rough edge left by the hacksaw and your modification is complete.

If you have done the job correctly, it should be possible to place the saw on top of the master strake and the screws against the edge without the blade touching this edge. The saw can be started and run along the master strake. Taking care to maintain pressure against it, this should

Figure 16. *A Skilsaw jig for ripping planking.*

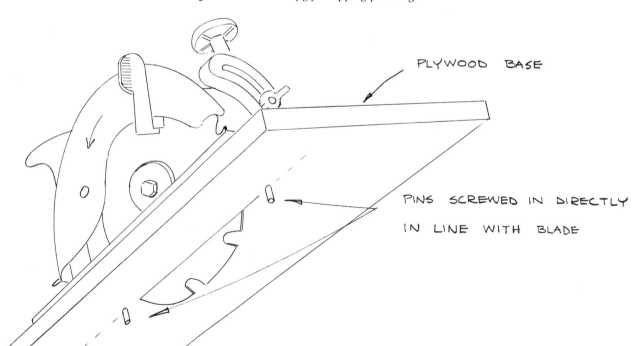

PLYWOOD BASE

PINS SCREWED IN DIRECTLY
IN LINE WITH BLADE

Applying the final skin longitudinally.

that they can be removed when the deck edge is later planed off for fitting the deck. If the topsides are to be varnished or finished clear, the fastenings should be countersunk neatly and plugged. When the planking is thinner than about 5/16 inch, it is better to counterbore for the screw fastenings and plugs after the glue has cured. This means that the screws or nails will have to be removed.

When the next strake is positioned, it may be necessary to bevel the edge slightly so as to fit the adjoining strake. With a little practice, this bevel can be anticipated and the amount can be planed off before the strake is tested in place. Use of bar or pipe clamps will allow the edges to be pulled together during the final fastening. Planing off the outer edges of the strakes to a 45-degree angle will give an attractive appearance of vee seams without the problems of caulking. This effect is often achieved later with a vee router bit, running the machine along a batten tacked to the hull.

It should be mentioned that after a few strakes have been secured, it may be necessary to true up the fastened plank edge with a rabbet plane to knock off any bumps that may have developed. Sometimes the master strake needs to be modified slightly, as even a slight error when multiplied can become noticeable.

If the shape of a boat were constant, as in a cylinder or a barrel, it would be possible to cut all the strakes the same shape. A boat hull, however, has many compound curves to it, and it is usually necessary to plank a section at a time, altering the shape of the strakes slightly to accommodate these changing curves. Hard curves will require narrower strakes, whereas the flatter areas, such as in the bottom, can be of wider stock. Once the turn of the bilge is reached, then, it will be necessary to develop another master strake.

Tack down a straight plank around the center of the reverse curve aft, and allow the plank to lie in a natural position as it runs toward the bow; a certain amount of judgment is required to decide the best position, but keep in mind that the line it takes should be symmetrical to

cut the stock just slightly wider than the master without damaging it. It is a good idea to cut the sheer strake wider than the other strakes, as some of the edge will be removed when the deck edge is planed down, thereby reducing the width. If the sheer strake wasn't wider to begin with, it would then look uneven. The remainder of the stock can be cut out without any marking. Sometimes the master can be edge-set somewhat to take advantage of some defect in the stock. Use of a sharp "planer" blade in the saw will leave clean, smooth edges suitable for gluing.

Draw equally spaced vertical lines on the diagonal planking to simulate frame positions, so that fastenings can be driven at these positions. Start planking at the sheer, using clamps to hold the strake in place. Temporary fastenings should be used along the edge of this sheer strake so the hull. In other words, the line of the planking should follow the run of the sheer and not be too high or low at either end of the boat. After tacking this strake down, divide up the gap between it and the fastened strakes to determine how many strakes you will have. The new master strake will be drawn out following the same procedures described earlier. Once again this strake is used as a pattern for the next group of planks, saving a great deal of tedious marking time.

Plugs are used to cover fastenings and are cut from the same material as the planking. Often erroneously called dowels or bungs, which have the grain running end on, plugs are cut with special cutter bits that must be used in power drills. Several types are available, and the prices differ considerably. The cheaper ones cut plugs that have to be broken out of the material with a screwdriver, but they have the advantage that the bit cuts a slight chamfer to the edge of the plug, which allows it easy entry into the hole. This type of cutter is slower if many plugs are required, but it's cheaper and offers good value. The more expensive professional cutters allow plug after plug to be cut and ejected out of the side of the bit. These do not chamfer the edge,

but if they are kept sharp, this is no problem. These bits also can cut long plugs for deeply recessed fastenings.

To glue in plugs successfully, it is essential to have the glue spread around the circumference of the plug, not on the end, which merely stops it from being driven in up to the fastening.

An easy way of gluing plugs is to use a flat plastic lid of the type used to seal cans after they are opened. These lids are made of plastic material that seems to defy most waterproof glues, including polyester and epoxy resins, for if glue is left to harden in them, it can be removed easily by bending the lid. Pour enough glue into the lid to make a puddle deep enough to dip the plug into. When removing the plug from the glue, wipe the bottom end on the edge of the lid to remove surplus glue. Drive the plug into the hole with a light hammer, keeping the grain direction in line with that of the strake. This seems a simple enough task, yet many amateurs have spoiled otherwise excellent jobs by poor plugging.

If the hull is to be sheathed with one of the modern synthetic materials, the fastening holes can be filled with a similar filler. There are several excellent products on the market of the

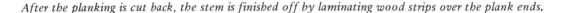

After the planking is cut back, the stem is finished off by laminating wood strips over the plank ends.

type used for filling dents in car bodies. These are usually polyester fillers, which harden quickly and are sanded easily.

The epoxy fillers are also excellent, but they usually take longer to cure and on some vertical surfaces will often sag, so it is necessary to cover the wet filler with masking tape to prevent it from draining out of the hole.

With the planking completed, there remains some preparation work before sheathing or painting can be started. The stem needs to be planed off so that some wooden strips can be glued over the end of the planking to form a rabbet and cover the end grain. This is best trimmed down with a power plane and trued up with an adjustable compass plane. The final skin must also be cut off around the transom, so it can be sanded and finished.

Another job at this stage is to cut off all the ends of the diagonal planking along the keel and clamp. The edge of the planking can be planed off along the keel line to prepare it for finishing strips or the ballast keel. The edge of the sheer,

of course, will be planed off after the boat is turned over.

If the vessel under construction is a power-boat, it is possible that some form of keel or skeg is required along the centerline. This is usually built up of glued laminations that are fastened to a flat area that has been prepared along the centerline. This flat section can be formed either by planing down the vee section along the centerline or by gluing layers of wood on each side of the centerline and then planing it down. The advantage of the latter method is that wider stock can be used in building the skeg and can later be shaped to a radius that allows sheathing material to conform to the shape more easily. The skeg laminations can be built up of two-inch material and glued and spiked into position.

Later, bolts can be drilled completely through to connect into transverse laminated floors, which should extend across the keelson to several stringers. This type of construction is also used in some of the modern fin keel sailing

Power sanding a cold-molded hull.

yachts, which have no reverse curve to the bilge.

A few designers, notably Laurent Giles & Partners of England, include a feature in their designs that is almost a trademark but that also has excellent construction practicality. This is the addition of what is termed a "thickened sheer strake," which stands proud of the remainder of the hull about 1/2 inch or so. This sheer strake increases the width of the landing for the deck, plus it is a good method of capping all the ends of the diagonal planking. Traditionally, the thick sheer strake gave increased resistance to problems of hogging in older vessels and also provided extra wood to fasten the chainplates to.

The underside of this sheer strake should have been lofted to determine its correct position. Noting from the plans the position at each station of this edge of the sheer strake in relation to the grid, measure these distances vertically to a spirit level and mark the heights on the planking. Tack a batten to the hull along these points and stand well back to see if it lies fair. The cutting out of this thick sheer strake will be similar to that explained for longitudinal planking, as it will probably take two or three strakes to make the desired width.

For sanding off the hull quickly and efficiently, the best tool for the job has to be a high-speed disc sander fitted with a flexible soft pad. This excellent machine provides the most satisfactory method of sanding down curved surfaces on wood or fiberglass systems. Industrial sandpaper is stuck to an 8-inch diameter flexible rubber disc, which is rotated at about 3,500 RPM. The pad is held flat against the surface instead of tilted, as with the normal disc sander. It's a dirty, dusty job, but use of these soft pads will save hours of work over other methods.

10

Variations of Cold-Molding

The term "cold-molding" covers a wide range of construction techniques, and the method that has been described here is only one aspect of it. In each case, however, the general principle of the system remains the same: the planking, or skins, are laminated with the use of waterproof glue in a variety of directions so as to lock up any movement and spread out the grain to form a one-piece homogeneous structure.

The method that I have described involves fastening the skins over a framework of stringers, molds, and bulkheads. This is perhaps the most basic method and one well suited to amateurs, for it does not require the time-consuming and costly construction of a male plug. Of course, there are variations in how the framework can be constructed. The one that we have used is relatively simple, using only stringers to support the skin. Sometimes the desire for super-lightweight construction has designers using a combination of framing supports. The most notable example I can think of is one of the designs from the board of Laurent Giles & Partners, who produced the super-lightweight cold-molded ketch *Blue Leopard*, using techniques developed in the aircraft industry. With an overall length of 111 feet, this vessel has a planking thickness of only 1-1/2 inches. Quite

obviously, some expert engineering went into the design of scantlings as light as this. The designers used a combination of framing by fastening the four layers of planking to bent frames, which in turn were supported by a series of longitudinal stringers. Bulkheads, transverse floors, and even the joinery were used as part of the structure of the vessel. The Giles method was also used in the smaller *Lamadine,* a 90-foot ketch, and the famous Dutch ocean racer *Stormvogel.*

Another construction method includes the use of a male plug, which consists of closely spaced, thin strakes fastened over station molds. This takes the place of the skeletal framework that we used; the skins are fastened temporarily to this form while the glue cures. A thin plastic film is placed over the plug prior to planking, preventing the glue from bonding the hull to it. The backbone timbers are laminated beforehand and temporarily fastened to the mold. A gap or slot is left in the mold to receive this structure.

The overall procedure is much the same as the one previously explained, except that the plug allows fastenings (which are usually small staples) to be placed wherever required, rather than only in stringers or bulkheads. As succeeding skins of veneer are applied, the staples

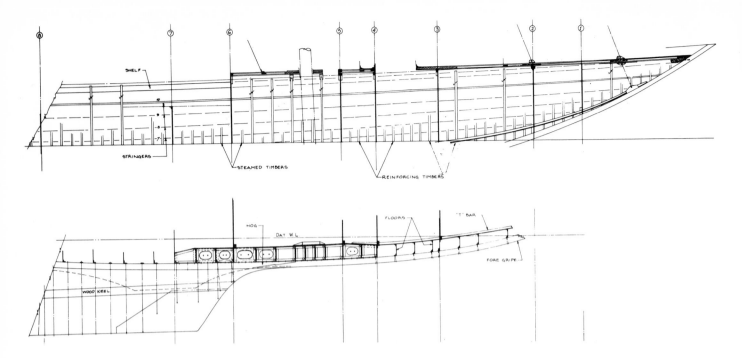

SHELF

STRINGERS

STEAMED TIMBERS

REINFORCING TIMBERS

HOG   DAT W.L   FLOORS   'T' BAR

WOOD KEEL

FORE GRIPE.

Blue Leopard has an intricate framework that makes it possible for her to have a thin skin for her size.

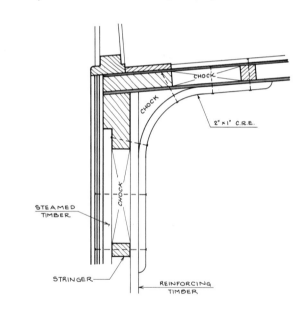

CHOCK

CHOCK

CHOCK

2" x 1" C.R.E.

STEAMED
TIMBER

STRINGER

REINFORCING
TIMBER

TYPICAL SWEPT KNEE
AT REINFORCING TIMBERS MARKED ✓

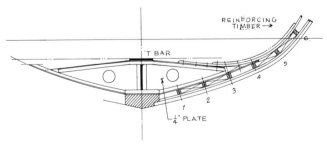

REINFORCING
TIMBER →

'T' BAR

¼" PLATE

MIDSHIP FLOOR

This dinghy was cold-molded by the author's sons using the male mold in the background.

are removed to leave a hull with a smooth exterior and interior. After the final skin has been fastened and has cured, the hull can be removed from the plug. The end result is an immensely strong one-piece hull that is very light in weight. The advantage of this method is that the plug can be built so that it can be used to build more than one hull.

My twin 16-year-old sons, James and John, used this method to build the eight-foot dinghy shown in the accompanying photo. The mold was built by setting up some solid plywood stations upside down on a grid, then planking the mold with thin longitudinal strakes, which in turn were planked over with two diagonal skins of 1/16-inch veneer. A gap was left down the middle of the mold to allow the keel and stem to be temporarily fastened into place. A curved transom of 1/8-inch mahogany plywood was bent around framing made from laminated mahogany veneer, which had been glued, shaped, and temporarily fastened to blocking attached to the aft end of the mold. The entire mold was covered with thin polyethylene sheet, leaving only the transom, keel, and stem exposed. Three skins of 1/16-inch mahogany veneer, each laid on opposing diagonals, were glued together with 3/8-inch steel staples used for temporary fastenings.

In such small craft, the planking is strong enough by itself and does not require framing material to support it. In larger craft, it is generally necessary to support the skin. This is done by installing extra stiffening, such as bent frames and bulkheads, after the shell is removed from the plug.

A method that has been gaining in popularity borrows from the two techniques discussed above. In this method, a skeletal framework, consisting of backbone timbers, clamp, bulkheads, and molds, is set up on a grid. The first skin is then strip-planked over the frame, the planks being glued edge-to-edge and fastened permanently to the bulkheads and other permanent members. Then thinner, diagonal skins are laid up over this longitudinal skin. This has the advantage that the fastenings from the diagonal skins will not project through to the inside of the hull, thus leaving a smooth interior that is easily sanded. Bent or laminated frames are installed later, wherever required. Some builders prefer to install the frames in the initial stages of construction, including them in the framework set up on the grid.

In constructing a cold-molded vessel, different builders have differing opinions as to hull thickness versus amount of framing required. Some prefer extensive framing supporting thin skins

while others prefer thick skins with minimal framing.

Among those who support the latter procedure is the well-known Gougeon Brothers firm. They advocate this approach because of the possibilities offered when epoxy is used as a sealant as well as an adhesive. Their WEST System (for Wood Epoxy Saturation Technique) involves applying three coats of WEST epoxy to the finished skin and results in a composite construction of wood and epoxy. The epoxy seals the wood, filling the voids and achieving some degree of penetration. This keeps the wood dry, which protects it from rot and preserves its strength. Not only does the epoxy keep the wood dry, it also greatly increases the strength of the wood. Its great compressive strength augments the weakness inherent in planking woods in this respect. By increasing the thickness of their hulls and taking into account the strength added to the wood by the composite construction, Gougeon Brothers have found that it is possible to build a rigid hull without much in the way of interior framing. This is clearly a case of adapting cold-molded construction to take fullest advantage of the materials being used.

I should point out that the use of epoxy as a sealant is not a new practice; some boatbuilders (including myself) had used it in this manner years before the WEST System came upon the scene. Gougeon Brothers just happened to be the first to fully appreciate (and then publicize) how epoxies might best be used for cold-molding, and how cold-molded construction might be adapted to exploit epoxy's virtues.

So far, I have discussed only techniques that employ thin veneers or strakes. It is also possible to use plywood for planking vessels that have chines. It is not recommended to plank round-bottom boats with plywood sheets because the sheets must be ripped into such narrow widths that there is a significant loss of strength.

For building chine vessels, sheets of good-quality plywood are sawn up into convenient widths and laid up, usually over longitudinal stringers. Because of the limitation of the length of plywood sheets and the expense, this method generally has been used only for smaller craft, yet the noted New Zealand designer John Spencer has built many large ocean racing vessels this way. The famous Spencer-designed racer *Infidel* has a well-deserved place in yachting history under her current name, *Ragtime*. Other super-lightweight designs of this type from John Spencer include the 73-foot *Buccaneer* and the 68-foot *New World*, both veterans of the international racing circuit. The hulls of these vessels are planked up with wide, vertically laid sheets of plywood of two or more skins fastened to stringers that are fairly closely spaced but not notched into the bulkheads and sawn frames.

By including a certain amount of curve in the topsides and bottoms of his later designs, Spencer has stressed the plywood and gained strength as well as a pleasing appearance, in contrast to the more usual slab-sided plywood hulls.

It may not matter greatly which construction method is chosen to build a wooden vessel, but you will realize from the foregoing that there are many variations on the theme. It is obvious that the development of waterproof adhesives was one of the most important advancements to benefit the wooden boatbuilder. It is indeed a great pity that yachts built to the 12-meter rule were never constructed with the cold-molded principle, as are many of the larger ocean-racing craft, which often sail thousands of miles to compete in various worldwide races.

Opposite: *A 32-foot Spencer design being planked with sheet plywood.*

11

Sheathing the Hull

Until a few years ago, sheathing a hull meant: (1) nailing sheets of copper over the entire underwater area of the hull to defeat marine growth and borers, or (2) nailing another skin of hardwood to the planking for similar reasons or for protection against abrasion by floating debris or ice.

Today, sheathing may be done for the same reasons, but the materials have changed. Modern synthetic materials are now available, and they not only serve some of the same purposes as earlier sheathing materials but they also offer additional advantages. The tough skin resulting from use of modern sheathing materials will waterproof the wood as well as protect it from attack by marine borers. A painted surface will last considerably longer on such a skin than on bare wood, which, due to its lack of stability, will break down the paint more quickly. The sheathing will also completely cover all the fastenings, leaving a tough, smooth exterior that is easily maintained.

One of the earliest of the modern sheathing materials used on wooden boats was fiberglass cloth or woven roving. Still used extensively today because of its relative cheapness, fiberglass does a remarkably good job if its limitations are realized. The chief problem with fiberglass is

that although it is very strong, the filaments of glass in the woven fabric will not stretch. When this fabric is bonded to an unstable backing, such as solid wood, which can swell and shrink due to changing moisture content, the glass material has to either hold the wood stable or give, which it cannot do, so it usually breaks at the point of maximum stress. Despite this limitation, there are many successful examples of glass-sheathed hulls. My own *Trekka,* which has circumnavigated the world twice, is sheathed with glass cloth. Several commercial catamarans built in Hawaii have been operated daily for over 20 years and they have glass-sheathed plywood hulls. There are countless other vessels that have been sheathed with the material.

To be successful, glass sheathing must be applied to a stable surface, such as plywood or cold-molded construction, where the underlying laminates of material (called cross banding in plywood) serve to lock up the movement. It is certainly no use using fiberglass as a sheathing material for a conventionally planked carvel-constructed hull. There is simply too much movement in the structure of a vessel with caulked seams.

For exterior surfaces such as plywood decks and cabin tops, fiberglass is still a good choice,

The completed hull ready for sheathing.

but better materials have been developed in recent years for the sheathing of immersed boat hulls. This also applies to the resins, which are used as adhesives to bond the cloth to the wood. Early fiberglass sheathing was done with polyester resins, which, though improved, still lack the flexibility and adhesion that the modern epoxy resins offer. Even a good job of sheathing with polyester and glass can still be torn off wood by hand if some material is left to grab hold of. There is no way you can do this with the modern epoxy systems.

Fortunately the average vessel does not travel at speeds that are likely to duplicate this treatment, but when a vessel is sheathed, most owners would like to think that the material will be bonded to the hull permanently. In this respect, it is hard to beat two materials that are currently available and have been used for several years: Dynel and polypropylene cloth, known as Vectra. Both of these synthetic fabrics have the advantage that they will stretch to

accommodate considerable expansion in wooden construction due to moisture absorption.

I first used Dynel in New Zealand during the mid 1960s. An American product, it was marketed by an Auckland chemical company that specialized in marine surfaces and finishes. Dynel and epoxy resin were used extensively in that country to sheathe many wooden cold-molded vessels. I saw a large cruising yacht that had been rescued from the clutches of a coral reef in Honolulu that had Dynel sheathing over carvel planking. After many hours of pounding by the surf and coral, a remarkably small amount of damage resulted, being confined mainly to one bilge and the bottom of the keel. As a professional builder and surveyor, though not involved with this case, I was most interested to note that even where the wood had been ground away, the material did not separate from the surrounding area. The vessel was insured and the owner requested that the hull be completely resheathed after repairs had been made. Although the repairs were easy, the removal of the Dynel was almost impossible, even with power sanders and blowtorches. The new areas were resheathed and damaged sections patched, but the original material was left as it was, still in excellent condition.

Dynel is a loosely woven, soft scrim material rather like cheesecloth. It does not cause a skin rash the way fiberglass materials do, and it can be formed around concave and convex surfaces considerably more easily than fiberglass. Because of its rather fuzzy texture, it does tend to need more resin to bond it to a surface than fiberglass cloth does. A squeegee similar to those used by window cleaners helps to level much of the fuzz, but often the hull needs to be sanded before another coat of resin is applied.

Polypropylene cloth, made of the same synthetic as the lightweight buoyant rope, has come on the scene more recently and has the same advantages as Dynel. In appearance it looks very similar to fiberglass cloth but is much lighter in weight. Due to its smooth surface, it requires less resin than Dynel, but it cannot quite match the easy way Dynel can be molded around awkward angles and shapes.

Another material that has been in use for sheathing boat hulls for several years is named Cascover. It is a nylon cloth sheathing developed in England by Lester Lovell of Southampton. Although a good product, it was considered by the makers to be too difficult for the average builder to apply, and the only way to have a vessel sheathed was to use the services of Lester Lovell's staff. Naturally, this had its drawbacks, and for this reason was unlikely to find much favor with builders situated in the U.S.A., New Zealand, or Australia, for instance. Instead of an epoxy-type resin being used as an adhesive for the material, a waterproof resin similar to resorcinol waterproof glue (also manufactured by Lester Lovell) was used.

With the variety of synthetic materials now available that have similar qualities to the ones mentioned above, many builders are using such unlikely materials as fly screen and shade mesh, which, after all, is a good deal more durable than the well-tried canvas used for decades. The adhesives used to bond these materials are often latex rubber-based products, and many builders have had excellent results with these cheaper systems. One in particular is named Arabol, which is a trade name for a synthetic resin that is much the same as the milky white P.V.A. glues. Arabol is manufactured by the Borden Chemical Company and is used mainly as an adhesive in applying lagging to engine exhaust lines. The adhesive will stick most fabrics to wood extremely well and is generally used with canvas, burlap, or some of the other synthetic fabrics readily available.

The techniques used in applying sheathing materials are usually quite straightforward, requiring little more than a commonsense approach. Some builders prefer to apply a coat of resin to seal the wood surface before the cloth is applied, and this is wise on some woven materials when it may be difficult to work the adhesive through from the outside. Generally, however, the material is of an open weave that is stretched over the prepared surface and held in position with staples while the resin is applied with a paint roller and evenly distributed with a squeegee. Most materials seem to come in widths of 36 to 60 inches so joints are necessary. A simple lap joint of about 1/2 inch is plenty, as it will be ground down with a sander to provide a smooth surface.

Because the topsides of the vessel will be subject to more scrutiny than the underwater areas, it is normal to sheathe this section of the hull from one end to the other without any joints. The adjacent panel of cloth will usually be lapped over the edge, but this will be below the waterline. Some builders prefer to lay the cloth vertically on the hull and sheathe the hull in sections. This reduces the area to more manageable sizes but generates quite a bit of extra work sanding the laps.

After mixing most polyester and epoxy resins, it is essential to spread them as quickly as possible before they change from a liquid to a solid state. Most of these resins are heat sensitive and will cure considerably faster if left in the

Wetting out Dynel cloth with resin and roller. Note that white pigment has been added to the resin.

mixing pot. For this reason it pays to mix small batches and transfer the mixed resin to a wide paint-roller tray. Use a short-hair roller to apply the resin, working from one end of the vessel to the other. If the cloth is stretched out well, few puckers will develop. Those that do may have to be eliminated by cutting the material and allowing the surplus cloth to form a lapjoint. Persistent bubbles or air pockets in the cloth due to creases are often removed easily when the resin is allowed to thicken. It will then be possible to stick down the cloth by applying pressure with a squeegee or brush.

Sometimes it is necessary to stop the sheathing at a particular line; for example, some builders will sheathe only the underwater areas and require the cloth to end at a definite point, perhaps the waterline or the top of the boot top. It is difficult to keep the selvage edge of the material straight enough to accomplish this, and a better approach is to mark in the waterline on the hull or apply masking tape to show the position, allowing the cloth to be wetted down a little over the line. When the resin has gelled considerably, the cloth can be cut along the desired line with a sharp knife or a one-edge

razor blade, which will slice through the cloth without pulling it out of position. Then the waste material can be removed and surplus resin carefully scraped from the wood.

During the sheathing operation, brushes and rollers may have to be stored overnight or for a period of a few days. With the current price of solvents, it is often cheaper to throw away such items rather than clean them. However, to avoid too much waste of solvent, it is possible to protect brushes and rollers by scraping as much resin out of them as possible before washing and placing them in a metal can with enough acetone or lacquer thinners to cover them. Use polyethylene sheet or a plastic garbage bag to cover the top of the can and secure it firmly with masking tape to prevent loss of the solvent through evaporation. Some plastic handles cannot stand this treatment and wooden handles on rollers and brushes are preferred for this reason.

Only natural-bristle brushes can be used for resin, and good sources of supplies for resins and related equipment are some of the surfboard shops, which stock fiberglass materials and most of the gear required for sheathing. The young men who build surfboards are real artists and

The sheathed hull ready to be turned over.

have developed the knack of working with fiberglass and rigid foam to a very high degree. They generally use fiberglass cloth, as they are sheathing over a stable core of foam, but the techniques used are not unlike those for skinning a boat hull.

Usually one or two more coats of resin are required to fill the weave of the material after it has been applied to the hull. It is often worthwhile adding a colored pigment to these coats, this making a good base for the paint and allowing the surface to be seen more clearly during finish sanding. With a clear resin, you tend to look through the surface to the wood below.

When you do final sanding will depend on the time required to cure the resin so that it will not clog the sanding paper—often a period of several days. During this period you will be able to make preparations for turning the hull over, which is described in the next chapter. The waterline or boot top can also be marked at this time; for several years I have used a method you may wish to consider.

A wooden hull usually has the waterline scribed into the planking with a saw kerf, or knife. This is undesirable when the hull is sheathed, for such a groove is easily filled in by the sheathing material. My solution is to reverse the method by applying a slight ridge along the hull. I stick a thin string made from nylon or some other synthetic line along the marked waterline. The job is done very neatly if masking tape is used on each side of the waterline for the full length of the hull. The gap between the strips of tape is about 1/4 inch. The string is held in position with short pieces of masking tape at intervals of several inches. When all is positioned correctly, resin is applied to the string between the strips of tape with a small brush. When the resin has cured and bonded the string to the hull, the short strips of tape can be removed so that the entire length of line can be recoated. This method will give you a permanent line to paint to, yet it is easily sanded off if the waterline has to be raised.

A good method of marking the waterline is to set up a horizontal straightedge at each end of the hull in the same plane as the waterline. Stretch a light line between these points and mark the hull where the string touches. The length of the straightedges can be considerably reduced if another one is set up midway between the end ones. This allows the line to be moved to conform with the hull shape. With enough reference points marked on the hull, a batten can be used to connect them into a true line. Before removing the straightedges, sight along them to check if the line is correct.

Many well-maintained vessels are spoiled by a carelessly painted waterline—it can ruin the whole appearance of the boat.

130

12

Turning Over the Hull

For the average builder, one of the main deterrents to building a hull upside down is the thought of turning over the finished shell for completion. Like most seemingly impossible tasks, it can be done relatively simply if the operation is planned for.

As with most jobs, the local circumstances of the situation will determine the best approach to the task. For the average amateur or small-time professional builder, the expense of hiring heavy equipment to perform this task will gobble up any savings or profits that could have gone into equipment or one's pockets. Sometimes this is unavoidable, of course, but so many vessels have been built upside down in recent years that it is no longer considered a difficult operation.

Large hulls have been quickly turned over inside webbed slings supported by one or perhaps two cranes, and some heavy equipment companies have become experts at it. When building close to the water, it may be possible simply to jack the hull over so that it falls into the water right way up. Some hulls are even flooded and rolled over with the use of a towboat. But none of these methods are much use to a builder who is not conveniently situated near the water or accommodating cranes.

I have turned over several hulls using the hoop method, which has the advantage that it can be done by one person at minimal expense.

Basically the procedure is to make up two half-hoops (usually out of wood) and fasten them to one side of the hull. The other side of the boat is raised with hydraulic car jacks and the hull is carefully eased over onto the hoops and then to an upright position. Some slight modifications are needed, however, if the hull is to be turned over inside a building or shed, as the hull will creep over the ground as it is being turned. This can be remedied by placing two planks, with pipe rollers between, underneath the hoops. The planks are "locked" together during the jacking process with clamps or bolts. When much of the weight has been transferred from the jacks to the hoops, it is possible to jack the top plank sideways to correct the position.

The shape of the hoops should allow the hull to be raised to the halfway position quickly, and some experimentation of shapes with cardboard and scissors on the plan of the body sections will show the best compromise. There is no set distance between the hoops, the position usually being decided by attaching them to the tops of bulkheads or mold cross spalls.

The attachment to the wooden keel is also important, and this can be done by bolting

Above: *Cranes must sometimes be used to turn over large hulls. (Sea Spray)*

Below: *The beginning stages of the operation: Jacks placed under the hull on the side opposite the hoops lift the hull onto its side.*

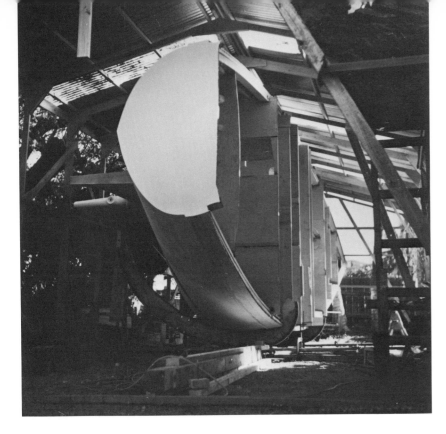

After the hull reaches the half-way point, jacks are placed under the hoops to let the hull down easily.

transverse framing or angle irons, across the keel and securing the ends of the hoops to them. Some form of diagonal bracing between the hoops is desirable to prevent them from collapsing, but generally it is the size of the hull rather than the weight that is the chief problem.

A simple way to build the hoops is to saw out the required shape from wide, one-inch boards, bread and butter style, taking care to stagger the joints, gluing and nailing several laminations together. Fairly rough general-purpose lumber can be used for this and can then be capped with some thin laminations of plywood or planking material, which will form a tire and hold everything together.

A couple of hydraulic car jacks placed under the opposite clamp (which should be protected from the rams with a flat steel plate) will supply the power to lift the hull. If the building shed is strong enough, it may be possible to get some support from a chain hoist hung from the roof, but this is seldom possible. As the hull is jacked higher, it is necessary to block underneath it so that the jacks can be reset.

The blocking can become unstable and dangerous however. For this reason I prefer to set up a couple of double-plank shores to a ceiling joist or rafter so that long wooden

bearers can be positioned inside them and under the boat and held with metal pins or bolts. The advantage of this system is that it becomes stronger as the boat is lifted higher. If two positions are set up, it is possible to place the jacks on the bearers and avoid much blocking; also, the jacks are set at the correct angle during the greater part of the lift.

As the hull approaches the 90-degree position, the weight on the jacks will noticeably decrease, and some blocking or shores should be arranged on the hoop side to prevent a "runaway" situation, which could be embarrassing. Eventually the position is reached where the center of gravity passes through the 90-degree position and the hull will want to turn the rest of the way without any further assistance.

From this point on, the jacks are used in the opposite manner, as brakes, by fully extending the rams and bleeding off the pressure to lower the hull carefully. Because of the much greater radius of the hoops, from here on the hull will have to be skidded over on the rollers quite often. It will save problems if the plank immediately under each hoop is long enough to accept the full length of the hoop tire, because it is often difficult to lift the lower side of the tilted hull to reposition the planks when weight

As the hull is lowered, the plank on which the hoops rest is shunted aside on the rollers to position the hull.

is on them. It is essential that the jacks be placed on these planks during the lowering of the hull, or it may be skidded on the rollers accidentally.

A significant advantage of the hoop method is that work can be suspended during the operation for rest or meals without tying up expensive equipment or having to rush the job. This kind of pressure often causes accidents to occur.

After the hull has been turned over, it should be set up level and chocked securely so that its position will not change during the completion of the interior finishing.

Part II

Finishing the Hull

Introduction

In Part I of this book we covered the procedures required to produce a high-quality cold-molded wooden hull, one of the best and most economical ways to build a one-off design. It must be realized, however, that many people today have neither the time nor the facilities to tackle the complete building of a hull and may compromise by either purchasing a stock hull or installing a new interior in an existing boat. Naturally this approach will enormously reduce the amount of time required to complete the project. However, before one decides upon such an alternate route, there are many points to consider. Most of us involved in boating have definite opinions on the subject, with the result that the novice is frequently confused by conflicting advice。

I, for one, am convinced that it is easier to install joinerwork in a wooden hull than in a hull constructed of fiberglass, steel, aluminum, or cement. The great advantage of building your own wooden hull is this: Much of the joinerwork can be installed relatively early on in the construction, with the result that the joinerwork is so much a part of a vessel's structure that it is not likely to come adrift at sea. And since most of a vessel's interior is wood, it is easy to join this interior to a wooden hull, using such methods as gluing, nailing, screwing, bolting, or cutting joints.

Such a wide range of techniques cannot be taken advantage of easily, if at all, by those who choose to finish off hulls constructed of materials other than wood. In finishing a fiberglass hull, the builder is often forced to fasten much of his joinerwork to bulkheads. This can be an unsatisfactory solution, as the bulkheads in fiberglass boats are often bonded in place by a tape and resin combination that has been known to fail in a seaway. Although there exist other methods of attaching bulkheads and joinerwork in fiberglass boats, such methods are costly and difficult. In the case of steel or aluminum hulls, the bulkheads are usually bolted to webbed frames. While this provides a strong attachment for fastening joinerwork, it is not as easy nor as versatile a technique as those available to builders who finish off wooden hulls.

Installing a new interior in an existing boat is often a worthwhile project. However, work of this nature usually takes far longer than originally anticipated because of certain problems often encountered. Quite often the vessel is already afloat, which involves getting all the materials to the job and attempting to work with them in a restricted space with limited equipment. In addition, the success of the project is at the mercy of the climate, as anyone who has completed such an undertaking knows. The size of the boat is also a consideration; generally renovations are more suited to a large vessel where it is possible to live on the job and set up a proper work area. However, marina and harbor authorities often view such projects sourly, and boat owners are forced to moor their vessels in out-of-the-way locations, which usually have poor facilities and add little to one's enthusiasm for the project.

In any event, whatever method you choose will require careful work and thought.

In the following pages you will find advice on how to finish off your vessel, as well as sprinklings of philosophy that have been handed down to me from some of those fine craftsmen (now sadly reduced in number) who have shared their knowledge and skills with me over the years.

13

Building the Deck and Deckhouse

Usually the first job after turning over the hull is to remove much of the temporary framing and molds inside the boat. To aid in this and the remaining construction, a ramp should be set up alongside the boat so that it is easy to walk up with tools and materials rather than make endless climbs up and down ladders. With a ramp setup, one man can carry sheets of plywood and other heavy items aboard. It is safer and quicker than ladders, and the time spent setting it up will soon be recouped.

While the interior of the hull is clear, it's a good time to sand the inside of the planking. If there are screw points protruding through the inside skin, the fastest way of cutting them down is with a disc sander using an industrial flexible metal grinding disc.

Screw points can also be cut off with end cutters or "dykes" where the stringers are too close together to get a disc sander in. Sometimes it's worthwhile to reduce the diameter of the disc, which will make considerably more space accessible for sanding.

If the height of the building shed will allow it, the next job might be the fitting of the ballast keel and remaining deadwood. Often, however, the builder faces the problem of little headroom and will be reluctant to raise the boat higher

while so much work remains to be done on the deck and interior. The keel can usually be fitted toward the end of the construction, and since this seems to be normal practice among other builders, I am leaving the description of this task to Chapter 15.

The selection of the next job will depend on the preferences of the builder. He can choose either to start fitting out the interior or to complete the deck. For several reasons, I generally prefer to get the deck on a vessel fairly soon after turning over the hull. The deck ties the whole structure together and will prevent any deflection in the hull shape. It also provides an excellent work space on which to set up sawhorses or even machine tools and lumber; this will help to cut down on the endless climbing in and out of the boat for materials. Another reason is that certain interior work needs to be done after the deck is in place, and by this stage the bulkheads are already installed.

DECK CONSTRUCTION

Before the deck is constructed, the sheer and clamp should be shaped to accept it. A portable electric plane is the best tool for this, and a useful aid during this operation is a wooden pattern with a hollow cut in it to the same shape as the tops of the beams. A straight, flat batten laid along the sheer and a good eye are the best tools for deciding if the sheer is fair. Stand well back and look along the sheer from several points to make sure this line is correct. An unfair line at the sheer will stand out like a sore thumb and ruin the appearance of a good hull.

The deck beams are usually laminated over a form rather than cut from larger material, which not only is more wasteful but also results in a weaker beam. They may be clamped together individually or glued from wide boards and ripped into suitable widths after the glue is cured. It is at this stage that the benefit of locating the top inboard edge of the clamp at the correct height earlier can be appreciated: the ends of the beams can now be checked into the clamp until the beams' top edges are level with the top inside edge of the clamp. The ends of the beams are often dovetailed into the clamp, but if the deck is to be covered with plywood, a straight notched joint is quite adequate and may also save a little time.

Because of their curvature, the correct length of deck beams is sometimes difficult for a novice to mark out accurately. The location of each beam should be marked on the top edge of the clamp. Then, to determine the proper length, turn the beam upside down so that its true forward face is in line with the forward position marked on the clamp. After allowing extra length (usually about an inch at each end) for the amount that will be checked into the clamp, mark the determined length on the beam. The vertical angle at which the deck beam will sit must then be marked on the clamp's inner face. By turning the beam rightside up and positioning it over the marks on the top edge of the clamp, this angle can be determined with a bevel gauge butted against the side of the beam and clamp.

The angle of the inside face of the clamp changes due to variations in hull shape, and this must be taken into account when cutting the beams to length. For example, where there is

A half-beam notched into a hatch carlin.

tumblehome, there will be a greater distance between the bottom edges of the two clamps than between the top edges. Because of this, you must be sure to cut the beam ends vertically, or else the beam will either be too long or too short, depending on whether there is flare or tumblehome. When installing the deck beams, always fit the longest ones first. Then if any should be cut too short, they can still be used elsewhere.

Half-beams in way of hatches are best fitted full width, and the positions of the short carlins should be marked in on the other beams at the same time. These matching half-beams will need to be half-checked into the carlins, which are often the same thickness or "molded" depth. (The terms "molded" and "sided" are often used to identify the measurements of structural members when the words "thickness" and "width" are confusing. The sided measurement of a transverse beam is the width of it in a fore and aft direction.)

Some builders go to great pains to keep the sides of the deck beams vertical, which technically they should be. In practice, however,

Fitting foam for a sandwich deck.

they are usually fitted in the "natural," which means that you set them square off the sheer, as described above, so that the top edges of the beams do not need beveling to receive the decking. The method used will depend largely on the size of the beams.

All the beams should be fitted "dry" so that their relative heights can be checked before final fastening. If the top edge of the clamp has already been properly beveled to fit the underside of the deck, and the deck beams have been fit in flush with the top of the clamp, this is sometimes an adequate check. However, it is not always possible to have the top edge of the clamp beveled off to the correct height before the beams are finally fastened. When this is the case, it is good to make a check with a stiff batten clamped over the top edges of the beams close to the clamp. The batten will ensure that the top edges of the beams are in a fair line so that the decking can be laid on top of them.

If the deck is to have a deckhouse, it will be necessary to fit carlins along the inboard edges of the side decks. I usually notch these into the tops of bulkheads or cross spalls and spring them to the required shape, checking the ends into slightly wider beams than the others. The half-beams between clamp and carlin are then fitted.

The correct height of the carlin can be checked by placing a full-width beam across the boat so that the underside at each end rests on the inboard edge of the clamp. Where beams are required to fit on each side of a bulkhead, it is possible to angle-cut a wide beam so as to allow it both to be glued to the bulkhead top and also to be set in the "natural" position.

If a clear deckhead is required, the undersides of the beams can be sheeted with plywood and the spaces between the beams filled with rigid foam. This not only insulates the deck but makes a sandwich construction that is very strong for its weight.

This type of deck requires careful planning and foresight, as all fittings and hardware mounted to the deck need to be blocked solidly and not fastened through the foam. Fittings such as stanchions, winches, decklights, and backstay levers all require solid blocking, and much work can be saved if it is installed at this time.

Sandwich decks can also be built by using sprung deck beams without laminations. One or more "strongbacks" are temporarily fastened longitudinally, and the beams are bent over them and secured at each end to the clamps. It is best to secure the ply to the underside of the beams first. This not only allows the rigid foam to be installed more easily, but it also allows the outboard edge of the ply to be well secured where it butts up against the clamp. A fascia piece, usually of teak or some other hardwood, is glued and fastened to the clamp immediately below the deckhead ply so that fastenings can be driven into the fascia piece from above, thereby fastening clamp and plywood together.

Sandwich decks are usually designed around the thickness of the available foam, with the usual sizes being in 1/2-inch increments, such as 1 inch, 1-1/2 inches, and 2 inches. Rigid foam is also manufactured in specific widths, and often it is possible to space deck beams so as to take advantage of these widths. The deck ply, being well supported with the foam, can be considerably thinner than with beams decked on top only. For ultimate strength, the lower and top plywood should be of a similar thickness, but in practice the top plywood is usually thicker, as it has to support sudden shocks of human feet or other mistreatment, such as dropped anchors.

Sometimes a thin deck is required because of headroom restrictions below decks. Thin decks can be made up of molded plywood laid over temporary longitudinal framing. It is usually best to start with a relatively thick first skin and fasten thinner plywood to it with nails, screws, or staples, so that fastenings will not penetrate all the way through. This type of construction allows considerable scope in the design of deck superstructures, which are often molded in place and are part of the deck itself.

In such cases, it is often necessary to scarf

wide panels of plywood together to make lengths longer than the standard eight feet. Scarf joints are easily cut with an electric portable plane; such a sharp cutter will reduce the amount of hand planing needed to make accurate joints, which again should be cut to the 1:12 ratio previously mentioned. A 3/4-inch sheet of plywood requires a scarf nine inches long, and if one is scarfing a full four-foot width, it is sometimes difficult to obtain sufficient even pressure over the entire scarf area. Many builders simply nail through battens on each side of the plywood. However, if the material is to be finished clear, as with hardwood facings, this is a somewhat crude answer to the problem of clamping.

A simple gluing press can be made up similar to the one in the accompanying illustration. It allows several sheets to be glued at the same time. When assembling, it is necessary either to drive two or three small nails through the glued joint or staple them together to prevent the scarf from moving when pressure is applied. If more than one sheet is to be glued at the same time, each sheet of plywood should be separated in the scarf area by polyethylene film or waxed paper.

Scarf joints should also be used when building a super-light deck on narrow beams. Usually if a

Figure 17. *A simple gluing press for scarfing plywood.*

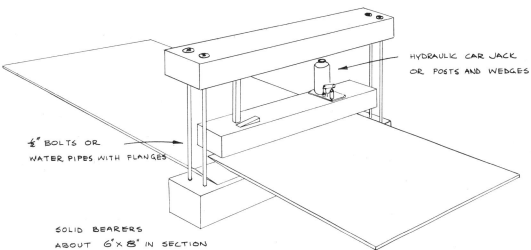

HYDRAULIC CAR JACK OR POSTS AND WEDGES

¾" BOLTS OR WATER PIPES WITH FLANGES

SOLID BEARERS ABOUT 6" X 8" IN SECTION

3/4-inch plywood covering is specified, it is assumed by the designer that two layers of 3/8 inch each will be used, with all joints staggered. When gluing large sheets of plywood together, it is essential to spread the glue quickly and get the top plywood down into position before the glue evaporates or sets. Some preparation work is wise and makes the task easier.

In the same way that screws are used to pull together the layers of plywood in a molded plywood deck, they are used here to pull the plywood together between deck beams. The top ply should be pre-drilled for these fastenings when it is dry-fitted. A grid of squares is marked on the exposed surface, and holes are drilled at each corner of the square, with one in the center. Satisfactory sizes for the squares are 7-3/4 inches for 3/8-inch plywood and 9-3/8 inches for 1/2-inch ply. These measurements work out well for fastening down a full 8-foot x 4-foot plywood sheet.

I use this system of fastening wherever the plywood thickness needs to be increased and large areas are covered, such as on coamings, superstructure, and molded coach roofs. Instead of leaving the exposed edge of the plywood showing at the sheer, which then requires more care when sheathing, it is better to cut back into the plywood 1/2 inch or so and glue in a long strip or fillet. After the ply has been glued down, the necessary material is easily removed with a portable saw or router. This makes a neat finish to the deck edge, and the top joint is often covered with a bulwark or toe rail.

BULWARKS

It is good to install the bulwark at this stage of construction because the interior of the hull is still bare and it is easy to get at the underside of the clamp. The bulwark also prevents tools that are on deck from falling over the side and gives the builder a feeling of security on a deck that may be several feet off the ground.

Some builders go to great pains to tie the planking to the keel, yet the deck edge joint to the hull often receives little consideration even though it is, in fact, one of the most important connections in the entire structure of a vessel. The addition of a bulwark can add considerable strength to the hull/deck joint when the deck is sandwiched between this member and the clamp, with bolts or long fastenings to tie it down. This results in a very strong, waterproof joint, in contrast with some techniques of mass production.

Generally, I prefer to make the bulwark part of the hull by gluing it bread-and-butter style to the plywood deck. Besides adding strength, a bulwark built by the bread-and-butter method has another advantage; it can be sprung to shape around temporary blocks or stanchions fastened to the deck. It often looks better if the bulwark is set back from the deck edge about 1/2 inch and either faded into the topside planking at each end of the hull or fitted with "knight-heads." It is necessary to plane off the underside of the first lamination so that the outside of the bulwark assumes the same angle as the topside planking. Further laminations can easily be added to make up the required height. Some designers specify a tapered section to the bulwark showing a greater thickness at the base than at the top. This again can often be done with the method described above, but using material that is beveled before it is fastened.

Occasionally the curve in the sheer is too great to bend material around, as with flared bows in a power vessel, and the laminations will have to be either sawn out of the solid or made up from thinner material and bent. Another solution to the problem is to bend several light planks around the temporary blocks and glue-laminate them together vertically.

The underside of the bulwark is marked and fitted by scribing an equal distance off the deck on both sides and removing the bent lamination so that the excess material may be removed.

Another way of making bulkheads is to build up the topsides higher than is necessary and drop the deck down inside the hull the required amount. Although this may appear to be an easy solution, it isn't, for this joint does not readily

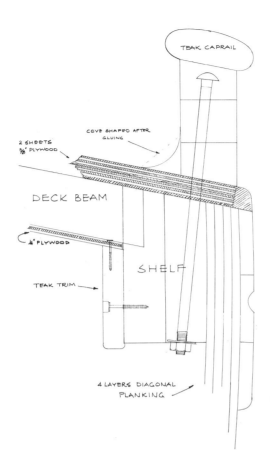

TEAK CAPRAIL

COVE SHAPED AFTER
GLUING

2 SHEETS
⅜" PLYWOOD

DECK BEAM

¼" PLYWOOD

SHELF

TEAK TRIM

4 LAYERS DIAGONAL
PLANKING

Left: Figure 18. *Deck-edge joint.*
Below: *Bread and butter bulwark*
laminations being bent around
temporary stanchions.

give the same watertightness and strength that the bread-and-butter method gives. Because the planking extends above the top of the clamp, it is difficult to plane the top of the clamp to fit the deck ply. Also, since the bulwark is not on top of the deck ply, there is nothing to help hold down the deck except for perhaps a small fillet. Glass tape can be used for this, but the strains from the flexing and working of the hull may eventually break this down. Needless to say, this method of construction requires careful work if you are to minimize its drawbacks.

The insides of the bulwarks on a yacht are often awkward to maintain. The area is difficult to sand and paint, as dirt and water naturally collect there. Sometimes I fit a curved fillet to the inboard face of the bulwarks where it meets the deck, which eliminates the hard corner and leaves a shape that is considerably easier to work on. This also adds support to the bulwark and allows deck sheathing to be extended to the underside of the rail cap. The top edge of the bulwark needs to be shaped to receive a rail cap. The vertical heights of the bulwark can be obtained at each station from the table of offsets or the lofting, but it will require a good eye for the final shaping to ensure that the line is fair.

The bulwark top also needs to be beveled so that the rail cap can be fastened at the correct angle. There are differing opinions as to the angle of the rail cap, with some designers maintaining that it should be level, parallel to the waterline in the body view. I prefer to shape the rails with plenty of curve to the top, but I plane the bulwark top parallel to the deck camber. This also allows drainage for trapped water.

After the top edge of the bulwark has been planed off, fasten some long bolts completely through at regular intervals so that nuts and washers can be located under the clamp. The rail cap is usually left until the end of the finishing work, as it is likely to be damaged if installed too early in the construction. For a description of finishing the bulwarks with the addition of a rail cap, see Chapter 17.

While the bulwark is left without a rail cap, it is advisable to protect the top edge of the bulwark by nailing down a batten in the area that is used for getting into the boat. If this is not done, materials dragged across the bulwark will soon split away the edges.

High bulwarks are seldom seen on modern yachts. They need sufficient support and usually must receive this with some form of wood or metal stanchion. The old method of securing wooden stanchions through the deck to the topside planking is not recommended. This practice contributes to troublesome leaks and subsequent dry rot, so it is better to design metal stanchions or brackets for this job.

The size and type of scuppers are usually shown on the construction drawings, but sometimes this is left to the discretion of the builder. The sizes of scuppers are largely determined by the height of the bulwarks. Obviously, low toe rails or bulwarks require little more than a drainage hole to keep water from standing on deck. In practice it is usually best to cut out more than one scupper hole, as it is often difficult to determine from the plans exactly where the lowest part of the deck is located. Also, many vessels are trimmed quite differently from what the designer intended, due to crew weight or the considerable amount of gear carried by many ocean cruising yachts. Usually a scupper placed at the lowest part of the sheer, with one ahead and one astern of it, will suffice, but with many designs, due to the deck camber, the lowest part of the sheer is not necessarily the correct location for a scupper.

Scuppers cut through the bulwark or toe rail may have to be cut after those members have been installed, due to the problem of obtaining a fair line when bending them into position after a substantial part of them has been cut away. The slots or holes that form the scuppers through the toe rail or bulwark should be marked accurately so that bolts or other fastenings are not positioned in the way.

From a seagoing point of view, scuppers cut through the bulwark are excellent, because they allow water to drain off the decks quickly and easily. But for vessels that are tied up in marinas and admired more than used, these scuppers have their disadvantages. They certainly drain off surplus rainwater, but with the dust and grime from populated areas, this rainwater can also wash a surprising amount of dirt down the topsides, leaving unsightly stains on otherwise clean paintwork. In this situation, the inboard scupper has much to recommend it—it locates a drain inboard of the bulwark and is connected by piping to a through-hull fitting near the waterline.

Often a combination of these two types is used: the holes through the bulwarks are located 1/2 inch or so above the deck line so that they will be effective when the boat is heeled, while the inboard type will handle rainwater when the vessel is moored.

The construction of the deckhouse is often done at this point if the vessel is large enough that interior joinerwork can be completed without inconvenience. It is generally advantageous to make and install tanks for fuel and water before the deckhouse is built, even if they could still be maneuvered through hatches and openings. Some thought should also be given to installing the engine at this point, for that, too, requires a good amount of space. These procedures will be covered later in Chapter 15.

FLOOR TIMBERS AND FLOORING

Before beginning construction of the deckhouse, it is often best to install the floors and floorboards so that work can be done more easily inside the vessel. The latter need not be installed permanently; at this point all that is needed is a platform on which to work and set tools.

Floor timbers are often required to help carry the loads imposed on the wood keel by the outside ballast via the keel bolts. If this is the case, they should be installed before the ballast keel is fitted; then the floors can be placed over the keel bolt positions, so that when the keel is installed, the keel bolts will come up through the floors, thus distributing the keel bolt loads.

Laminated floor timbers on the racing sloop Improbable. *Note centerline stiffening. (Mallitte)*

On a cold-molded hull with longitudinal stringers, these floor timbers are often laminated into position across the keel and secured to the stringers in much the same way that a leaf spring is made up. Besides being strong, they are easily installed.

Laminations of 3/8-inch-thick by 3- or 4-inch-wide material can be nailed across the centerline, allowing the ends to extend past several stringers. Sometimes a fitted block similar to those used in the construction of knees is required on top of the keel; this allows the laminations to conform to a natural bend. As the thickness of the floor is built up, the ends of the laminations can be shortened so that a tapering section is built into them. Fastenings driven into the

A laminated floor timber with keel bolts coming up through it.

stringers should be laid out in a definite pattern so that succeeding nails are not driven into heads underneath.

Once the first lamination has been fastened, it is possible to use C-clamps to hold the laminations together during the gluing. Some pressure is generally required in the center, and this can often be achieved with a well-placed shore or post wedged from the deckhead.

The floorboards are usually supported by transverse bearers, but if plywood is used, the bearers can be run in a longitudinal direction if desired. The addition of bearers to the faces of the bulkheads will allow bunk or seat fronts to be fitted in the future.

Three-quarter-inch plywood makes good temporary floorboards and has the advantage that when the interior has been finished, it can be covered by carpeting, tiles, or strips of hardwood and used for permanent floorboards.

DECKHOUSE CONSTRUCTION

The attachment of deckhouses to decks is done in a variety of ways. Sometimes poor practice in this respect is responsible for much unnecessary work later, when attempts are made to correct the problems.

The old-fashioned attachment of trunk cabins to the inside of carlins is not recommended. This was one of the major sources of leaks in many of the older offshore cruising yachts. It is not even very strong construction, as any blow from a big sea will tend to drive the house side inward, away from the carlin. I am strongly in favor of having a sill glued and well fastened to the plywood immediately above the carlin. A house that is fastened outside this sill has much better support than the other method. The ends of the sills should be half-lapped and glued.

In recent years a great deal more angle has been given to what used to be vertical house sides. This generally looks better, is less susceptible to damage, and allows more working space on deck. If you wish to build a deckhouse of this type, it is a simple matter to accommodate the sills to the angled sides by planing the outer side of the sills to the required shape.

Few materials offer better strength for house and coach roof structures than plywood. It is stable, lightweight, strong, and easily worked. Owners who prefer varnished house sides can either purchase hardwood, veneered, waterproof plywood or face the material with a thin layer of hardwood. Again, teak is one of the most suitable choices for this.

The construction of deckhouses in plywood is relatively simple. High sides may require permanent or temporary "studs" to make a framing for the plywood to be bent across and fastened to. It is often necessary to combine sheets of plywood to make up the desired thickness, and this can be done in much the same manner as with the deck. Usually a thinner outer layer is fastened to a thicker one, so that fastenings will not penetrate to the inside. To allow the plywood to lie in a fair line, it is best to cut out all windows and openings after any glue-laminating has been done. This is not difficult with a portable jigsaw, and rabbets for window glazing can be cut with a router, using a stop fence clamped to the base of the machine.

For adequate landing of the roof, it is necessary to fasten a clamp or beam shelf along the top edge of the house sides. This clamp performs much the same function as the clamp at the

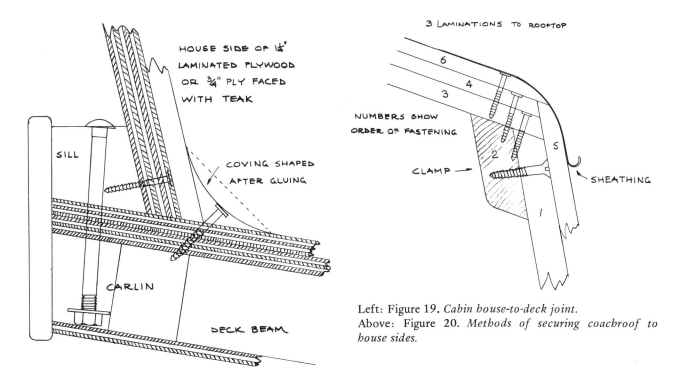

HOUSE SIDE OF 1¼"
LAMINATED PLYWOOD
OR ¾" PLY FACED
WITH TEAK

COVING SHAPED
AFTER GLUING

SILL

CARLIN

DECK BEAM

3 LAMINATIONS TO ROOFTOP

6
4
3

NUMBERS SHOW
ORDER OF FASTENING

CLAMP →

2

5

SHEATHING

1

Left: Figure 19. *Cabin house-to-deck joint.*
Above: Figure 20. *Methods of securing coachroof to house sides.*

Below: *Curved deckhouse sides built of several layers of 1/4-inch plywood.*

deck edge; it can be used to secure the ends of the roof beams and the covering, which is usually plywood.

It is good practice to give additional support to the house with the use of tie bolts or rods. These are often easily installed by allowing them to lie against the inside of the house side and securing them by drilling holes through the deck sill and carlin at the bottom and the roof and clamp at the top. Wood studs or knees can be grooved in back and fitted over the rods, which thus can be completely hidden and will not require long holes to be bored for installation.

Another aid in securing the house sides to the deck adequately is a coved fillet glued to the corner where the outside of the house sides meets the deck. This can be done by preparing triangular material and gluing it down into position, then shaping it to a concave section with a round plane after the glue has cured. The addition of sheathing material, which can be used over the complete deck and house, will make an absolutely waterproof job.

A coach roof can be built of stressed plywood without beams, using the same method described for a deck. Usually the forward and aft ends of the house are cut to the desired curvature or crown, and longitudinal strongbacks are set up between these ends to allow the plywood to be bent over them and secured to the house sides and clamps. It is often necessary to fasten temporarily a stout batten to the outside of the house side so that C-clamps can be used to pull the plywood down at the edges. If the house side is to be built up of more than one sheet of ply, it is possible to form a lock joint as described for the transom construction by fastening the outer sheet of the house side over the edge of the roof, and in turn fastening the last sheet of the roof plywood over the edge of the house side. These corners should be well radiused, which will allow sheathing to lie evenly.

Laminated hanging knees are sometimes required to stiffen the deckhouse or deck wherever the spans between bulkheads are too great. These knees are made at the workbench by bending thin laminations over a simple sawn form. The procedure has already been described in regard to building transom knees in Chapter 7, and the only change you might consider is to groove the back edge of the knee so that it can be fitted over a tie bolt.

It is advisable to make some provision for future removal of any large equipment and fittings, such as engine and tanks, through deckhouse and hatch openings. Sometimes this can be accomplished by installing a loose cockpit bottom or roof panel that is bolted into position but sealed with glass or Dynel cloth tape. Many owners have cursed builders for omitting this consideration. Engines break down, tanks develop leaks, and often their removal from the vessel costs far more than the repair bill.

14

Metal Fittings

The average vessel requires a great number of metal fittings that have a multitude of uses. Much of this hardware is bolted on deck (cleats, fairleads, stanchions, stemhead fittings, etc.), and an excellent selection of these items is available through marine hardware dealers. Frequently, however, the builder is unable to find a fitting that will suit the particular job, and his only solution is to either change the boat to fit a standard piece of equipment or make up a special fitting to suit the boat. This latter choice is a common enough approach to the job, and this special hardware is produced either by having it fabricated—that is, cut out of plate or sheet and welded—or having it cast in a foundry.

It is good there is a choice, for it is often difficult to decide which method of producing fittings is best. The neighborhood sheet-metal worker or welder who will fabricate fittings usually requires accurate drawings, measurements, and angles, which are often difficult to produce on paper. Nevertheless, this is usually the best method if making one- or two-off fittings.

Sometimes, however, the other approach is best, and this will mean making a wooden pattern of the fitting so that a foundry can cast it in the required metal. The advantage of this latter method is that the fitting is first made up in wood and can often be set in place to check that everything fits.

PATTERNMAKING

Patternmaking is the skill required to make these accurate wooden patterns, and like many other trades, it is not learned quickly or in one chapter of a book. The average boatbuilder, however, is quite capable of making simple patterns if he understands a few basic rules. (The making of a pattern or "plug" to allow the casting of a ballast keel is part of the patternmaker's job—this was described in Chapter 8.)

The patterns required for casting small bronze fittings are often easily made, but they require some knowledge of the principles involved in foundry work. Wooden patterns are made so that they can be placed in a special sand that is molded around them. The removal of a pattern leaves the impression of the shape and forms a mold into which molten metal can be poured to produce the desired shape.

The art of foundry work dates back centuries before the early Greeks and Romans, who produced many beautiful bronze artifacts, the pride of collectors and museums. Most of that bronze work was made by a process known as the "lost-wax method." A pattern—or statue, if you like—was first made in wax, then placed in molding sand and baked in an oven to melt the wax. The resulting cavity was the exact shape of the pattern and formed the mold into which molten metal could be poured.

Modern foundries still employ this technique for mass-producing cast fittings by having a mold that will cast an endless supply of wax patterns. The average boatbuilder, however, will not be too interested in this method, as a wood pattern generally is more suitable, but this method is used sometimes to produce a bulb-shaped keel, which would otherwise require a complicated pattern to allow its removal from the mold. Instead of using wax, a pattern can be made up from rigid foam plastic and placed in the ground so that cement can be formed around it. When the cement is cured, the foam is broken or burned out, leaving the desired mold shape for the molten metal This process is also known as investment casting.

The main requirement of a wood pattern, aside from producing the correct shape, is that it be made in such a manner that it can be withdrawn from the molding sand. Simple patterns may not require much consideration in this respect, provided the pattern is made with "draw" allowed. Draw is the taper required of a pattern to enable it to be lifted from the sand without damaging the impression or mold.

To illustrate this point, let us assume we wish to cast a shape similar to a small pyramid. A one-piece pattern would do the job, because the shape has excellent draw if turned upside down and placed in the sand; a sphere or ball, however, would be a different proposition, and to cast this shape it would be necessary to use a molding box, sometimes called a flask. This would allow the ball to be placed on the bottom half of a box (the drag) filled with molding sand and positioned so that the sand was level around its greatest width, which would be an imaginary equator.

The molder, the man doing this work, then sprinkles the sand around the pattern with powdered chalk and places the top of the molding box (the cope) into position. This box has no top or bottom, so it just forms a wall around the pattern. The box is filled with sand and packed hard against the pattern, a process known as "ramming." Due to the powdered chalk, the top of the molding box can be removed from the bottom and will separate perfectly at the joint. The ball is removed from the sand and the top is replaced, which leaves a complete round mold in the sand. The molder would make provision for a channel through the sand for the molten metal to flow into the mold, but that essentially is the process.

On many shapes it is not always easy to determine where the equator is, so it is better for the molder if he has a "split" pattern. This means making a pattern that would separate into two halves at the equator. Now all he has to do is ram up the sand level to the joint, sprinkle the chalk, add the top half of the pattern, the molding box, and sand, and when the box is lifted off, one half of the pattern can be removed from each half of the mold. One of the benefits of this arrangement is that one pattern can be used for many castings.

Simple patterns, such as cleats and fairleads, are usually split vertically along the centerline so that they can be placed on their sides in the molding box.

The two sides of the pattern have to fit together in exactly the right position, and one side is fitted with two or more tapered dowels, which engage with holes on the other side. These dowels have to be fitted carefully, as they must align the two sides accurately yet allow for easy separation.

The professional patternmaker has many skills and aids not available to the amateur, who will probably approach the job in a different manner. One of the most trying tasks for the beginner is to position these tapered dowels accurately after he has made the two sides of the pattern. The professional uses special metal dowels that are easily aligned by first fitting the

Above: *Simple wooden patterns for foundry work.* Below: *Bronze castings for mast step and keel bolts.*

female section and leaving it slightly raised, so that when the other side of the pattern is positioned and pressure is applied, the print from the female section will show the exact place to fasten in the male dowel. The amateur patternmaker will often do the job the other way around, first fitting the dowels to the material before any cutting out or shaping is done.

Close-grained, stable woods are the best choice for good pattern work. White pine and Honduras mahogany are generally used when available, but other woods such as Douglas fir and good-quality plywood are good alternatives.

Most marine fittings are cast in a bronze alloy that is largely composed of copper and tin but often contains a small proportion of other metals, such as manganese, aluminum and iron.

153

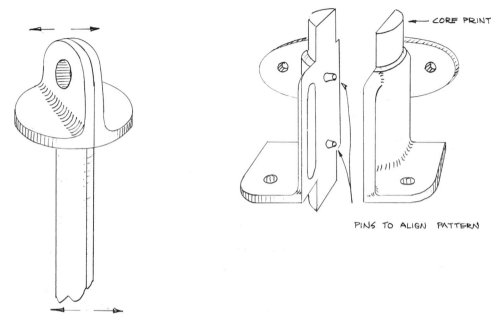

SPLIT PATTERN FOR EYEBOLT
CHAINPLATES

CORE PRINT

PINS TO ALIGN PATTERN

Figure 21. *Split patterns for metal fittings.*

Some of these alloys are extremely strong and are excellent for resisting marine corrosion. Underwater metal fittings, such as rudder pintles and gudgeons, seacocks and skin fittings, propellers, etc., are usually cast in bronze; all these items have to be made from a master pattern.

It is best to check with the foundry beforehand to know the shrinkage to allow for your patterns; usually the patterns are made 3/16 inch to the foot larger for bronze castings.

In the description of making the keel plug, I mentioned "coring" the pattern so that holes could be formed in the lead for the keel bolts. The technique of coring the pattern becomes much more important when the castings are to be made in bronze, as large holes will not be easy to drill later. Another consideration is that castings are usually priced by their weight, so the more unwanted material you eliminate, the better. Don't make your pattern too complicated, or the foundry will have to charge for the molder's extra time in making the mold.

Let us suppose you wish to make a simple

cored pattern to cast several bronze stanchion bases. These fittings will require a body or casing to support the stanchions, plus a base that will allow it to be bolted down. The body requires a one-inch hole through it for the stanchion pipe, and as shown in Figure 21 this is provided for by fastening a core print at each end of the pattern where the hole is required. When this pattern is placed in the molding sand, the shape of this print will also be duplicated in the mold. However, when the pattern is removed from the mold, the molder will insert a special sand core into the print that will fill the mold space where the hole will be, allowing the molten metal to flow around it to form the casing. The prints are used, therefore, to support the core in the mold while the top of the mold box is removed.

Foundries usually have standard cores that they can make to the required length, but sometimes the shape through the casting may not be a round hole but a square or rectangular one. It may be necessary to make a "core box," which will enable the molder to pack sand into the box, allowing him to make a core to fit the print left in the mold. Simple core boxes are usually little more than a piece of plywood with a wood enclosure nailed to it to form the outline shape of the print. The molder will "ram up" the sand in the shape, then turn it over to empty it out in the form of the core.

The molders have many clever techniques that allow patterns of the most impossible shape to be removed from the sand. One of these is the use of carbon dioxide gas, which, when blown through the sand, will set it up almost as firm as cement, making the mold and any cores quite firm. It will also assist the withdrawal of the pattern if some draw or taper is made in the print when a core is to be installed in a vertical position in the mold.

Wood patterns need to be protected from splitting or warping out of shape, and for this reason are usually painted. Orange paint is regarded as the standard color to identify the parts of a pattern, and the cores are indicated by painting them black. The insides of core boxes are sometimes painted red to show what they represent. Instead of using orange paint, some patternmakers finish their patterns by varnishing them with a quick-drying shellac, which can be sanded very smooth and leaves a clean impression in the sand.

By knowing some of the principles involved in foundry work, the boatbuilder can often make one pattern that will reproduce countless castings, so he should keep all patterns for possible future use.

With some of the alloys available today, castings offer an excellent solution to the problem of the many special fittings required for marine use. It is unfortunate, therefore, that many of the smaller foundries that specialized in this type of work have been put out of business by antipollution laws. The last foundry in Honolulu closed for this reason while I was building the *Sunrise*, which meant that patterns for the castings had to be sent overseas—in this particular case, to Auckland, New Zealand. It pays, therefore, to think well ahead if delays in supplies are to be avoided.

CHOICE OF UNDERWATER METALS

Most boatowners eventually come up against a phenomenon usually referred to as "electrolysis," which is a general term used to describe the chemical decomposition of metals by the action of an electrical current passing through a liquid electrolyte, such as battery acid or seawater. The word "electrolysis" is also used to describe "galvanic corrosion," which is the destruction or deterioration of underwater metal fittings by an induced electrical current flowing between metals of different potential or degree of "nobility."

The effect of electrical currents on underwater metal fittings of all types of craft can be serious. Cases where propellers and rudders have completely disintegrated are common around repair yards, and damage of this nature is a matter of considerable concern to boat owners. To combat this effect, certain practices have been adopted, sometimes with beneficial results. Among these is the use of sacrificial zinc blocks attached to the submerged metal fittings, thereby encouraging the less "noble" zinc to corrode instead.

Another practice, which is possibly the most desirable approach, is to have all submerged metal fittings of the same material so that they have a similar "galvanic value" to minimize any current flow between them.

Some authorities believe the answer is bonding, where all the underwater fittings on the inside of the hull are electrically connected by copper wire or strap, thereby making a common ground.

Unfortunately, there is no clear remedy for the situation, as electrical current does not always conform to manmade rules, and each boat requires different treatment to effect a cure.

The main cause of electrolysis is undoubtedly the presence of live electrical current on the vessel. This may be from a leak in the D.C. battery system due to a short, or perhaps the incorrect connection of some item of equipment. The more serious cases are usually caused by similar leaks, but they are from the higher-powered A.C. shore current, which may be leaking through the boat to "earth"—in this case, the water the vessel is floating in. Use of nonmarine battery chargers plugged into shore power is another frequent cause of severe electrical leaks, and the remedy is to trace them and correct the situation.

The galvanic corrosion caused by dissimilar metals is a problem that may be the fault of a boatbuilder who used materials of widely differing values on the galvanic scale, and it is often difficult to tell the difference between this type of corrosion and the electrical leak kind. Sometimes it is a combination of both.

Following is what is known as the Galvanic Series, which starts with most passive or most noble metals, which are cathodic.

TABLE OF GALVANIC VALUE IN SEA WATER

1. Platinum   [Most noble, cathodic end]
2. Gold
3. Silver
4. 316 Stainless Steel (passive)
5. 304 Stainless Steel (passive)
6. Monel K (66% nickel, 29% copper, 3% aluminum)
7. Monel (67% nickel, 30% copper)
8. Nickel (passive)
9. Silver Solder
10. Titanium
11. Copper Nickel alloys
12. Silicon Bronze (87% copper, 4% silicon, 1% tin, 4% zinc, 2% iron, 1% aluminum, 1% manganese)
13. Aluminum Bronze (82% copper, 4% iron, 9% aluminum, 4% nickel, 1% manganese)
14. Gunmetal (90% copper, 10% tin)
15. Manganese Bronze (88% copper, 10% tin, 2% manganese)
16. Copper
17. Red Brass (85% copper, 15% zinc)
18. Yellow Brass (65% copper, 35% zinc)
19. Naval Brass, Muntz Metal (60-64% copper, remainder zinc)
20. Nickel (active)
21. Tin
22. Lead
23. Lead Tin Solders
24. 316 Stainless Steel (active)
25. 304 Stainless Steel (active)
26. Cast Iron
27. Wrought Iron
28. Mild Steel
29. Cadmium
30. Aluminum
31. Zinc
32. Magnesium   [Least noble, anodic end]

Most of the metals used for underwater boat fittings—such as the propeller, the shaft, and cast fittings—are usually some type of bronze alloy. On commercial wooden craft, which are sometimes galvanized-fastened, there is often a mixture of metals: steel for rudders, bronze propellers, perhaps stainless steel shafts.

The use of zinc blocks may or may not add to the confusion. Although it is impossible to connect zincs to all the hull fastenings, these often manage to survive in craft that were built over 50 years ago. In some cases this is true even of wrought iron fastenings, which the above table shows to be far down the scale of resistance to corrosion.

Some years ago I had the opportunity to salvage some specimens from the hull of the first European ship to be wrecked in New Zealand waters. This wooden vessel, an 800-ton East Indiaman named *Endeavor* (not Captain Cook's ship), struck a rock and was abandoned in Dusky Sound in 1790. Many of her fastenings were iron and the planking was copper-sheathed, nailed to the teak planking with hand-forged sheathing nails. I found the copper to be well corroded, but the sheathing nails had lasted perfectly and seemed to be of a different metal, since they were harder and more yellow in color.

There are similar examples of bronze cannon being perfectly preserved after lying alongside heaps of iron cannonballs on the ocean floor for hundreds of years. Many bronze artifacts of great antiquity have been preserved in seawater for thousands of years without the benefit of modern technology. Why should these metals survive for such long periods of time when the underwater fittings on relatively new craft show extensive corrosion after quite short periods of time? Could it be that we create the corrosion problems by attaching zincs to the underwater fittings? Many people with years of maintenance experience in boatyards feel strongly that this practice often has a detrimental effect and will accelerate corrosion problems, in effect creating a battery.

There are many complex factors to take into account, and it is often impossible to figure out why fittings of the same metal from the same pour, when bolted alongside each other on a vessel's bottom, will show completely different rates of corrosion.

The quality of the seawater definitely has considerable bearing on the life of marine fittings: the more polluted the water, the higher the rate of decay. The higher temperature of tropical seas also has a large effect in advancing corrosion. The rate of flow past these fittings is another important factor, as it will affect the presence or absence of oxygen in the water. Stainless steels, in particular, require good aeration in the surrounding water if they are to remain "passive." If you put a stainless steel shaft or fitting in polluted water where there is little oxygen, the steel may become "active," with only slightly better resistance to corrosion than ordinary steel.

The resistance of stainless steels to corrosion is believed to be due to a thin hydrous oxide film on the surface of the metal. Under stagnant conditions, oxygen is depleted rapidly and the "film" cannot repair itself, so the steel becomes active and starts to pit. ("All types of stainless steel are likely to pit or groove in seawater and the stainless alloys as a group are far more susceptible to localized attack than the copper-based and nickel-based alloys." Page 557, Vol. 1, *American Society for Metals Handbook.*)

Another possible reason for deterioration of underwater fittings is the area relationship between the dissimilar metals. Bolts and fastenings

may be attacked by the larger mass of a less noble metal—for example, when large metal fittings such as ballast keels and shaft struts are installed. Generally, the safest way for a boatbuilder to avoid electrolysis problems is to choose metals that are of the same type and have a similar galvanic value. The greater the difference in value, the more chance of corrosion. The practice of attaching sacrificial zincs does not always have a beneficial effect, and there are enough boat owners around to support that statement.

The choice of stainless steel for underwater fastenings such as bolts and propeller shafts is at best a bit of a gamble, and it is usually more reliable to select a bronze shaft to match a bronze propeller.

It must also be realized that bronzes are copper alloys, and many of them contain large percentages of zinc, as in the case of the yellow metals and some manganese bronzes. These alloys may corrode in a process called "dezincification," where the particles of zinc waste away, leaving a porous weak mass on the metal surface that eventually penetrates the alloy and causes it to fail. For maximum longevity, it is best to choose alloys without zinc; the boatbuilder who makes his own patterns and has them cast in a foundry will have a better chance of obtaining suitable underwater fittings than if he buys standard fittings of unknown alloy content from a marine hardware store.

One of the best choices for resistance to corrosion is gunmetal, also known as phosphor bronze. It is not as strong as some of the other bronzes, so the size of the fittings may have to be increased somewhat. Another excellent, though more expensive, alloy is nickel aluminum bronze, also known as propeller bronze. This metal, with a tensile strength of about 90,000 p.s.i. and a yield of 38,000 p.s.i., is very hard and strong.

Determining the difference between galvanic corrosion or electrolysis due to stray electrical current is often impossible unless all electricity is disconnected and the vessel is removed to unaffected waters. Electrical leaks can often be traced and measured with sophisticated meters, and this is frequently done around modern boat harbors, where stray A.C. current may be leaking from nearby craft and docks.

Sometimes the only solution is to remove your craft to a more favorable location, but as with many things in this life, the advantages are often outweighed by the disadvantages, and one must expect a certain amount of aging with any material. The corrosive environment of sun and salt water will attack even the best-built craft, and it is but a delaying battle we fight against inevitable odds at the finish.

15

Installation Work

A large part of the boatbuilder's time is spent installing all types of articles and hardware. Some of it is simple, some quite complicated, but it all has to be accommodated in a limited space so that it will function in harmony, becoming a complete entity. It requires a certain amount of dexterity to bring all this to a successful conclusion, for the commencement of many jobs is dependent upon the completion of others. For instance, much of the joinerwork cannot be started until after the installation of the tankage. In turn, the plumbing system cannot be completed until after much of the joinerwork (especially around the head and galley) has been completed. The same goes for the engine and its allied control systems. Thus much of the installation work detailed in this chapter and the finishing of the interior and exterior of the vessel must go hand-in-hand in a parallel sort of fashion.

It is often difficult to decide during the construction of a new vessel the best time to commence much of this installation work. Even an experienced builder will have problems in solving the correct job sequence for the completion of the overall project. The problem is that, unless a design is being built over and over again, as in a stock production setup, each vessel will probably require an individual approach due to the differences in design. For this reason there is no definite pattern for the installation work to follow, which may seem somewhat haphazard to the uninitiated.

I have mentioned the engine and tanks, but there are many smaller installation jobs that, though not as large, are equally important and will have to be considered before the joinerwork is done. The rudder and steering gear, particularly in a center-cockpit sailing vessel, is best installed before cabinetwork is fastened, or the builder will regret the space limitations or lack of strong attachment points for this vital equipment. Obviously experience of previous jobs will greatly assist in this respect, and about the best advice I can give to a novice is to install as much of the large, awkward components as possible early on, making sure that it is possible to remove them from the boat at some future date if necessary.

ENGINE INSTALLATION

Few jobs open up more options than the installation of a vessel's engine, which, in the course of a vessel's construction, involves all kinds of tasks—the aligning of the engine and propeller shaft, the plumbing for fuel, cooling, and exhaust systems, the installation of the electrics and battery storage, and the connection of all the instruments that monitor the overall performance of the entire system. It is usually best to begin installing the engine before the deck or deckhouse is completed, as it is easiest to get the major components into the hull at this point.

Engine Bed

The engine bed installation is often the most difficult task, which is why I recommend doing this while the vessel was still upside down. An engine foundation needs to be solid and stable, particularly in small craft with one- and two-cylinder engines, which often have vibration problems.

Engine beds are sometimes made up in steel using angle bar or "I" beams that are welded together and bolted to bulkheads or other substantial framing. Generally, however, the engine beds are well-supported wooden members that are tied into bulkheads, often passing completely through them and providing support over an extensive area of the bilge. This is particularly true of power vessels, in which the engine is the only form of propulsion and thus is considerably larger and heavier. In fact, the engine bearers in powercraft are often designed and built as part of the overall structure of the hull, as opposed to sailing vessels, where in many cases they are almost afterthoughts.

Rather than use heavy, unstable balks of lumber for the beds, which may cause misalignment of the engine when subjected to warm engine-room temperatures, I prefer to laminate these members of smaller kiln-dried material, forming a core that is sandwiched between plywood cheeks glued on each side and well nailed.

This construction makes an excellent engine foundation and can be handled in other ways as well. The beds can be reduced in weight by making up a framed core and leaving areas hollow or filled with rigid foam, some of the

sides can even be cut out in lightweight applications.

It is usually best to make the beds smaller than the finished height, so that extra material can be added after they are permanently fastened.

Boring the Shaft Hole

The next stage of the operation is boring the hole for the propeller stern tube. This job is much easier if you already have a pilot hole through the centerline for a boring bar and have made provision for keeping bolts clear of the hole. A pilot hole is necessary so that a fine string or wire can be set up midway between the beds and at the correct angle the shaft will assume. You may not have been able to bore this hole until now, as would be the case in a twin-engine power vessel with shafts out through the planking on each side of the centerline. The hole is drilled from the inside of the hull after its correct location has been established by using the string stretched tight from a known position forward (usually shown on the designer's plans at a precise position on a bulkhead) and parallel to the engine beds.

After this hole is drilled, the string must pass through it and be set up outside the hull in the exact shaft line position. This outside termination of the string should be well back from the hole exit and solidly positioned, because the string will have to be reset when bearings for the boring bar are lined up.

The boring bar is used to enlarge the pilot hole to the finished size and correct alignment. The bar is easily made up from a length of old shafting that has had one end turned down to fit into the chuck of a slow-speed power drill. The cutter is located about midway along the bar; it projects from a hole drilled through the bar and is held with a setscrew. This cutter is normally a small tool steel bit of the type used for machine work, but suitable cutters can be made up from good-quality steel items such as an old Allen wrench or a round- or square-section file. The length of the bar depends on

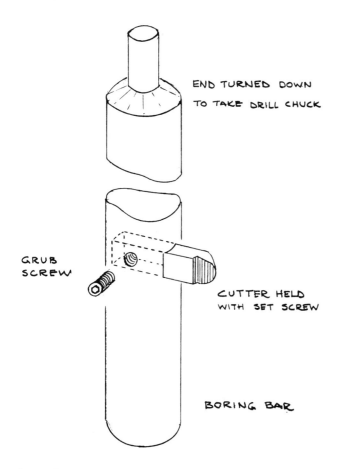

Left: Figure 22. *Boring bar.* Above: *Boring the propeller shaft hole.*

how far apart its supporting bearings are set. These bearings usually consist of holes drilled through hardwood boards that are clamped or bolted into place.

Setting up these bearings is the next job. To do this, the string will have to be released and passed through them. There is usually one bearing situated at each end of the hole, with one more positioned at the end of the bar to prevent it from whipping excessively when turning. It also helps to drill a 1/4-inch hole through the top of the bearing so that oil can be fed to the revolving bar to prevent the bearing from deteriorating too much. Bearings inside the hull usually are fairly easy to secure by clamping some form of cross braces to the engine beds. Outside bearings are usually a problem, as there is little to support them. It may be necessary to wedge a firm strut from the ground to the horn timber or to the planking for the bearing support. The bearings are aligned by using a pair of inside calipers and measuring from the taut

string to the sides of the bearing, which also needs its face set at 90 degrees to the shaft line.

The string is now removed and the bar inserted into the bearings. The cutter should be set to make a minimum cut. The drill needs to be a slow-speed model and the boring bar should be fed gently into the hole, as the bit only cuts on one side of the bar. Several passes will be necessary to open the hole out to the finished size. Use the calipers to check the measurements.

Usually the hole is bored out to accept a stern tube, which has a bearing threaded in it on the outboard end. The inboard end has a stuffing box and sometimes a bearing also. A power vessel with twin engines will require a slightly different procedure, as the outboard ends of the shafts will probably be supported by bearings located in metal struts. These struts should be made up before the pilot hole is enlarged to the finished size for the shaft log.

The struts can be fabricated or cast in bronze,

161

which will require a pattern. These patterns are tricky, as the boss is in a different plane from the angle of the strut feet. This type of pattern is normally split in a transverse direction, with the feet split also to allow removal from the molding sand. The shaft logs also are often cast in bronze, but they require patterns of a less demanding nature. The finished struts are bolted to the hull using the string to align them; to do this, shims usually are necessary under the feet.

The boring of the planking for the shaft log installation can be done from the inside of the hull, using a temporary bearing in the struts to support the bar.

Drip Pans

It is generally advisable to provide for a substantial drip pan under the engine. Stainless steel is excellent, but good pans can be made of 1/4-inch plywood sheathed with fiberglass. If the job is to be done by a local sheet-metal worker, it will be necessary to make up templates of the sections required. A drain at the low part of the tray should allow for a pump that can be connected to remove any oil or water. Sometimes the installation of the pan is such that it leaves no clearance between it and the stringers for a hose to be run down to the bilge at the side of the drip pan. In such cases an entry should be made through the bottom of the drip pan. If a large section of tubing or sheet metal that will surround the hose is welded to the bottom, it will allow the hose to be withdrawn if required.

Hoisting the Engine

The difference in weight between a 500-pound engine and an engine weighing half a ton matters little, for almost any engine will require careful handling if it is to be hoisted 10 or 15 feet into the hull. There are various ways of doing this, and quite obviously much depends upon the circumstances.

For a professional builder it is usually not worth the time to rig a makeshift arrangement, and if he has no facility for lifting this kind of weight, he may hire a portable crane. Occasionally the engine is so large and heavy that it is not placed on its bed until the vessel is in the water. If this approach is contemplated, all the other engine components, such as fuel lines, electrics, exhaust and cooling systems, should be arranged beforehand so that the actual engine installation consists merely of connecting a few bolts, cables, and piping. Generally, however, the power plant is secured first during construction and its ancillary equipment is set up around it.

The amateur builder with time on his hands may decide to do this work himself without hiring professional help, and there are various ways he can do this. Naturally, if there is a reasonably substantial roof over the boat, it is usually possible to rig a lifting device such as a ratchet-type lift (sometimes called a "come along"). I have lifted a 1,200-pound diesel using block and tackle and utilizing a large sheet winch for power. As an alternative, perhaps an anchor winch can be temporarily set up to provide lifting power. Props, either off the boat or the ground, may be necessary to support the roof, but if that is impractical it may be necessary to rig a horizontal beam of wood or steel with one end supported on the boat and the other by an A-frame adequately braced.

It is a good idea to remove much of the equipment bolted to the engine, such as the alternator, starter, and perhaps even the heat exchanger piping and filters. This will help to reduce weight, but, more importantly, these parts will be less likely to be damaged by the lifting slings or chains. In many cases, removing the gearbox will almost halve the total engine weight—as always there are a few options to choose from.

Securing the Engine

An engine must be held down securely, and there are several ways of doing this.

Sometimes bolts are run through the beds and

out through the bottom of the hull, where they are counterbored and plugged. However, this seems a rather extreme measure, even if the nuts are difficult to install. Another method is to bolt down two sections of angle iron along the top of the beds and drill and tap these for the holding-down bolts, using shims under the feet for correct alignment. The advantage of this is that some bolts can be run through the beds horizontally, thus supporting the engine over a wide area.

One of the most satisfactory arrangements is also quite simple and is common on large vessels. Four pads of about 3/8-inch to 1/2-inch steel plate are made to fasten to the engine feet. Three holes are drilled—one at each end and one in the center that will be tapped to take the engine holding-down bolt. These pads are bolted to the engine feet and the engine is placed on the beds. The remaining holes in the pads are used for long lag bolts—also known as coach screws—which have excellent holding power if pre-drilled to the correct size. The engine can be aligned by placing shims between the feet and pad, or between the pad and bed.

It is also possible to cut out the beds where these pads will be and install a 1/2-inch to 3/4-inch-thick firm cushion of neoprene rubber, which still allows for a solid mounting but dramatically reduces vibration and noise.

The engine is aligned by installing the propeller shaft and coupling. If you have done your job well, the rear flange on the engine should engage, but the use of a feeler gauge between these flange faces will show how true the engine is lying. For this reason, any holding-down lag bolts are drilled only when it is obvious that the engine will not have to be moved sideways. The other vertical adjustments can be done with shims.

It is also possible to drill and tap each of the engine's feet with a fine thread to take a small bolt. If these bolts are screwed in, the engine can be raised or lowered easily until the correct alignment is obtained and the size of shims decided.

It might be wise to say a few words about the coupling attachment to the shaft. This is often

done so that it is almost impossible to remove, particularly if it becomes frozen due to corrosion. The coupling should be the split type that can be spread slightly for removal; these are always keyed on and usually have a pin completely through as well. An arrangement I particularly like is to have the coupling made so that it is secured to the shaft with a tapered fit and keyway exactly the same way as for the propeller. This arrangement allows easy disassembly and also makes it possible to reverse the shaft when it becomes worn. A coupling machined in this manner will usually require a spacer collar between the two flanges to cover the shaft nut and allow a locking pin to be installed. With some hydraulic gear boxes, it is necessary to have a form of brake on the shaft to keep the propeller from turning the shaft when the vessel is under sail; the coupling collar is a good place to put this brake.

Once the engine is bolted down and lined up, the main part of the installation work is completed. The exhaust system is shown on the plans and is usually run over the side or to the stern using the engine cooling water to cut down the temperature so that rubber hose can be used for much of the distance. When siting seacocks for the seawater inlet and the exhaust, try to place them in a position where they can be reached and serviced easily. Owners of vessels being passed for survey by the U.S. Coast Guard may be surprised to know that cone-type seacocks will not be accepted. The ordinary common gate valve, which often has brass stems, is recommended by that authority, and many builders are puzzled at this logic, since the cone type is generally a far superior fitting.

Be sure to include a section of flexible piping in the exhaust line from the manifold to the muffler, or engine vibration will eventually fracture this section.

Vibration is one of the main bogeys of engine installation. While it may not be apparent in the early breaking-in period, if you have not taken this problem into account, you can be sure that sooner or later you will have to pay the piper for your negligence.

Everything that is attached to the engine

should have a flexible section in it close to the connection point. This applies especially to the saltwater inlet, which is usually connected with hose but is sometimes done with copper tubing. Make sure that any copper tubing has a section of hose where it connects to the engine's saltwater pump.

Fuel lines are often piped with copper, but the last section should be flexible or it will eventually fracture, even if the tubing is looped to prevent this. There are some excellent fuel line hoses available now with all kinds of end fittings that will allow connections to copper tubing if desired.

Make provision for a couple of good primary fuel filters and mount them in a position where they can be checked easily. This will save no end of problems later.

FUEL TANKS

Because of space limitations, it is usually best to install the fuel tanks before the engine is placed on its bearers. Normally these tanks are made up by a sheet-metal worker. They are generally of welded construction, made with ordinary mild steel sheet or plate, or stainless steel. Since the labor content is often the largest factor in the overall cost, there is not necessarily much difference in price between the two materials. Mild steel tanks are quite acceptable if they are well painted and protected from seawater on the outside. The 50-gallon drums used by major oil companies are proof enough of the durability of steel, and many commercial vessels have these drums mounted permanently as low-cost tanks.

Most small pleasure craft will have specially made fuel tanks that will fit some particular space, often outboard of the engine so that the tops can be used as shelves. Custom tanks require accurate templates, which should be cut from suitable material such as 1/4-inch plywood or hardboard. Shapes of each tank end should be fitted. If there are to be baffles inside, it will often assist the sheet-metal worker if you develop these shapes for him.

It is best to have a mockup of the templates to make sure everything fits. Light battens can be nailed in between the ends to represent the plating, and this allows you to check that the tanks can be positioned without the need to cut out hatches or doorways. If you are conscious of the cost of the tanks, it pays to keep in mind that steel, like plywood, comes in 4' x 8' and 4' x 10' sheets. When designing tanks, therefore, check the sizes carefully; it's often possible to save yourself from joining sheets together or welding on narrow strips to make a size that could have been changed slightly to save considerable expense.

Frequently it is more convenient to have two smaller tanks without baffles than one large tank with them. The smaller tanks will require slightly more material, but they may be easier to make and perhaps more easily installed in the boat. The capacity of tanks can be calculated by measuring the cubic area. This is sometimes difficult with a tapering tank, but if you measure at midpoint, you can obtain an average section that when multiplied by overall length will give a fairly accurate answer. The section on weights and measures in the appendix gives figures to work with for this purpose.

It is well worthwhile to have lugs welded to the sides or ends of tanks so that the tanks can be bolted to bulkheads or special members installed to secure them in position. New techniques now are being used to secure tanks in position using foam-in-place resins. These resins are mixed on the job and poured in behind and around tanks to fill the voids completely and literally glue the tanks into position. This has the added advantage of protecting the outside from corrosion, deadening sound, and insulating the insides of the tanks from the condensation that can form.

The tanks require a number of pipe fittings to be attached to them, and these should be located in a convenient position, such as close to a bulkhead, so that piping may be secured to it. Most of these fittings can lead out of the tank top with standard pipe threads, which are easily adapted to hose, metal, or rigid P.V.C. I prefer to draw fuel out of the top of a tank that is made with a standpipe inside extending to about 3/4 inch from the bottom. This arrangement eliminates sediment or water from being drawn into the fuel lines. The tanks should have a petcock installed at the lowest position to allow periodic drainage of any impurities. It is also possible to connect a small, clear vinyl hose to this petcock, securing it vertically alongside the tank. This makes an inexpensive fuel sight gauge when the cock is opened.

Each tank will require a fuel filler, a fuel exit, and a breather or vent hole. The filler cap should be positioned on deck where it is easy to get at with a fuel hose, but it should be clearly marked so that some unfortunate person will not mistake it for a water tank filler. The normal size is 1-1/2 inches in diameter in small vessels, but it should be larger if the tanks are over about a 50-gallon capacity. Tank vents must exit outside to the atmosphere, particularly if the fuel is gasoline, but they can be quite small if the filler opening is large enough to allow air to be expelled from the tank as fuel is being added. Vents are often located on the outside of a coaming or at the stern where any fumes are unlikely to be noticed.

WATER TANKS

The construction of water tanks will probably be done at the same time as the fuel tanks and requires similar procedures for making the correct shapes. Water tanks today are generally made in stainless steel, since there is little difference in cost between having them made of mild steel and having them galvanized later.

Many amateur builders have made fuel and water tanks using plywood and fiberglass. While these tanks are usually easily built, they do have certain drawbacks in that the plywood walls are rather thick in comparison to metal ones. Also, with water tanks, the resin can taint drinking water stored for long periods of time. Nevertheless, this type of construction is feasible and usually economical.

The normal way of making these tanks is to make up the shape required, minus the 3/4-inch waterproof plywood top, but with allowance for the top to be secured later. The inside of the tank is sheathed with cloth and resin and the loose top is also similarly treated. When sufficient coats of resin have sealed the cloth completely, the exits, usually in the shape of through-hull fittings, are fastened into position. The top is then secured with either a thiokol-type sealant or resin putty mix to make the joint waterproof.

Fiberglassing inside a box is not the most pleasant task for even the most avid boatbuilders, so some experienced tank builders prefer to apply the glass cloth and resin to 4' x 8' sheets of plywood before cutting them to size. This allows all the large areas to be coated evenly, and the corner joints then can be taped or coved after the tank is assembled. Few professional builders can make up tanks in this manner to compete in price with the sheet-metal worker, but sometimes this method can be a means of solving some difficult situations.

One of the most expensive items in tank construction is the manhole cover that is sometimes provided but so little used. If a tank is made so that it can be removed from the vessel, it is doubtful if a manhole is justified, as a tank can usually be cleaned ashore with a hose and detergent better than when secured in the boat.

All water tanks—like fuel tanks—require a filler, a breather vent, and an exit. The first is usually 1-1/2 inches in diameter and the others are 1/2-inch B.S.P. fittings, which allow a variety of choices for plumbing connections. As with the fuel tanks, it is good to have some lugs welded to the tanks to allow for adequate fastenings to secure them.

Try to avoid placing tanks under bunks; a half-filled water tank can be surprisingly noisy when the vessel is underway, and condensation from tanks can cause damp mattresses.

Fresh water is a necessary but heavy item on a long-distance cruising vessel, so the material and location should be considered carefully so as not to affect adversely the trim of the boat and the quality of the tank's contents over extended periods. The tank itself should be adequately supported by bearers or posts to prevent buckling and possible leaks.

Breather vent exits are usually located below deck and above the level of the deck filler if possible, so that a hose may be left unattended during filling and water can spill out on deck when the tanks are full.

FITTING THE BALLAST KEEL

The chief problem in fitting the ballast keel is the difficulty of drilling holes through the wood keel to match the holes in the casting, because it is often impossible to get enough clearance for a long drill to bore up from below when the ballast keel is in place. It is usually necessary to have a pattern or jig that will allow the positions of the holes to be marked on the outside of the wooden keel so that they can be drilled and aligned accurately without the ballast keel in place. After a plywood template is made of the casting top, holes are cut to match the bolt positions. This can be done using a router straight-shanked bit fitted with a ball race of the same size on the end of the cutter. Depending on the thickness of the wooden keel and the size of the bolts, it may be possible to bore the finished-size hole in one operation by carefully checking the angle of each hole in the casting and using a helper to hold bevel gauges to line up the drill.

With large keels where there is to be considerable thickness plus floor timbers, this method may not be accurate enough. It is safer to bore a pilot hole large enough to accept a boring bar so that the ballast keel may be placed in its correct position and the boring bar inserted into a hole. A couple of collars of the same size as the ballast keel holes are fastened to the bar with countersunk setscrews. This will align the bar correctly in the ballast keel, enabling a temporary bearing to be set up inside the boat. The fly cutter should be set to open the hole gradually to the desired size, thereby allowing the bar to be realigned if necessary.

Keels are sometimes cast with the bolts set into them, which means that it is impossible to remove them for inspection. This presents difficulties in keeping the bolts set up parallel during the casting operation, and it complicates the dressing off of the keel top. The method has certain merit where several similar keels are to be cast, because a special mold can be made that reduces the molder's job in setting up cores, but this is seldom practical in a one-off situation.

The bolts for fastening a lead ballast keel should be chosen carefully to prevent problems of galvanic corrosion. The galvanic series table on page 156 shows that lead is well down the list, yet because of its mass, there is normally little corrosion evident after a considerable period of time. The most common choice for bolts is one of the various bronze alloys, preferably one of the types without zinc content. Stainless steel is often used, but it is unreliable in underwater locations and I would not recommend its use.

The ballast keel may be bonded to the hull with one of the modern sealants, such as P.R.C., or even a suitable epoxy resin that has a substantial amount of talc or fiber filler added to give it body. If it is necessary to shape the lead to fair it into the hull, this can be done quite easily with a wooden plane, provided the bottom and cutter are lubricated regularly with oil or kerosene. The same technique works with a power plane, but care is required because the shavings are quite heavy and will be thrown from the machine with considerable force. Use of an eye shield is advised.

The keel casting may need to be built up to match the hull, and epoxy filler is excellent for this because it can be shaped easily with a disc sander when dry. I prefer to encase the whole keel in Dynel, which allows for a super finish.

Fin keels of the Star boat type are fitted to large ocean racing yachts (*see Buccaneer* plans) and they may be iron castings as with the Stars, or steel fabrications, which may include fuel tanks as well as lead ballast. This type of keel is generally easier to install, because the bolt holes are usually drilled through a flange alongside the fin itself. The main disadvantage is that this

Above: *Moving the lead keel into position.* Below: *Keel fabrication on* Buccaneer. *Note holes in flange for attaching keel to hull. (Sea Spray)*

type of keel will probably have to be made by someone other than the vessel's builder. It also requires that the vessel itself be lifted quite high so it can be bolted into position.

RUDDER ASSEMBLY

The steering system and rudder assembly is one of the most important components of any vessel. Careful building and installation work are required to produce a trouble-free arrangement.

The rudders on powercraft, usually of relatively small area, are often cast in bronze to patterns made up by the boatbuilder or perhaps welded together out of sheet or plate supported by internal or external webbed framing. When they are to be cast, the rudder stocks are often made of shafting that has been tapered and drilled. When made separately like this, the shafts can be placed in the rudder molds so that molten bronze can be poured around them to make the rudder blades. This method saves quite a lot of machining over having the stock cast with the blade and is generally stronger also.

On high-speed powerboats, rudders and struts are often shaped like wedges instead of airfoils, which can make the patternmaking somewhat easier.

Sailing vessels, with their larger-proportioned rudders, depend on metal hardware like the pintle and gudgeon hinges that allow an outboard rudder to be hung and turned on, and the blade itself is generally of wood.

Rudder fittings usually are designed at the same time that all the other necessary pattern work is done, so that the foundry will be able to do the lot at one time. These rudder fittings are often quite simple, being a U section that allows the wooden blade to be inserted between the two arms, which are then bolted or riveted together. The pins of the pintles usually are made of rod or shafting and are installed by threading them into the finished castings. This is strong and also allows for future replacement. The casting straps are often set flush into the blade if the blade is thick enough, so it won't be weakened. This looks neat but it is not as strong.

A yacht with an inboard rudder will require a different approach, as the blade will need to be attached to a metal stock. The steering mechanism, which in its simplest form is a tiller, then is attached to the metal stock. A metal rudder stock is connected to a wooden blade in a variety of ways, and the most suitable method may be shown on the designer's plans. There are certain factors to consider, however, and the builder may decide that the method shown is not suitable for his requirements.

Quite often the plans will show a long rudder stock that will take considerable effort to get in place. For the average rudder set on the trailing edge of the deadwood or sternpost, it is necessary either to have the stern of the vessel high enough so that the stock can be inserted into the bearing gland in the horn timber or a hole will have to be dug in the ground so that the rudder can be lowered far enough to do the same job. The latter can present problems with a cement floor. One solution would be to reduce the length of the stock by connecting a separate section with a muff coupling inside the hull to make the required length. An alternative is to install a flanged coupling outside that would allow it to be joined with bolts to a similar coupling on the rudder itself.

The installation and removal of a rudder should not be a difficult operation, and some thought on the matter of the heel fitting may solve this. The heel fitting receives the pin on the lower end of the rudder, and unless it is removed, it will prevent the rudder from being dropped down. This heel or gudgeon is sometimes designed so that it can be unbolted, allowing the rudder to be lowered sufficiently to withdraw the stock. There is often another bearing midway between the gland and the heel fitting—this is usually just below the propeller aperture. This fitting is sometimes split so that when the securing bolts or rivets are removed, the straps may be separated and lifted out of their recess.

The attachment of the stock to the wooden blade is most important and is done in several ways. Sometimes castings are made that are recessed into each side of the blade and attached

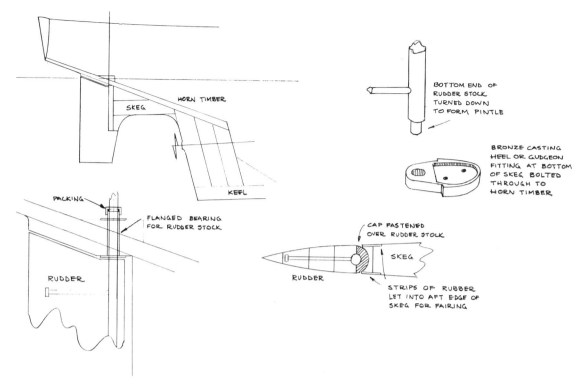

HORN TIMBER

SKEG

KEEL

PACKING

FLANGED BEARING
FOR RUDDER STOCK

RUDDER

BOTTOM END OF
RUDDER STOCK
TURNED DOWN
TO FORM PINTLE

BRONZE CASTING
HEEL OR GUDGEON
FITTING AT BOTTOM
OF SKEG BOLTED
THROUGH TO
HORN TIMBER

CAP FASTENED
OVER RUDDER STOCK

SKEG

RUDDER

STRIPS OF RUBBER
LET INTO AFT EDGE OF
SKEG FOR FAIRING

with a keyway to a solid stock. A similar method is to bend straps around the stock and weld the joint to tie it together. A very good system with a large stock is to drill and tap two or three rods into the aft side of the stock so that the blade can be bolted to the stock and nuts and washers can be recessed into the trailing edge of the blade. With a thick rudder blade, this arrangement allows a cap to be glued over the leading edge of the stock so that the metal work is buried inside the blade. Some rudders require the stock to be bent around the aft end of the propeller aperture; this means that a template must be made of the required shape so that the stock can be heated and bent to match it. Sometimes it is easier and better to make up a pattern and have the stock cast to the correct shape. This allows the aft edge of the stock to be made square so that the blade can be bolted to it without hollow shaping.

The bearing through the horn timber is usually a section of bronze pipe with a flange brazed to the outside and threaded at the top to allow a collar to be screwed down to secure it. A stuffing box is screwed on the same thread to make the tube watertight, or else the pipe is extended sufficiently to make this unnecessary.

The bearing through the hull is an important one, so it is worthwhile to fit one of the modern

Above: Figure 23. *Rudder installation details.*
Below: *A long rudder stock is sometimes difficult to install. (Sea Spray)*

bearing materials inside the pipe to obtain minimum friction. Teflon, Micarta, Tuphnol, and nylon are all suitable materials for this. The boring of the hole through the hull for this bearing requires a similar approach to that described for boring the propeller shaft hole. A pilot hole is first bored to enable a boring bar to be set up and aligned on temporary bearings; this procedure is explained on page 161.

CONTROLS AND ELECTRICAL SYSTEM

After much of the heavy installation work has been carried out, there remains to be completed the supporting systems that monitor and control some of these pieces of equipment. Although some of this work can be started as soon as the major components have been installed, much of it must wait until the interior and deck finishwork are farther along.

Steering System

Wheel steering controls are installed in a variety of ways, one of the most popular of which is the quadrant and cable system. This requires a quadrant to be secured to the rudder stock and connected with wire cables that lead through pulleys to a steering pedestal. This pedestal has a horizontal shaft set in bearings with the steering wheel attached at one end. Secured to the shaft is a sprocket, over which passes a length of chain that is connected to the steering cables. A turn of the wheel will pull the chain and thus move the quadrant.

The quadrant and cable system has many advantages and is adaptable to most craft, but the installation of pulleys needs to be done carefully so that the alignment is accurate. When designing a system, the aim is to use as few pulleys as possible to eliminate undesirable friction and bends in the cables.

All pulley assemblies need to be well bolted to substantial structural members, and when the steering system has to be fastened in areas where there are interior accommodations and cabinet work, it is often easier to build this finishwork after the steering system has been installed.

Other types of steering systems include the use of shafts to push and pull a tiller arm mounted on the rudder stock. This kind of steering employs a mechanical gear box that may be controlled by a sprocket and chain or revolving shafts set in bearings. Many successful and inexpensive steering systems have been built by cost-conscious amateur builders using suitable steering boxes from wrecked automobiles and trucks. These often can be purchased for a few dollars in junkyards, and I know of several such units on world-cruising yachts that are now steering across oceans after their lives on the highways of the world had ended. Most religions predict a life after death, and these units would appear to have attained a logical heaven.

Hydraulic steering systems have much to recommend them—they are easily installed and positive in action. Most types require a tiller arm mounted on the rudder stock connected to a slave cylinder set at 90 degrees to it. The steering wheel is mounted with the master pump unit, which can be installed in a pedestal or behind a bulkhead so that the necessary hose lines for the fluid can be connected between the two components.

When any kind of steering gear is installed in a pedestal, it is necessary to use nonmagnetic materials to avoid compass deviation.

The professional builder will usually obtain steering systems from one of the several companies that specialize in this equipment, but the cost-conscious amateur builder can save considerable expense by making up his own gear along the same lines. Patterns for casting the necessary parts for a quadrant and cable system are not difficult to make, but automobile steering boxes probably offer the best value.

Engine Controls

The engine controls for throttle and gear shift may be for hydraulic or manual gearboxes. With the excellent control units available on the market, few builders need to make these except for the manual gearboxes of larger diesel engines, which often require considerable effort to engage gears.

The controls are done in a variety of ways, depending on the proximity of the engine to the steering position. Since the handle on the gear box usually moves forward or aft depending on the desired direction, some form of push rod connection can be arranged with a vertical shaft from the cockpit alongside the pedestal down to the proximity of the engine. An arm can be fastened at the bottom of this shaft so that it can be rotated forward or aft. Sometimes a sprocket is fastened instead, and motorcycle chain is set up and connected to the gear-box handle. This type of control often takes some puzzling out before the answer is found, because it may need to be built with heavy parts to avoid too much play or flexing. The handle for the gear shift in the cockpit is usually made so that it can fold down when not in use, which will gain some space and keep people from damaging themselves and the system.

The installation of the engine instruments is straightforward, but the position of the dials is worth consideration, because when installed near the bottom of a cockpit, they can be kicked in or soaked with seawater. You should assume that if the dials are left exposed in a cockpit, they will eventually need to be replaced. A waterproof acrylic plastic cover often solves these problems.

Rather than depend on warning lights, or engine temperature and oil pressure gauges, I prefer to use the Murphy safety switches, which can be wired into an alarm bell and command instant attention when there is a malfunction.

Don't forget to connect the oil pressure gauge with a flexible hose, or you may have to replace the copper sometime, perhaps after all the oil has been pumped out of the engine!

Electrical System

With an increasing demand for reliable electrical systems on small vessels, it is very important that provision be made in the installation work for adequate storage and protection of the heart of the electrical system—the vessel's batteries. Because of their weight, batteries are too often placed down low in the bilge area and generally ignored until there is no power and the engine won't start. Batteries should be stored in acid-proof boxes and, in a sailing vessel, mounted in a fore-and-aft line to prevent acid from leaking out of the filler caps.

In the past, battery boxes were usually lined with sheet lead, but an alternative is to make them with 3/4-inch plywood and sheathe it with fiberglass to protect the wood from spilled acid.

Lids may be fitted to the battery boxes to protect the tops from being damaged or shorted out, but it is important to allow adequate ventilation for batteries, because they give off explosive hydrogen gas while being charged. If the sides of the box are extended two or three inches above the top of the battery, some of the side tops can be cut out, leaving ventilation slots under the top. An alternative is to make the box with longer corner posts and support the top on these. Whatever method is chosen, make the box so that it can be secured well and the battery can be removed without too much trouble.

The location of the battery box is important—a good location for it will largely determine the reliability of your entire electrical system. It should be close to the engine to avoid using great lengths of electrical cable with their resultant voltage drop, and it needs to be in a place that is accessible for checking the battery's electrolyte levels. However, because of space limitations, many engines must be installed under companionways, where they are liable to be exposed to salt water. This can harm the electrical system, so every effort should be made to place the various components associated with the engine—batteries and alternator—in a protected location. It is no easy task to meet all these requirements, and usually a compromise has to be made.

There is nothing particularly difficult about wiring a boat, but it is not an operation that should be taken lightly (no pun intended). The entire system should be planned out beforehand so that wires are not run haphazardly. Most engine manufacturers will supply a wiring diagram of the basic charging system showing the correct connections into the various controls. Color-coded wire will assist in identifying the various circuits, and modern crimped terminals make the connections simple. For marine work it is advisable to solder these crimped connections to make permanent contacts.

The remarks here are only of a general nature based on my experience of installing marine wiring in deep-sea cruising boats. There are several good books on the subject of marine wiring for the novice electrician.

The electrical system should be composed of two separate banks of batteries connected with a master switch, which allows both banks to be charged together yet isolated in use. The wiring from this master switch can then go to buss bars, which are two copper strips mounted on insulated material. These buss bars, either purchased or made, will provide a means of connecting all the individual circuits around the vessel.

A good electrical system will have a switch-board with either fuses or circuit breakers. This switchboard is located between the buss bars and the various electrical circuits throughout the vessel. Everyone has his own idea of the best electrical arrangements, but you won't go far wrong if you run all your wiring high up under the beam shelf or clamp through P.V.C. tubing. This arrangement has several advantages: it provides a neat, secure method of holding the wire and it protects it from dampness and drips. Use tubing large enough so that additional wire can be fished through later if necessary.

Each side of the vessel's interior lighting should be on a separate circuit; electrical equipment should not be wired into these but into their own individual circuits. The average 40-foot cruising boat with normal electrics aboard—such as interior lights, navigation lights, spreader lights, pumps or fans, perhaps an echo sounder or radio—will probably need a switch-board with about 10 to 12 circuits on it.

It pays to use good-quality stranded wire, which can often be obtained from auto parts stores that specialize in low-voltage wiring and connections at reasonable prices.

16

Finishing the Interior

With the deck and deckhouse substantially complete and major components such as the engine and tanks installed, the finishing of the vessel's interior can be undertaken. This involves one of the most interesting aspects of the construction process—the cabinet and joiner-work. Joinerwork is necessary to build such things as doors, drawers, bunks, shelves, etc.

No matter how well the hull has been built or how many hours of work have been spent installing structural members and standard equipment, such as engine and tanks, etc., the quality of your vessel will be judged by the way your finishwork has been done. Finishing may be the least important task as far as the performance and ability of the vessel are concerned, but it is by far the most outstanding feature that will be noticed by 99 percent of the people who inspect your vessel. This is of the utmost importance if you are building a vessel with the intention of selling her. Everyone will admire a well-finished interior, even though it may not be the most practical layout.

While much attention should be given to good joinerwork if you are to have an attractive interior for your boat, it should not be allowed to distract one from achieving a well-laid-out interior as well. A cruising sailing vessel's interior requires careful thought to make it a practical, seagoing layout. You should take a long, hard look at the proposed layout, with an eye for its suitability for use at sea. Sinks that have to be pumped in order to drain; cupboards that will shower their contents into your face; dinette tables set to one side with transverse seating—these are some of the arrangements that should be avoided, as they are unsuitable when a boat is heeled 25 degrees.

Even if you find the layout of the vessel shown in the accommodation plans to be satisfactory, do not depend on the plans to show all the details of how the interior should be built. Much of the interpretation of the plans is up to you, the builder. While this gives you considerable latitude, it also leaves the door open for omissions. In reviewing your plans for the interior, then, you must be mindful of all the detail that is necessary to fill out the plans. For instance, keep in mind that it is desirable to allow air to circulate in the bilge areas, behind seats, and under bunks, and that floorboards that are fit too closely to the hull will restrict this circulation. Vertical or horizontal slats fastened with a gap between provide air circulation and also make an attractive ceiling or hull liner. Interior handholds are often overlooked;

these should be provided so that it is possible to get a firm grasp when moving about the vessel.

A good interior, then, is the result of the marriage of good joinerwork and careful, well-thought-out planning, as we shall see in the following sections.

Of all the stages in construction, finishing offers the most headaches to the professional builder, for here is where the economic position of the vessel is won or lost. Good finishwork is time-consuming, and it requires a lot more ability from a workman than sloshing wet fiberglass into a mold or nailing strips of glued wood together. Frequently the only way a builder can compete and stay in business is to adopt schedules that include as little time as possible for the interior finishing. As a result, the yachting public often accepts shoddy interiors that are poor imitations seldom worthy of being called joinerwork.

Many trades are required in the building of a yacht—there are the specialists who install plumbing, electricity, and engines, to name a few—but the old-time ship's joiner was and still is regarded as the most important artisan on the job. The very name "yacht" implies gracious accommodations and fine woodwork, and is it left to the joiner to see that the owner of a vessel is satisfied with the quality of the interior accommodations and cabinetwork. Fine joinerwork is still in demand by those owners who appreciate it and can afford it, but unfortunately the men capable of doing such work are few.

The craft is being lost due to the lack of adequate apprenticeship programs for the young men who wish to learn. Working conditions have changed enormously in the 30 years since I was a young apprentice. In those days it took five years of training, working 54 hours a week, to acquire the status of "journeyman," which implied that a man had learned his trade and was entitled to a top pay scale.

Apprentices today have better working conditions and earn a fortune compared to what we received, yet they cannot hope to get adequate training and skills from a two- or three-year program, working 40 hours a week with a yard that mass-produces boats on an assembly-line basis. Somewhere during those five years, we apprentices learned to have some pride in the work we were doing, even though it may have been a relatively simple task. I strongly believe that there are still young men around who would sign up for such a training program if it were available today. Often employers are hamstrung by the demands of labor unions, and the responsibility of running an apprenticeship program is just not worth the headaches involved.

During my first few days as an apprentice, I learned boatbuilding's three Golden Rules, not necessarily in this order. 1) Buy only good tools and keep them sharp. 2) Keep your ears and eyes open and your mouth shut. 3) Do it right, or do it again until it's right.

Rule One was covered in the second chapter. The old saying, "A poor workman blames his tools," dates back to times when each craftsman had an extensive kit of tools, and a poor job then, as now, was due to the workman rather than his equipment. A beginner has enough going against him without the additional handicap of poor tools.

Rule Two was sound advice for a young apprentice; he often learned a good deal more by observing the way a craftsman tackled a job rather than by asking foolish questions. The old methods were good for the materials and circumstances of those days, but any person worth his salt realizes that improvement is always possible. The materials and tools available today should allow work of even better quality to be produced by craftsmen who have pride in their work. Use your brains and imagination to upgrade your ability. Remember that there is usually an easier and better way to do a job—it's just a matter of finding that way.

Rule Three was dependent largely on the other two. It was a no-compromise rule and should be the aim of a beginner in any job, but particularly if it concerns building a vessel.

If I have digressed somewhat from the subject at hand, it is because I wish to stress the

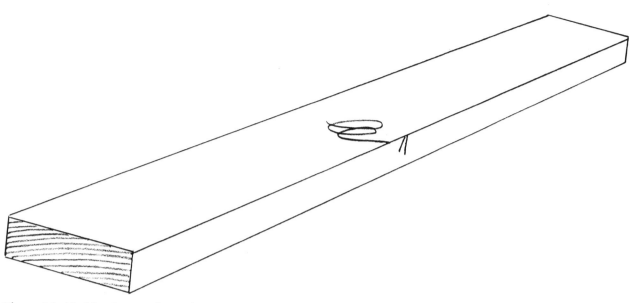

Figure 24. *Marking face marks on lumber. Mark the best side and edge on material for joinerwork and do all marking from there.*

importance of good joinerwork and cabinet-work. There are certain basic procedures in producing quality work, and at the risk of offending the reader, it might be best to start with some of them.

"You can't make a silk purse out of a sow's ear" is another old saying; likewise, you cannot expect to make fine joinery out of poor-quality lumber. The material used should be well seasoned, clear, vertical-grain stock. If you look at any piece of dressed lumber carefully, you will note that one side is better than the other. Obviously, this should be the side that is used and seen most, as with a table top or door front. The same applies to the edges: one may have a straighter line or better grain than the other. Every piece of lumber chosen for a particular job is selected as suitable and then marked to show the best side and edge. This marking is usually done somewhat as shown in the diagram. It indicates which is the good edge when only the "face" side is seen, and vice-versa. Marking-out with squares and marking gauges should always be done from the face side or face edge. By doing this, the good, visible side of the work will be accurate and level, even if the material varies slightly in thickness or width.

The novice joiner is often confronted with the problem of choosing a suitable joint to fasten together two pieces of material. There are many ways to accomplish the basic requirement of joining wood together, from the plain butt joint to the secret dovetail. Naturally, much depends on the workman, his experience, the particular job, and the material being used. Above all, though, the aim should be to construct the work with the best side of the material showing and a *minimum exposure of end grain.*

Another important consideration to be taken into account, is that much of the work will be finished bright, and the joints and material will be clearly visible. Any poor workmanship or practices will, therefore, be noticed, and nothing looks worse than poor joints that have been filled. An old rhyme springs to mind from apprentice days, "In glue and dust, we place our trust." This should not be your motto; you should strive to cut close-fitting joints that do not need to be filled.

Sometimes, however, even well-cut joints deteriorate, open, and fail, and this can be distressing to someone who has taken care to mark out and work his material accurately. The

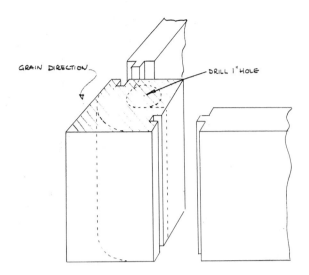

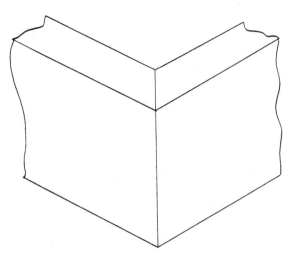

A PLAIN MITER JOINT HAS LITTLE STRENGTH

GRAIN DIRECTION

DRILL 1" HOLE

Above: Figure 25. *A tongue-and-groove joint with a rounded corner cut from a solid block.* Right: Figure 26. *Miter joints are less suitable than other joints for joiner-work, but they can be improved if they are modified as shown.*

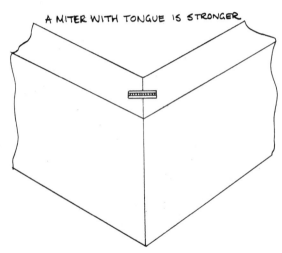

A MITER WITH TONGUE IS STRONGER

most common reason for this failure is lumber that is not fully seasoned, which results in a joint that shrinks. The same thing can happen if seasoned wood is later swollen due to excessive moisture, so it pays to keep in mind that lumber swells and contracts with changing weather conditions. The illustration from the U. S. Forest Service on page 46 shows shrinkage of lumber that has been taken from different parts of the log. It can be seen that vertical-grain lumber is less prone to movement than flat grain, which is why boat lumber is normally cut in this manner. Some woods are more stable than others, but they all react to a certain extent to moisture, with the minimum shrinkage being across the grain.

The confusing number and types of joints in woodwork relate to these shrinkage problems and to the need to hold two pieces of material together permanently in a variety of positions, from joining ends together (a scarf joint) to angled joints, such as half-laps, mortises and tenons, etc.

I have already stated that one of the basic joinery rules is the avoidance of end grain, and

because of this, the plain miter joint is often used at the corners of trim and cappings, around door frames and windows. The plain miter joint is popular because it is simple to make, but beware of using it in boat joinerwork. This joint is one of the worst offenders when it comes to shrinkage, and it is seldom possible to hold it together permanently. When joining capping, a half-lap miter joint (page 191) or plain half-lap is stronger and less likely to fail. When joining vertical corners together, as with hatch coamings or edging on countertops, shelving, etc., some form of tongued joint may be used, which is a better choice than a plain miter, though still not as good as a dove-tailed joint.

With these general rules in mind, we can now go into the specifics of producing top-quality joinerwork for the interior of your vessel.

DOORS

Doors, are always built so that the outside members, called "stiles," run the entire length. The cross members, called "rails," are fitted between so that their end grain cannot be seen when the door is opened. This is the outside framework for a door that has its center filled with a lumber or plywood "panel." Large doors often have more than one panel; sometimes they are divided by a central rail, which would make a two-paneled door. Because wide panels are subject to shrinkage, these are sometimes divided by the addition of a vertical member parallel to the stiles and called a "mullion" or "munnion." These members are always fitted between the rails so that their end grain is hidden and the strength of the rails is maintained. This elementary rule should be followed wherever it is necessary to construct doors or framing to surround them. These latter assemblies are called "face frames" in cabinetwork and are used to cover the edges of cutouts for cupboards and partitions that form compartments in a vessel.

To fit the individual stiles, rails, and mullions together to form a framing for panels or doors, it is necessary to cut some suitable type of joint that will allow them to be assembled and held together permanently. The joint most commonly used for this is called a mortise-and-tenon joint; the slot of the former is termed the female and the tenon the male. In the past, these joints were cut so that the tenon on the rails protruded through the stiles and was held in place with two small wedges driven at each end of the mortise. To do this without weakening the stiles too much, it was necessary to cut off part of the tenon so that it did not extend the full width of the rails at the ends of the doors. A short piece of the cut-off tenon was retained, however, to fit in a shallow slot called a "haunch." Wherever

wide rails were fitted, such as at the bottom of a door or where a door was divided into panels, haunches were cut to reduce the length of the mortise in the stiles. With the use of modern glues, this technique has largely disappeared and been replaced by a simpler mortise-and-tenon joint having a shorter tenon that doesn't penetrate through the stiles.

When marking out the material to make doors or face frames, it is best to leave the stiles about an inch longer than necessary, so that the mortises are supported at their outer ends. The "horns" are cut off after assembly and after the glue has cured.

Usually, the joinerwork required in the average small vessel does not amount to very formidable proportions. The large divisions and partitions, such as seat and bunk fronts, the sides and ends of cupboards, etc., are best done in plywood, with face frames used to cover the edges. Some builders take shortcuts and use the plywood itself as a face frame by cutting square holes in it for doors and leaving the edges of the cutout unfinished. This is a cheap and tacky solution and is to be deplored.

For the face frames and doors in the average small vessel, 3/4-inch-thick material is usually quite adequate. The width of the stiles and rails will largely depend on the size of the framework. Here again, there is a general rule if the door or framework is long and narrow: increase the width of the bottom rail by about half as much again as the sides and top. Often a frame used in facing a workbench or counter will be considerably wider than it is high. In a situation like this, it is permissible to increase the width of the stiles to three or four times the width of the top rail. This is done to eliminate excessive width in the doors.

To make up an average small frame, a door would require 1 x 2 (3/4" x 1-1/2") and 1 x 3 (3/4" x 2-1/2") material for both face frame and door. The face frame is marked out first. Determine the height required and mark the overall length onto the stile material. Using a square, mark the width of the top and bottom rails to give you the length of mortise required. For the average small frame such as this, a simple mortise or slot about 1/2 inch deep with a width of 5/16 inch would be about right. These are easily and quickly cut with a router, using a straight-fluted cutter and a fence to guide the machine. The length of the rails will need to be one inch longer than the finished opening, so that a 1/2-inch tenon can be cut at each end. Because the tenon thickness can be changed easily, mortises are always cut first so that they can be used to determine the correct size of the tenon.

Most tenon machines are pretty expensive pieces of equipment that are seldom seen in a boatyard. However, tenons can be cut well enough on a table saw by holding the material vertically and against the fence, allowing it to be cut by the blade, which is projecting through the table exactly 1/2 inch. Use some scrap material of the same thickness to cut a sample tenon and saw off the outside "shoulders" with a hand saw to see how well the tenon fits the mortise. Some adjustment is usually necessary; they should not fit too tightly or splitting will result.

A fine-toothed crosscut saw blade is needed for sawing the shoulders of the tenons. The fence is reset so that the distance from it to the outside of the saw blade is 1/2 inch, and the blade is lowered until it cuts the shoulder but not the tenon.

Some table saws have a slot in the table top for an adjustable fence to be slid along it. If one of these is not available, it is best to cut a 3/4-inch plywood jig exactly square, and place one side against the rip fence, allowing the rails to be held along the front edge at 90 degrees to the fence, so that the rail and jig can be pushed across the saw blade.

If you have a router, you may also cut the tenons with this versatile machine by using a simple wooden jig as shown in Figure 27. The material is slipped between the jig sides and placed in a vise or clamped together securely. Adjusting the cutter depth will change the length of the tenon; the thickness can be altered by adjustments of the router fence.

Tenons can be cut by hand, of course, by sawing the end grain with a hand saw and cutting the shoulders with a tenon or back saw, but if many are to be cut, it is a daunting

Figure 27. *A simple jig used for cutting tenons with a router.*

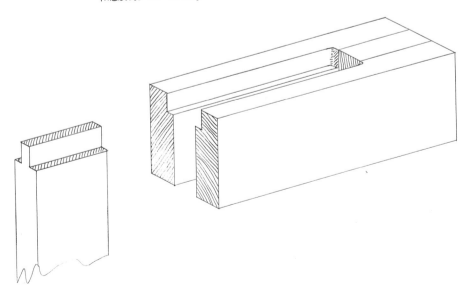

PLACE STOCK BETWEEN JIG SIDES AND HOLD WITH CLAMP OR VISE, ADJUST ROUTER FENCE TO SUIT THICKNESS OF TENON.

prospect. The door itself can be made up in similar fashion with a panel filled into slots in the rails and stiles. This is often done with hardwood-faced plywood, which makes an excellent panel because it does not shrink. If 1/4-inch plywood is used, the face edges of the stiles and rails will need to be grooved to allow the panel to fit inside. This type of door can be made on a table saw without using a router to cut the mortises, as the groove cut for the panel can be continued right to the ends, with the tenons for the rails cut to fit this.

Panels can be made up in a variety of ways, and the type chosen will depend on the builder's or owner's ideas. Some door panels are made up from wide stock and cut down at the edges to fit in the framing groove. Other alternatives are vertical slats, woven wood strips, and various kinds of wallboard finishes. The choice is endless. Sometimes it is necessary to make a door with a panel that is to be fastened in later. To do this, it is necessary to prepare your stiles and rails by cutting a rabbet in them before they are assembled. This means that one shoulder on the tenon will have to be cut longer than the other. On a small door, a rabbet about 5/16 inch deep would be satisfactory, as it will be necessary to fasten some small "beads" to hold the panel in place. The beads are usually placed on the inside of a door, unless they are exposed to the weather, in which case they are often on the outside, which makes the panels more waterproof. Doors with beads have an advantage in that a panel can be removed or replaced if it is damaged. For this reason, beads are often fastened with flat- or oval-headed screws. This means that caulking compound should be used to effectively seal panels in exposed positions.

DRAWERS

A yacht interior should have a certain amount of drawer space, an item sadly lacking in many production craft and often badly made in those that have them. Drawers always used to be constructed with dovetailed joints, which were

the mark of quality in any joinery. These are not difficult to make and will give your work that touch of class if made well.

Drawers are constructed of several pieces of material. They have a front, two sides, a back, and a bottom. Self-locking drawers that have to be raised slightly to be opened are often the best choice, but this type requires that the front be made "lip and bullnose" style, so that the protruding lip conceals the necessary gap required for lifting the drawer front. Ordinary flush drawer fronts generally look better, but they require careful fitting.

Whichever method is decided upon, the front is made first. The flush-type front should be fitted to the opening in the face frame; the lip-style front is rabbeted only on the sides and top before fitting. The amount of overlapping lip should be about 5/16 inch to 3/8 inch square, so the front total thickness should be about 7/8 inch to 1 inch to allow the drawer sides to be joined adequately.

The drawer sides are usually made of 1/2-inch-thick clear lumber, but they can also be made of plywood. These sides should be cut the correct width and length to fit the height and depth of the opening. The sides for the flush-type front will need to be about 1/4 inch shorter than the lipped-front type, so the side dovetails will not be visible when the drawer is closed. The lip on the other type will cover these ends. It is best at this stage to cut a groove in the sides and front, which will allow the bottom of the drawer to be fitted. Usually 1/4-inch plywood or perforated hardboard is used for the bottoms, and a groove the same width as the thickness of this material is cut about 1/2 inch up from the bottom of the drawer on the inside of the sides and front members. This groove need only be about 3/16 inch deep or the sides will be too fragile.

The dovetails are marked out on one of the sides first. Since the ends of the drawer front are of end grain, and since you will want to conceal as much of the end grain as possible, the dovetails are made considerably larger than the pins. That way, the dovetails will cover up a greater

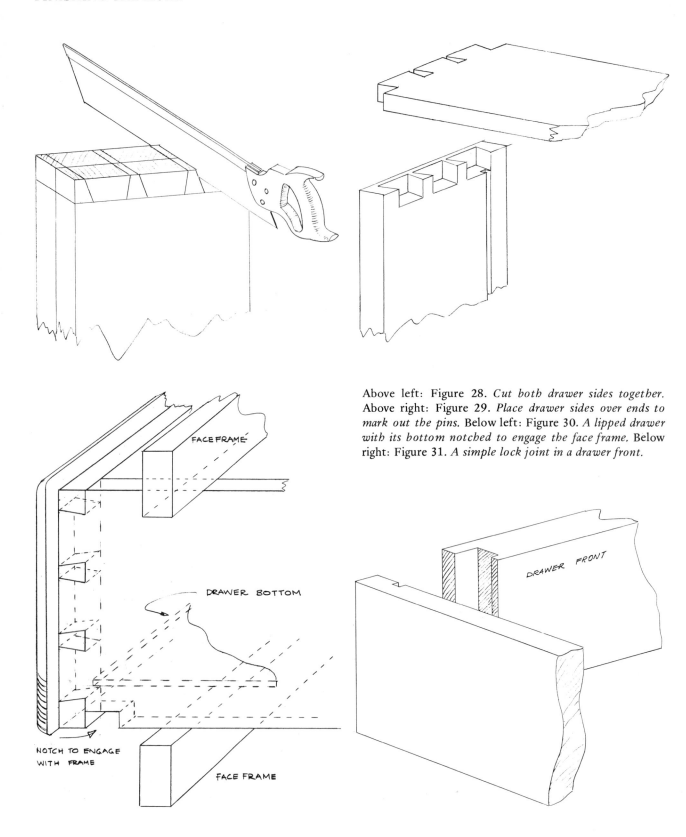

Above left: Figure 28. *Cut both drawer sides together.* Above right: Figure 29. *Place drawer sides over ends to mark out the pins.* Below left: Figure 30. *A lipped drawer with its bottom notched to engage the face frame.* Below right: Figure 31. *A simple lock joint in a drawer front.*

FACE FRAME

DRAWER BOTTOM

NOTCH TO ENGAGE WITH FRAME

FACE FRAME

DRAWER FRONT

amount of end grain than the pins will expose. Thought must also be given to positioning the dovetails so that one of them conceals the groove cut in the drawer front for the bottom.

The two sides are aligned, tacked together, and placed vertically in a vise so that they can be sawn at the same time. The spacing of the dovetails is marked square across the ends, and a tenon saw is used to cut down the dovetails to the required depth. Once this has been done, the sides are separated and the apertures where the pins will go can be removed with a small chisel worked with a mallet. Cut from both sides toward the center to avoid damaging the edges.

Place the drawer front in the vise, end on, with the inside toward you, and lay the correct drawer side on the end of the front so that the positions of the pins may be marked in. These marks will have to be squared down the back side of the drawer front 1/2 inch to fit the thickness of the drawer sides. The pins are cut out in similar style to the dovetails, using a tenon saw but only cutting one side at a time. The saw can be used to cut only part of the full depth, and the remaining chopping out is done with a chisel. It should now be possible to see how well the side fits into the end of the front. If the dovetails have been well cut, they will require only glue to hold them in place. The usual beginner's problem is that everything is too loose.

The drawer back is usually secured in a vertical slot or dado cut in the sides the same depth as the groove for the bottom. This back is narrower than the sides, extending from the top of the groove to the top of the sides only. This allows the bottom to be slipped into position after the drawer is assembled. The back is usually located about an inch from the ends of the sides so that the dado has more strength. This back is usually secured with finish nails through the sides. The addition of the bottom will make the drawer square, and the back edge will have to be nailed to the drawer back.

This is the general principle of making drawer dovetails, sometimes called blind dovetails because the front ends of the sides do not show. The description takes somewhat longer than doing the job. Your first attempt may be slow, but it's surprising how quickly the job can be done after a little practice.

The lipped drawer is made in a similar fashion to the flush-front drawer, except that when it is completed, the sides will be recessed to form the lip on the ends. A notch is cut out of the bottom of the sides immediately behind the drawer front, which allows the rail of the face frame to engage it.

There also are a couple of points worth mentioning that apply to any type of drawer.

All material used for making a drawer needs to be cut squarely or the finished product will wind or twist, which will prevent it from fitting or sliding easily.

The drawer runners are usually made from rabbeted hardwood so that they not only support the closed drawer but act as guides, allowing the drawer to remain square to the face frame. Some form of guide is also required to prevent the drawer from tipping when opened. Sometimes a thin guide is positioned in the center so that the back of the drawer will ride up against this. When there are to be several drawers on top of each other, the runners often are made so that they are the same depth as the rails on the face frame. This allows the runner to form a guide for the drawer immediately below. A variation on this is to cut a groove along the outside of each side of the drawer and fasten a batten, which fits the groove at the sides of the cabinet for the drawer to slide on.

There are, of course, many other methods of assembling drawers. It might at this point be a good idea to mention the most typical method. The sides of the drawer are simply fastened with "iron dovetails" by nailing the sides into rabbets in the ends of the front. The rest of the job remains much the same. Although "bronze dovetails" upgrade the work slightly, drawers made in this manner often come apart after only a little use. A lock joint can be machined into the drawer fronts to engage with a small dado in the sides. This is a better approach to the problem of attaching the front to the sides.

Dovetailed joints are the best solution from the point of view of strength, and if only a few drawers are required, they will not take much longer to make than the mass-production method. Attachments are available for a router that will machine a form of dovetail quickly and accurately, but often it takes too long to set up the machine, and unless many are to be cut, this may be impractical.

Ordinary open, dovetailed joints have many uses in marine cabinetwork, and after you have grasped the principles of cutting these joints, you will find yourself using them in many situations where you wish to avoid a cornerpost, such as a hatch coaming or a deck box.

It is possible to use dovetails to make good corner joints for sheet plywood; if you are accurate in your marking and cutting, much of this work can be done with a band saw or even a jigsaw.

BUNKS AND SEATS

With a nation of young people growing up who are often considerably taller than their parents, it seems foolish to build bunks that are too short. Many builders forget the taller people who find bunks of 6 feet 2 inches and 6 feet 4 inches uncomfortable. Bunks are frequently very narrow due to a widespread belief that they are better at sea. This is simply untrue—few people wish to sleep as though strapped down to a stretcher, and a bunk width of less than 24 inches just is not good enough. If you like your bed, and most of us do, make it a comfortable one. Allow for a 6-inch-thick mattress and make sure it is wide enough so you can sleep with bent knees instead of stretched out like a corpse. Small bunks are often provided because the builder or designer was reluctant to give up those few extra inches, which were often only used to extend the floor area—and for what purpose? Seats in a saloon can also be used as bunks and you should allow for them to be long enough and of sufficient width for them to be used as such. Forward bunks, though comfort-

able in port, will often be untenable at sea, and the saloon seats offer a good substitute.

The fronts of seats and bunks are usually fastened to bulkheads and other transverse divisions. Plywood is a good choice of material for this work, since it requires little more than cleats fastened vertically to the bulkheads for securing the ends of the fronts. Longitudinal stiffening is also required; a bearer at the bottom inboard side will do this and support the cabin sole.

Saloon seats require some additional considerations in their construction. If floor space is limited, extra space can be gained by raking the fronts outboard at the bottom. This gives more foot space and makes the seats more comfortable when sitting up to a table. Seat heights will often vary from one end to the other, since the cabin sole is not level. The average height of seats should be about 16 inches to the top of the cushion, so allow for cushion thickness when building the framework. Four inches of plastic foam suitably covered makes a good seat and is also comfortable to sleep on. The seat tops are often slightly lower at the outboard side, which makes a good lounging seat, but too much slope will be uncomfortable when sitting upright, eating, or perhaps writing at a table.

Edges of bunks and seat fronts will require some form of capping to finish off the edge of the plywood. This can be done in a variety of ways, from a simple parallel horizontal strip to the curved cutaway profiles common with bunk fronts. A combination of paint and brightwork often looks better than too much of one or the other. Large painted surfaces can be broken up by combining varnished cappings, drawer fronts, and cupboard doors.

Obviously, everyone has different ideas on how an interior should be finished. Remember that a change of upholstery materials can completely alter the tone of furnishings. The wonderful selection of fabrics now available often makes a choice difficult. Vinyl fabrics are not recommended for sleeping, however, due to their tendency to sweat. Canvas or some of the modern materials such as Vivatex or Acrilan are better choices.

Treasure's *saloon.* (Anderson-Sea Spray)

SALOON TABLES

Saloon tables are built in many different ways, and the table construction often depends on the type of vessel. About the only thing they will have in common is the height, which is usually 28 to 30 inches. They are normally made with two central legs but may be supported on only one if it is substantial.

Another method of securing table tops is to hinge one end to a bulkhead with a folding bracket or leg support. The pipe stanchion arrangement is another alternative—the table can be raised up to the deckhead out of the way or set at any height.

Generally a centrally mounted table will have folding leaves to allow the area to be increased but allow easy passageway when stowed. This can be done with the drop-leaf style, which has sides that are hinged to the central portion and can be raised and supported by brackets or sliding bearers. This is a popular arrangement, but it has drawbacks in a small vessel because the stowed leaves often restrict knee space when the seating is occupied. An alternative to this is to hinge the leaves so they fold over on top of the table. This usually means that a wider central portion must be provided, as each leaf can be only half the table width. One disadvantage to this arrangement is that unless special hinges are made, it is difficult to make a top that is completely level when fully opened. The usual butt hinges will project slightly and will need the extra support of thicker leaves. This can be done in the form of a fiddle.

The saloon tables of sailing vessels are often gimbaled, which has much benefit at sea, as it provides a level place to lay out a meal. If the central leg or legs can be well supported, it is relatively easy to mount a horizontal bar with straps fastened to it and attached to the underside of the table top. A couple of 1/2-inch rods

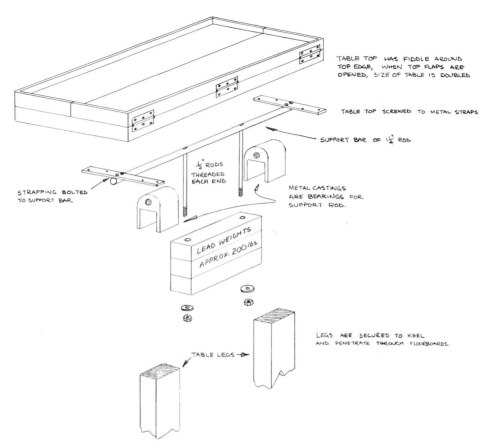

TABLE TOP HAS FIDDLE AROUND
TOP EDGE, WHEN TOP FLAPS ARE
OPENED, SIZE OF TABLE IS DOUBLED

TABLE TOP SCREWED TO METAL STRAPS

SUPPORT BAR OF 1¼" ROD

½" RODS
THREADED
EACH END

STRAPPING BOLTED
TO SUPPORT BAR.

METAL CASTINGS
ARE BEARINGS FOR
SUPPORT ROD.

LEAD WEIGHTS
APPROX. 200 lbs.

LEGS ARE SECURED TO KEEL
AND PENETRATE THROUGH FLOORBOARDS.

TABLE LEGS

Figure 32. *Gimballed table on* Treasure.

about 15 inches long are tapped into the shaft at 90 degrees to the straps. These are used to secure lead pigs that have had holes drilled through them. The ends of the rods need to be threaded so that nuts and washers can be screwed on to hold the lead. Although more weight is required the table will have a better action, eliminating a pendulum effect and possible foot injury, if the weight is kept close to the table top instead of down low. About 200 pounds of lead will be required for a table 24 inches wide and 3 feet 6 inches long, but even with this weight, it is advisable to attach fiddles to the table to prevent dishes from sliding over the edges.

GALLEY

The finishwork in the galley area needs careful thought. Lockers and shelves for storing cans and jars of food need good fiddles about three inches high if containers are to remain upright. Divisions (which should be easily removable for cleaning) will often keep food containers from sliding about in cupboards and prevent accidental spills, which will also upset the cook. There are usually enough forces rocking the boat without involving an angry cook. Remember also that many a vessel has foundered on the rocks of matrimony.

Surfaces in the galley should be easy to keep clean from grease splatters, and this is particularly true behind cooking stoves, which are often difficult to remove. The cabinet space around a stove should be kept clean and also should be insulated from excessive heat. Rather than use a painted surface for this area, a laminated plastic such as Formica, or a stainless steel sheet, would be a better choice. Mount the stove so that it can be removed for cleaning. Often this is done easily by using flexible fuel lines that don't require disconnection of the fuel supply.

The top of cooking stoves are usually

Treasure's practical galley. (Anderson–Sea Spray)

made to fit what you have rather than built in random sizes. Some large locker space for the storage of pots and pans and a special cupboard for a garbage pail are other necessary requirements for a galley. If possible, try to include a couple of drawers for the cutlery and other cooking hardware and equipment. A pull-out cutting board can often be placed immediately over a drawer and will save work tops from the edges of knives.

Galley sinks on a seagoing vessel need to be deep and relatively small to prevent washing-up water from slopping about and spilling. If possible, they should be located close to the center-line of a sailing vessel and kept above the waterline, so as to drain without use of a pump. Often this cannot be avoided, but it leaves a galley slave with a lot of useless work.

In the past, galleys often were situated in dark, gloomy interiors well forward in the vessel, where the motion was worst. Fortunately, designers have realized the importance of the galley area, so now this is usually positioned near a companionway hatch, where there is plenty of light and ventilation. Give the galley some careful thought when fitting it out. It is possible to build a good-looking yet functional area where hot meals can be prepared even in adverse conditions. In many respects, the remainder of the accommodations should be built around the galley.

HEAD

The building of a toilet compartment also requires careful consideration. Ventilation is very important, and the space behind toilets requires a surface similar to that described for a cooking stove. Unpleasant odors due to the difficulty of cleaning such areas are often an embarrassment to boat owners. By mounting a toilet in a specially prepared recess that has been lined with Formica or sheathing material, it is possible to wash out the area occasionally with a hose or a bucket of water. The whole floor of the toilet compartment can often be made completely watertight so that it can be used for a shower or

mounted level with surrounding work-top areas. In a galley with standing headroom, these tops are usually 36 inches above the cabin sole. Fitting in enough work-top space for dishing out food is one of the chief problems in a small-boat galley. Sometimes it is possible to fasten hinged work tops to bulkheads or divisions so that when required, extra space can be set up quickly and then folded away after use. Formica is a good choice for surfacing these work tops. However, other work-top areas, such as bureaus and chart tables, should be of plywood faced with a hardwood veneer or lamination to achieve a look of good quality. All work tops, regardless of use, should be fitted with adequate fiddles to prevent spills.

Racks for the storage of crockery and dishes need careful thought and the divisions are best washing area. The floor may be made of a stainless steel tray covered with a grating (constructed in the same manner as is the cockpit grating detailed in Chapter 17), or plywood covered with one of the sheathing materials previously described. When building a plywood floor, remember to tilt it somewhat to allow for drainage to an exit that can be connected to a pump.

Any builder constructing a new vessel would be wise to consider the increasing number of antipollution regulations, which often forbid the pumping overboard of untreated sewage. Self-contained portable toilets or holding tanks are now required by law in certain areas of the world, and this equipment is installed far more easily when the interior is being built rather than when left for later.

Any toilet installation should allow for easy removal so that it can be taken ashore to be worked on. The use of bolts with the nuts exposed offers the best means of doing this. The plumbing should also be easily removable, and this is often achieved with short lengths of hose secured with hose clamps. P.V.C. piping and fittings have greatly simplified the builder's work in this respect.

The installation of a washbasin in the toilet compartment will usually require a cabinet to support it. The space under the basin, which includes the plumbing for taps and waste, often has the discharge seacock for the toilet located there also. The washbasin water is usually allowed to empty into the toilet bowl and can be pumped over the side or into a holding tank. When a washbasin is mounted alongside a toilet, it is sometimes possible to install a hinged flap that can be used to form a vanity top over the toilet when washing. This flap can be secured up against a bulkhead or the vessel's side when the toilet is in use. Like the galley, the toilet compartment requires cupboards for the storage of supplies. A mirror mounted above the sink is desirable, and it can be installed on the front of a cupboard door or other convenient location. If a toilet compartment has a waterproof floor, the space will probably be used for storing wet

Treasure's head. Note the lift-up vanity top. (Anderson-Sea Spray)

clothing, oilskins, and sea boots. Some provision for hooks or racks to hang up this gear will often solve the problem of where to keep these items.

FLOORBOARDS

Mention has already been made of installing temporary floorboards. Finishing them is usually left until the last of the interior joinerwork and painting is completed; they will almost certainly be scratched or marked if done earlier.

There are several ways floorboards can be finished—from simply covering them with sheet vinyl or carpeting to gluing down cork tiles or hardwood. One of the smartest-looking cabin soles is the teak-deck look, with seams done in white. This is done by laying down solid teak

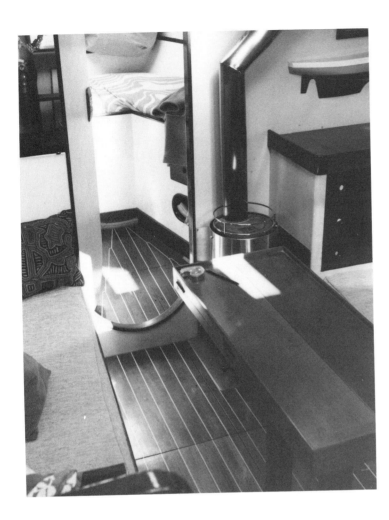

A teak strip and epoxy filler cabin sole.

boards with thin strips of a white wood between. In the past, holly was often used, but this is almost unobtainable today, so other woods have been substituted, but these are yellow or off-white and do not look as well. I prefer to use either a white polyester or epoxy filler, which does not stain, is easy to apply, and saves a lot of work.

The procedure I adopt is to fasten thin strakes of teak about 3/8 inch by 3 inches to 3-1/2 inch to the plywood with a gap of about 1/8 inch between them. I use nails and glue, taking care to line up all the fastenings and continue the run of the strakes onto the next floorboard if necessary. The nails are counterbored and plugged, and when the glue is dry, the teak is carefully cut to slightly more than the length of the plywood. Masking tape is stuck across the

ends of the teak to form a dam and prevent the white filler from running out. The filler can be made up from polyester or epoxy resin with pigment added. This can best be applied with a putty knife. Make sure the seam is completely filled.

After the resin has cured, the whole surface of the floorboard can be sanded off with a soft pad sander and the ends finally trimmed to the correct length. Instead of locating lift rings in the floorboards, which sometimes becomes expensive and unsightly, I make a small, 1/4 inch x 1/2 inch slot in the board to accept a special "key" made from a piece of 1/4-inch rod with the end bent over 90 degrees. An alternative to this is to use a 1/4-inch bronze carriage bolt with the sides filed away to form a tee, which can be inserted into the slot and turned.

A simple wooden handle is secured with a nut on both sides of it and will allow it to be grasped firmly, as opposed to the lifting ring pattern, which often allows only the end of a finger to be used.

The outboard edges of floorboards may collect dust and grit that can scar the surrounding joinerwork when the boards are lifted. For this reason, base trim or skirting boards are sometimes fitted to seat and bunk fronts. This trim will also save painted surfaces from scuffs and marking.

There are several excellent finishes available for floorboards that are to be finished bright. Usually a one-pot synthetic finish is the easiest to use, and the type that has been developed for gymnasium floors provides a beautiful surface without being slippery. Cork tile is another excellent floor covering, being light and having a pleasing appearance. It cannot take the punishment that a hardwood floor can, but this is seldom a problem in a yacht.

COMPANIONWAY STEPS

The entrance to the vessel's interior is often via a steep ladder. Since it frequently has to be negotiated when the vessel is heeled, it makes sense to provide a strong, well-secured set of steps that will not fold up at the wrong moment. The proportions of stairs in a home ashore can seldom be used in a small yacht. Often a ladder will need to rise more than five feet with very little amount of distance measured in a horizontal plane, resulting in a steep, almost vertical climb. Good handholds are essential, and often the steeper ladders are safer than the ones that people try do descend on the heels of their feet without being able to hold on securely.

Stepladders are made up from two outside members called "strings," which are usually notched to support the treads. If you made a temporary stepladder while the interior work was being completed, it may be necessary only to duplicate it in good-quality hardwood. The best procedure is to make up a pattern of the strings, obtaining good fits at the bottom and top before marking out treads. The amount of "rise" from the cabin sole to the top step is measured and divided by the number of treads required. The rise between treads should be between about 9 inches and 12 inches, measured vertically, and is easily marked with a bevel gauge or steel roofing square. The width of ladders is largely a matter of choice; in small vessels it is usually about 18 inches inside the strings. The treads should be notched into the strings about 1/4 inch to 3/8 inch and secured with plugged fastenings from the outside of the strings.

An alternative that looks better is to cut two small tenons in the ends of the treads and fit them into mortises that are cut completely through the strings. If the outside of the mortise is widened slightly on the top and bottom, the tenons can be firmly secured by driving in two small wedges that are glued into place. Sometimes the tenon itself is saw-cut horizontally so that a single wedge can be driven into the small slot, which will spread the tenon so that it is wider on the outside of the string and firmly held in place.

A nice effect can be built into the treads before they are assembled by cutting a series of deep grooves in the tops and filling them with deck seam compound or inserting strips of neoprene rubber so that they stand slightly proud of the surface. Slots in the strings can be cut to form handles between the treads that are often very useful for handholds for young children.

The finished steps should be well secured. This can be done efficiently by making up an arrangement using brass or stainless angles rather than using some of the fittings listed in marine hardware catalogs.

17

Finishing the Exterior

By the time you start finishing the exterior, you should be beginning to see light at the end of the tunnel. Not only is most of the work behind you, but you have undoubtedly become quite skilled in working with tools and have gone a long way toward mastering the techniques involved in using all the various materials. If you have gotten this far, the remainder of the work should not be difficult, for you will be using tools and techniques that you have already encountered.

HATCHES

Few builders today make good, strong, waterproof hatches. Some of the ones seen on production boats often appear to be made of the section that was cut out of the deck, with perhaps an addition of some 1 x 2 screwed to it for framing. Quite obviously, whoever designed work of this nature never had to sleep beneath it at sea, or if he did, he definitely has a grudge against boat owners. A hatchway is often a large opening, since it is used for the passage of sails, gear, and often crew members. Depending on the size of the vessel, there may be several of these openings through the deck or coach roof,

and poor construction sometimes causes severe leaks, with consequent spoilage of interior furnishings, food, supplies, and equipment, not to mention the disposition of the unfortunate person whose bunk is situated underneath. When so much work has been done to build a waterproof hull and deck, it seems ridiculous to pay so little attention to the large hatch holes that are covered by flimsy lids often incapable of supporting the weight of even an average person.

The chief cause of hatch leaks is due to the reluctance of the designer or builder to raise the coamings high enough so that water running along the deck cannot wash under the lid and over the top of the coaming. Rubber moldings and gaskets will often solve this problem temporarily, but the real problem lies in the basic design, which often leaves so much to be desired.

A hatch coaming performs the same function as the sides of the superstructure or coach roof, but because a lid with surrounding lips has to be fitted over the top, the overall size of the lid is usually considerably larger than the opening. It is the amount of this difference that is one of the chief ingredients of sensible hatch design.

Basically, there are two kinds of hinged hatches, the single-coaming type and the double-

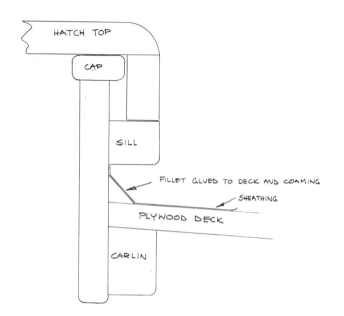

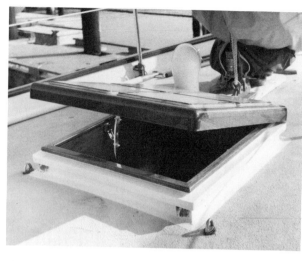

Above: *A single coaming hatch.* Left: Figure 33. *Single coaming hatch details.*

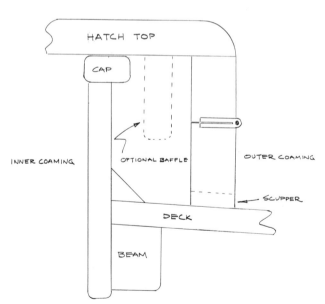

Above: Figure 34. *Double coaming hatch details.* Left: *A double coaming hatch.*

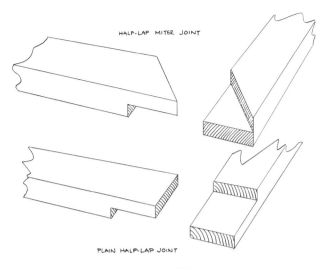

HALF-LAP MITER JOINT

PLAIN HALF-LAP JOINT

Figure 35. *Half-lap joints.*

coaming type. With the former arrangement, the hatch lid is secured to the one coaming. The latter type has an inner and an outer coaming, with the hatch secured to the outer one.

The double-coaming type is undoubtedly the most reliable for waterproofness. It has a lot more going for it, but it does have the disadvantage that the overall measurement of this type is significantly greater. For the average vessel, a well-made single-coaming hatch will more than meet the needs demanded of it.

The decision as to how the coamings should be fitted will depend on the space available and the builder's choice. I usually fit four pieces of material for a coaming to each side of the opening, that is, inside the two carlins and deck beams. These are then dovetailed together at the corners and fitted down into the opening, where it is glued and fastened into place.

A wide capping is fitted to the top of the coaming, using half-lap miter joints (*see* Figure 35) similar to half-laps to hold the corners. The outside of the coaming is further joined to the deck by nailing and gluing a triangular fillet, which can be simply mitered at the corners. Sometimes the fastenings are removed, and I plane a hollow in the fillet to form a cove, which looks a little neater. The hatch is then built so that its lips extend well below the level of the

coaming capping. The hatch top may be built of plywood and covered with teak or sheathed. If light is required below, a framework can be made up for industrial panes of Lucite, or a complete sheet of it can be used for the entire top.

The hatch is placed over the coamings, then a "sill" is fitted against the lower edge of the hatch lip and secured to the coaming with the corners half-lapped together. This makes for simple, accurate fitting. Hinges are fastened to either the fore or aft sills, depending on which way the hatch is to open. This arrangement is quite good. The hatch can be secured easily from below deck by using a clamp-type hatch fastener or simply by holding it shut with staple and hasp on deck. For ultimate strength it is hard to beat the system that uses a bolt that projects down from the center of the hatch lid and is secured to a cross beam placed across the underside of the deck opening. A washer and nut are used to tighten the lid down.

The double-coaming hatch is made in much the same way for the first part of the job, but instead of the hatch lid being hinged to the sill on the inner coaming, it is fastened to an outer coaming, which is set about three or four inches out from the inner one. This outer coaming has scuppers for draining any water that managed to penetrate the joint. Sometimes a baffle is fitted to the underside of the hatch to deflect this water down to the scuppers.

The double-coaming type hatch fulfills the requirement of stopping much of the water that runs along the deck, but often a single-coaming type can be modified to do this almost as well by fastening a coaming to the deck on all the sides except the hinged side. This coaming should be fitted so that there is a minimal gap between it and the hatch lid. If the deck slopes down toward the hinged side, there is no need to cut scuppers, as the water will simply drain out this side.

Hatches come in all sizes, but they should be large enough to be used for escape in an emergency, so they should not be smaller than about 18 inches square.

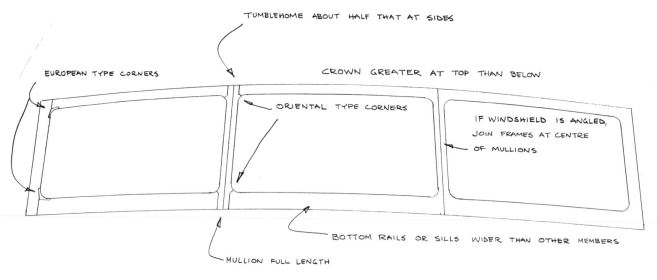

TUMBLEHOME ABOUT HALF THAT AT SIDES

EUROPEAN TYPE CORNERS

CROWN GREATER AT TOP THAN BELOW

ORIENTAL TYPE CORNERS

IF WINDSHIELD IS ANGLED, JOIN FRAMES AT CENTRE OF MULLIONS

BOTTOM RAILS OR SILLS WIDER THAN OTHER MEMBERS

MULLION FULL LENGTH

Figure 36. *General rules for windscreens.*

WINDOWS

The approach to window construction is usually indicated on the designer's plans. The rules for making wooden frames for windows are much the same as for doors. All stiles extend to the full height and rails are fitted in between, with the bottom rail being wider than the top. The glass is bedded into a rabbet and secured by fitting window beads, which are also installed with bedding compound. If the window is raked, it will be necessary to design the beads so that water will drain off them. Sometimes the rake is so much that this is not practical, so some windows are made with a little scupper in the shape of a small piece of copper tubing inserted through the bead at the lowest point and draining out lower down the rail. Opening windscreens on power vessels are difficult to make tight, and for this reason are seldom specified in seagoing craft.

Windscreens in particular are often constructed to somewhat complex shapes. There may be several panes of glass, each set in its own frame to be fitted together into the required shape. These windscreens are usually fitted on top of a cabin roof, which has a certain amount of crown to it. The top of the windscreen will also be curved, usually with slightly more crown

to give the windows a better appearance. Often the outboard frames also have a certain amount of tumblehome and the front is angled too, so there can be enough different bevels and curves to confuse even an experienced builder.

The best way to tackle a job like this is to make a mockup of the desired shape by cutting and fitting sheet plywood to represent the finished frames. The three-pane windshield with a center frame and angled side frames needs to be marked out carefully. Start first by establishing a centerline and measure equal distances out from each side for the joints to the side frames. If there is tumblehome on the cabin sides, there should also be a certain amount to the sides of the center frame, so that the glass will be narrower at the top than at the bottom. The amount is usually about half of the cabin side tumblehome. If these mullions aren't angled, they will appear to be wider at the top, even if made parallel.

If plywood is used for the mockup, it is possible to mark the positions and sizes of the various members that will go to make up the finished windscreen. The top and bottom rails will be curved, and probably angled too, and the side stiles will become mullions when the frames are fastened together.

At this stage it is best to mark how the joints

will be made. These are generally done mortise-and-tenon style, and due to the angled shapes involved, they will require careful marking and cutting. If the corners of the windows are to be curved, this shape should also be marked on the plywood so that you can decide how to cut the various members. There are two good ways to make these curved corners, one being the traditional European method and the other what I call the Oriental way, as it is done on many yachts built in the Far East. This latter method does use more lumber, but there is only one joint to fit in each corner instead of two. By the same token, the European method is stronger, as a separate block is glued into the corner with plenty of area for a good glue joint, whereas the Oriental joint has pieces with end grain butting together. The choice will depend on the amount of radius to the corners and the angles involved. Remember that to look right, the radius must be decreased if one corner of the window has a considerably narrower angle than the other corners.

Teak is certainly the best choice for this kind of work, but it is essential that it be well seasoned or the corner joints will surely shrink when the boat is exposed to hot sunshine.

Generally the rabbet for the glass is cut on the outside and beads are installed, as for framed windows. A router is an excellent tool for cutting these rabbets, particularly when the corners of the framework are radiused. I have made a small, adjustable, curved fence that is bolted to the bottom of my router. This allows the machine to cut a rabbet around an inside curve (*see* illustration).

Windows are often cut to irregular shapes in the sides of cabinhouses and doghouses. The irregular shapes frequently have arcs in the corners and curves in between. The making of beads for these shapes is sometimes delicate work, as they have to be sawn out of solid material, and the inevitable short grain does not tolerate clumsy fingers. The curved corners of windows are normally marked out by builders in a rather unique way that is known in the trade as a "paint-can radius." There are two common

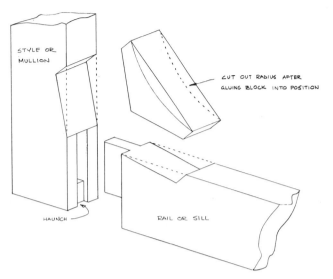

Figure 37. *European corner joint.*

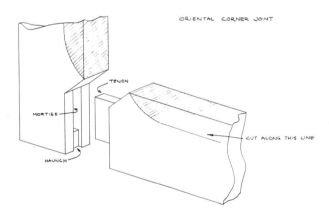

Figure 38. *Oriental corner joint.*

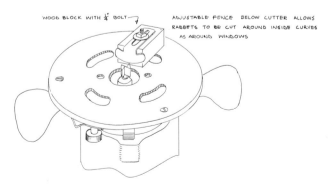

Figure 39. *A modified fence on a router.*

193

sizes for these arcs, the larger one being marked by using a round gallon can, placing it on the lines, and drawing around its bottom edge to join up the corners. A smaller radius is drawn by using a quart can in the same manner. It is surprising how many fellow boatbuilders use these handy shapes rather than compasses.

If one size of radius is used, all the corner beads can be cut out at the same time, using an accurate plywood pattern to mark the shape onto the material. A small band saw with a 1/4-inch blade is ideal for this work, but a good jigsaw will also do the job. The beads are first fitted "dry" and secured with screws into counterbored holes, leaving the correct amount of gap in the back of the rabbet that will allow for the glass and ample bedding compound.

When the beads have been fitted, the corner curved ones can be sanded in place using a small

drum sander of the type that will fit a 1/4-inch electric drill. These little sanders are very useful for smoothing inside curves. With coarse paper, material can be trimmed down surprisingly quickly.

Rather than make beads, some builders and owners prefer to have metal rings around the outside of windows. These are sometimes cast in bronze but are usually fabricated out of stainless steel and then polished. The metal frames need to be wide enough so that the screws or bolts that are used to hold them in place will miss the rabbet and glass. When securing windows to a thin cabin side, it may be necessary to glue extra material around the cutout to form a rabbet. An alternative is to use acrylic glazing, fastening the metal frame directly to the outside of the house side through holes drilled in the window. This arrangement can be made to look very neat if

Installing window beads.

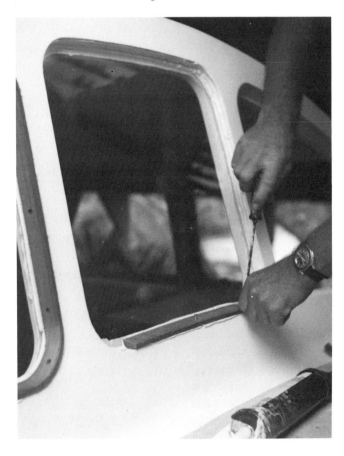

the acrylic window is cut about 1/4 inch larger all around the frame and the edge is beveled to about 45 degrees. Countersunk fastenings look better than round heads, although the latter involves less work. There is no doubt that this type of window is strong, neat, and waterproof; however, is is not everyone's choice.

Some builders install window beads on the inside of the superstructure, which also looks nice, particularly on the varnished sides of a coach roof or trunk. In the past, this practice was an invitation to leaks, but with the use of modern bedding compounds, this is no longer a problem. It must be kept in mind, however, that a window is not supported as well with the beads on the inside, and there is danger that a blow from a sea could stove in the whole lot.

The choice of glazing material is often difficult. Acrylic sheet is an excellent product, being light, strong, and often considerably cheaper if windows of irregular shapes have to be cut. The material is easily cut on a band saw or portable jigsaw, but it is easily scratched and will deteriorate if subjected to constant sunlight. Safety glass, the type used in automobile windows, is a laminated sheet glass and can also be used here. It is not cheap, however, and you will have to supply a pattern of the required shape if it is anything other than rectangular. As its name implies, safety glass will not shatter into jagged pieces when broken, but it really is not very strong, and if used, it would be wise to have protective shutters if the panes are large and the vessel is going offshore.

Another type of glass is usually reserved for the glazing of windshields or large exposed windows. Known as armored or tempered glass, it is a plate glass that is heat-treated and cooled rapidly to make it almost indestructible. As you might imagine, it is not cheap, for the tempering process requires specialized equipment, and the glass usually has to be sent to a factory for the treatment. The glass must be cut to size before tempering, as it is impossible to do so later. Armored glass is an extraordinary product and will often solve the problem of some glazing dilemma, but generally the acrylic or safety type will suffice for the average small vessel.

A Dorade ventilator made of sheathed plywood. Note the baffles inside.

VENTILATORS

Hatches and opening windows or ports cannot be expected to be adequate sources of ventilation when a yacht is at sea. Often a yacht encounters conditions when offshore that do not allow hatches and ports to be left open. If fresh air is to be brought below in all weather conditions, some sort of waterproof ventilators are needed.

A good water trap arrangement—usually known as a Dorade ventilator after the famous Stephens-designed ocean racer—is an easy way of accomplishing the separation of water and air. However, in extreme conditions it is wise to have some means of closing off all holes through the deck or deckhouse, even if they are designed to be waterproof.

Water traps can often be built into the deckhouse using hollow coamings or trunk cabin ends. The modern P.V.C. plumbing tubing (and fittings) is an excellent means of ducting air from outside to various parts of the vessel's interior.

Dorade boxes often are made of teak or sheathed plywood and built with a couple of baffles to prevent water from entering the standpipe through the deck. They are sometimes made with a clear acrylic top, which allows added light below to dark interiors. The acrylic may be either sand-blasted or sanded with an orbital sander to make it translucent, which will offer privacy if desired. The boxes need to be well fastened down, as they are often kicked or caught up with lines, and for the same reasons they should have well-rounded corners.

FINISHING THE DECK

Before any fittings can be bolted down on deck it will be necessary to complete the deck surface finish. This may be skinned with a suitable material, as with the hull, or planked with laid teak or some other suitable wood.

Sheathed Decks

The skinning of a deck and deckhouse requires much the same approach as that described in the section on skinning the hull and needs no description here. However, such a deck surface should be nonskid, so the following procedure may be of use.

Assuming that the plywood has already been skinned, the edge of the deck close to the toe rail or bulwark should be masked off with tape. The lower edge around the superstructure and hatches should also be masked so that the nonskid surface is not applied to the areas that will be painted.

There are several types of nonskid material. I generally use a sharp sand, which is readily available and does not wear out. However, crushed walnut shell and cork granules are other alternatives. If using sand, it is best first to sift it through a strainer to remove any small stones.

The nonskid material is stuck down to the deck using either polyester or epoxy resins, the latter type being the best. Colored pigment can be added to these resins; it will save subsequent painting for many years. The resin should be spread evenly over the required area with a wide roller, and while it is still wet, it should be covered with plenty of sand. Do not sweep the

sand about or touch the deck, or the marks will be visible later. Put plenty of sand over the resin, until no damp spots can be seen. Leave the resin until it is completely cured, at which stage remove all the loose sand with a soft hand broom or brush. The remaining sand should have a uniform texture if you spread the resin evenly.

Two more coats of colored resin are needed to seal the sand and lock it to the deck. When it is dry, remove the masking tape by carefully peeling it away, which will leave a ridge of sand that is a good edge to paint up to.

If you use walnut shells or cork, they are probably better applied with a sprinkler made out of a perforated can.

Teak Decks

A laid teak deck glued onto a subdeck of plywood provides a waterproof deck that is both handsome and light in weight, as the teak is seldom more than 3/8 inch thick.

The design of the layout largely depends on the shape of the deck. A wide, flared bow on a power vessel requires either a straight deck with the ends nibbed into the surrounding cover board or a half-sprung deck with the ends nibbed into both the cover board and a king plank. Most sailing vessels with less shape around the deck will use the fully-sprung deck, where the strakes are parallel to the sheer and are nibbed into a king plank. It should be recognized that a teak deck is chosen for visual effect rather than a practical surface, as it can never equal the nonskid surfaces of sand, etc. Because of the traditional look, it is usually best to lay the deck down without the use of glued, scarfed joints in the long deck strakes or covering boards. Plain butted joints or stepped scarfs that will be filled with seam compound will look better generally. The material should be all vertical grain to minimize movement and danger of splinters to bare feet.

Begin by making templates of the deck edge for cutting out the shape of the wide cover-boards. It is possible to allow a gap between the

A straight-laid teak deck.

A fully-sprung teak deck.

outer edge of the coverboard and the inside of the bulwark, leaving a shallow scupper that may be painted later. This has a pleasant effect and is often done on steel vessels.

If the deck is to be sprung, similar margin pieces will need to be fitted around all hatches and trunk cabins, and perhaps around any deck fittings, such as the anchor winch or stove pipe fitting. The king plank is also fitted and may be fastened temporarily for ease of cutting the nibs if desired.

The teak is either screwed or nailed to the deck, with some type of sealant used between it and the plywood. The choice of this sealant and the manner in which it is used is important, because water must not be trapped in any voids under the teak or seam compound. Teak laid with resorcinol glue must be done quickly or else the solvent in the resin will evaporate before the joint is made. For this reason, a more reliable choice is a filled epoxy resin, which has more body to it and also allows more time for assembly. The use of P.R.C. sealants are also good choices, although they are filthy materials to use for a job like this. Deck plugs over fastenings should be glued in with either resorcinol or epoxy glue. Sometimes the plywood is

sheathed with fiberglass or Dynel before the teak is fastened. However, the purpose of that is defeated if fastenings are driven through it later.

All the margin pieces that do not have to be nibbed out to receive the teak strakes can be fastened down permanently. The fitting of the strakes depends on the particular layout, but a fully-sprung deck is planked from the outboard side toward the center; a straight-laid deck is planked from the center out toward the deck edge; and a half-sprung deck is planked from the house side out toward the deck edge, then in toward the center to fill in the remaining areas on the foredeck and after deck.

The nibs are easily marked out, being set into the margin pieces about 1/2 inch to 5/8 inch to nothing, depending on the width of the strakes, which for a sprung teak deck should not be much wider than 1-1/2 inches, unless the deck occupies a considerable area. These nibs can be cut out with the margin pieces permanently fastened if a router is used with a collar attachment and a simple plywood jig, or they may be cut out with a jigsaw by removing the temporarily installed margin piece.

Thin strips of wood are spaced at regular intervals to provide the correct gap between each strake and its neighbor. These gaps should not be less than 3/16 inch wide so as to allow enough compound in the seam to shrink or expand in changing weather conditions.

To look right, the strakes should be fastened as though all the plug holes are located in a line with the deck beams, so the deck will have to be marked accordingly. When cutting nibs into a king plank, make sure both sides are the same. Sometimes you will have to steal a little by slightly narrowing the strakes on one side to conform to those on the other.

Two-pot P.R.C. seam compounds are preferable to the single-pot cartridge types, as the former will cure within a couple of days without shrinkage and enable the decks to be sanded within a week. A soft pad sander is the best tool for this job.

This type of deck can be applied to such areas as cockpit seats and hatch tops to break up large expanses of nonskid decks, and a mixture of the two types often looks better than a solid diet of either.

RAIL CAPS

Few pieces of finishwork are noticed more than a rail cap. Its appearance often reflects the builder's skill and pride in his work. On an older craft, it can give a good indication as to the condition of the vessel and how it has been maintained. By far the best material for a rail cap is teak: few other woods will stand up to the weather better, particularly if the rail is to be varnished. Many boats in tropical climates have teak rails and other finish trim that are left bare. For such lack of attention, teak is undoubtedly the best choice.

Mahogany is often used as a cheaper alternative, and on workboats and commercial craft, other tropical hardwoods such as greenheart and ironbark are good choices.

The rail cap is either bent or sawn to shape; the latter method is the least desirable, because it wastes much material, requires careful work to make it fair, and has to be joined with several

other sections to complete the shape. A bent rail cap can be made up full length and fastened to the bulwark, provided its section is not too big.

A good method for obtaining the correct shape for a sawn cap is to make a pattern of the entire length out of 1/4-inch plywood that has been cut into convenient widths so as to extend beyond the edge of the bulwark. These strips of ply should be fitted with plain butt joints and tacked down with small nails so that the top surface of the plywood is flush. This plywood pattern should then be rested atop the bulwark so that the shape of the bulwark can be transferred to the pattern. By measuring from underneath the ply or by using a "preacher" (a piece of wood cut with a long slot that can be slipped over the edge of the plywood and butted against the bulwark), the position of the bulwark can be marked on the top surface of the plywood. A full-length batten can then be tacked to the ply, allowing it to conform to a fair line with the correct amount of overlap on each side of the bulwark.

The width of a rail cap often varies to suit certain requirements. The outside edge is always a fair line and the inside is often changed by swelling it toward the bow and stern. Often the width is increased in the area of the chainplates. With the shape of the rail cap marked out, the plywood can be removed and cut to make a template.

The position of scarfed joints can be marked according to the available lengths of hardwood to be used. This way of marking out the rail caps takes the sheer of the hull into account, which is not done when consulting the plan view of the lofting.

On several yachts I have built wide rail caps laminated into position. Most of these caps have been between 3 inches and 4 inches wide, but the same procedure is possible with wider or narrower material.

The desired width of the rail cap is divided by three, and hardwood material is cut and scarfed to provide full-length stock. The three lengths of hardwood should have staggered scarfs, and it looks neater if the joints are vertical, the same direction as the glue lines in the laminations.

The center lamination is the first to be fastened. It can be screwed or nailed down at regular intervals. The line must be fair, which is best ensured by some temporary nailing where permanent fastenings will be placed later. The inner and outer laminations can then be glued and clamped to the center one, starting at one end and working toward the other.

There are a couple of ways of making the rail cap in this manner, and one evolved from the other, so they are offered here for your choice. The center lamination can be fastened down on top of waxed paper or a strip of polyethylene sheet so that the whole cap can be removed for final shaping. If this is done, it is best to fasten the laminations together from the inside edge with some long screws that will allow the outside lamination to be held also. These screws can be driven while the clamps are on the glue still wet. They should be spaced midway between the central fastenings, and all of them are plugged later. This fastening method can be used with both systems, so the job can be completed with a minimum of C-clamps. When the rail cap has been shaped, it should be bedded down onto the bulwark with a good sealant, such as P.R.C.

The next method is quicker and also makes an excellent job. Instead of removing the laminations for shaping, the cap is worked in position and glued down to the bulwark to become part of it. The center lamination is glued down first and allowed to set before the outer ones are added. The under outside edges of these laminations should be rounded off before they are glued to the central one and the bulwark top. If it is necessary to swell the rail toward the ends or at the chainplates, do not round off the edge in this area, as more material will need to be glued on when the cap is in position before final shaping is done.

A rail cap across a curved transom can be made in the same manner as that described above, except that it will probably be necessary to use thicker material so that it can be split horizontally after gluing to allow it to conform to the crown in the transom, which often is too

hard to bend. Knees are usually fitted where the bulwark and transom caps meet, allowing the two to be blended together in a pleasing line.

The junction of the two rails at the bow can be made herringbone fashion and fitted with a short wedge that forms a breasthook. The stemhead fitting will probably cover this anyway.

It is important that the rail caps and other varnished brightwork be made with future maintenance in mind. Keeping varnish in good condition requires regular attention, and the shapes of the various cappings and decorative trim can greatly affect the amount of work and time needed to complete the job.

Turned wooden posts supporting a monkey rail around stern bulwarks, or similar turned spokes on a steering wheel, may look impressive, but they are frequently a real headache when it comes to revarnishing them.

Shape your brightwork so that it can be sanded and varnished easily. Avoid square edges or complicated moldings if you have to maintain them, unless you are prepared to spend the extra time for this work. Inexperienced helpers will often sand completely through the varnish of these irregular shapes, causing an unattractive, blotched, mottled effect. The simple oval and rounded shapes for trim and cappings are not only easier to maintain but usually look better too.

DECK HARDWARE

The installation of necessary hardware, such as chainplates, fairleads, winches, stanchions, etc., should present little difficulty to the builder if, during the construction phase, he has considered how these are to be attached and made provision for them.

Chainplates can be made in a variety of ways other than the use of long straps of metal secured to the outside of the planking. With cold-molded construction it is possible to attach rigging to fittings that are bolted to the deck clamp or to bulkheads. In recent years I have had aluminum bronze castings made up in

Above: *Chainplate installations on cold-molded hulls.*
Below: *A sturdy stanchion base bolted to deck and bulwark.*

the form of large eyebolts that are long enough to bolt through the rail cap to the underside of the clamp. This type of chainplate allows the necessary holes to be drilled after all the finishwork is completed, and the eyebolts also assist in supporting the bulwark rail. Because of the tremendous loads involved, large bronze plate washers must be used under the nuts.

It is also possible to make up long U-bolts welded to a plate near the base of the U, but this requires two holes and does not offer the best support for the clevis pin in the base of the rigging screw.

Fairleads may be of the open or closed type and are often set into the bulwark itself with a double casting that is bolted together.

Stanchions need to be well secured because they are often subjected to unfair strains, such as from helpers fending off by grabbing hold of them. Because of the necessity of keeping the stanchions outboard to allow greater deck space, stanchion bases are often poorly secured from such inward strains imposed on them. For this reason, they should either have a broad base with at least three bolts to secure them to the deck or have additional support by being bolted to the bulwark as well.

Mooring bitts should be secured to solid material in the deck and placed so that lines from fairleads are easily led and made fast.

The anchor winch, which also needs to be well secured, usually is bolted to extra material fastened to the underside of the deck—often laminated pads of plywood set between or over beams. The winch should be positioned so that the chain will lead square on to the wildcat or gypsy to keep the chain from possible slipping or jumping.

Sheet winches often have to be secured to thin roof tops, where the nuts and washers of the holding-down bolts may be exposed. A neat and strong way of doing this is to cut a circular metal plate about the same size as the winch's base and then tap holes in this plate to allow the bolts to be screwed directly into it without the use of nuts.

Cockpit coamings should be fitted with scuppers that allow water trapped on the lee side to drain. If the seats are level or higher than the deck, copper or P.V.C. pipe can be let into the coaming and fitted with a rubber flap valve outside. Seats lower than the deck level will require scuppers connected into the cockpit bottom drains.

Treasure's deck layout. (Anderson)

COCKPIT GRATINGS

It is often necessary to provide a teak grating for the bottom of a cockpit floor. Making one involves quite a lot of time and material, yet a well-made grating will considerably enhance any cockpit. (They can be useful in shower compartments as well.)

There are many slightly different methods of making gratings; each builder uses the tools he has available, which often means he has to compromise. In the past, all the notches were cut by hand with tenon saw and chisel, but few people today have the time or patience for this, and machine tools are used wherever possible.

To look right, most gratings must have a frame around the outside. The size of this frame, however, is dependent on the size of the criss-crossed center, so before cutting up material, some marking out will be necessary.

The size of the square holes is usually between 3/4 inch and one inch. Anything larger is uncomfortable to stand on with bare feet. The grating material will also be the same width as the square holes.

Begin by marking out on a batten the pattern of alternating holes and material so that you can easily identify which is which—perhaps a crayon mark in the center of a division can represent a solid. The overall dimensions of the grating, including the framework, are now marked on another batten, or, if you prefer, a sheet of plywood, so that the positions of the notches can be superimposed on it to show how wide the framing has to be to fit it.

The inside of the framework has to begin at the end of a hole in both width and length. Mark the position of the framework so that you can double-check this. This outer framework is usually of fairly solid material—about 1-1/4 inches to 1-1/2 inches thick and 2-1/2 inches to 4 inches wide. The corners can be half-lapped or half-mitered together. Keep in mind the old rule that length fore and aft is much the same as height in joinery, so the sides of the framework should appear to go full length and the ends fitted between, as with rails, if half-lapped joints are used.

Before gluing the framework together, mark out around the inboard edge the positions of all the notches that must be cut to receive the notched rails and stringer slats. These notches are easily cut with a straight-shanked router bit using a collar attachment around the cutter bit, and a simple plywood pattern that is used to guide the machine (*see* illustration). These notches should be between 3/8 inch and 1/2 inch deep and will extend back from the frame edge the same amount as the width. When cut with a router bit, these notches will have rounded corners, as opposed to squared ones if cut with a chisel. They can, of course, be trimmed up square if desired, but they look just as well if left rounded. At this stage, the outside frame is glued up so that the rails can be fitted. These rails will have to be cut to length from the back of a rounded notch to the opposite side, then marked on the underside to form the shoulder for the lap joint, which must be fitted into the notches. If the notches were cut with a router, the lip ends of the rails will need the corners rounded slightly to fit. A chisel or a disc sander held on edge will do this.

When fitted, all the rails can be glued into position for the next job, which is to notch them for the stringers. It is here that other builders may decide to use different tools for the notching. A crosscut saw (also called a radial arm saw) fitted with a dado head can be used to cut accurate notches across the rails. If so, this would be done before gluing the rails to the frame. I generally use a portable electric saw with a fine-toothed crosscut blade to cut the sides of the notches. A straightedge clamped down acts as a guide. This has to be done carefully, for a mistake can ruin the job.

With all the saw cuts made, the center of the notches are removed with a router so that the stringers can be fitted. If a slight taper is planed on the bottom edges of the stringers, they will fit into the notches easily once the stringer ends have been rounded. With this completed, the stringers can be glued into position; when dry, the surface is sanded off. An additional touch is to drive a small, brass, round-headed nail, sometimes called an escutcheon pin, into the center of the stringers

Right: *Cutting stringer slots with a straight-edge and an electric saw.* Below: *A simple plywood jig is used with a router for cutting notches for the grating rails and stringers.*

where they cross the rails. This adds traction and used to be the way everything was held together before the days of waterproof glue.

Cutting the stringer notches in the rails is the tricky part, and another way of doing this is with a table saw, cutting across a wide board that, after notching, can be ripped up to make rails of the right width. There appears to be no easy way to make good gratings, which probably is why they are seldom seen today.

STEERING WHEELS

Steering wheels can be made up by the amateur builder, who possibly has more time for this type of finishwork than the professional. The type illustrated on page 205 shows a smooth-rimmed wheel I have made on several yachts. It is constructed of laminated teak strips and usually consists of three layers of material 3/8 inch thick by about three-inches wide. The shape of the wheel is marked out on a sheet of

3/4-inch plywood. I usually make up a six-spoked wheel, as it allows each lamination to have one straight-through spoke without a joint at the center, which makes for added strength. I now superimpose the shape of a six-spoked hexagon (which has to cover the curved lines) over the shape drawn on the plywood.

Begin by placing the teak (or whatever material you select) over the spokes, keeping the center of the material in line with the center of the spokes. The ends of the material have to be cut to an angled point where it will butt up against the inside edge of the straight rim material. As each piece is fitted into place, it should be tacked down with small finish nails to hold it in place. The outer rim pieces are cut out—all the same shape, of course.

That completes the first lamination. The center lamination is changed somewhat to allow the joints to interlock. Start by fitting the outer rim but staggering the joints so that they butt against each other in the center of the outside lamination segments. These, too, will all be the

203

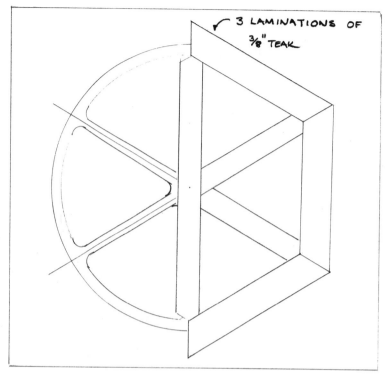

Figure 40. *Mark out shape of steering wheel on sheet of 3/4-inch plywood. Then fit thin laminations over shape, staggering joints.*

same shape as before. The center spokes are fitted in between, allowing the straight-through spoke to be placed across one of the divided ones underneath it.

The last lamination is fitted the same as the first, the only difference being the straight-through spoke, which should go over the last remaining divided spoke. The wheel is now ready to be glued together, but some means of clamping is required. This can be done by placing a sheet of plywood on top and adding plenty of weight, or drilling holes and bolting the plywood on for added pressure.

A polyethylene sheet will prevent the teak from sticking to the plywood during the gluing operation. The nails should be positioned so that they can be withdrawn later when the shape is cut out.

The final shape can be cut with a jigsaw or by hand, but it is done far more easily and more quickly with a router if a pattern is made up for one of the cutouts. A collar attachment is re-

quired on the base of the machine, and a template of 1/4-inch plywood is cut out in the shape of one of the segment openings. Drill a 1/4-inch hole through the center of the wheel and bolt the template to the wheel so that it can be moved around to each segment for cutting.

Before machining the segments, it is best to cut the outside of the rim. This can be done by boring a hole in the template to allow the router collar to be inserted into it. The template is revolved with the machine and a perfect circle can be cut. It will probably take two or three passes with the machine to cut the final depth. The same technique is used with the segment cutouts, but the template is clamped down during the machining of each opening. With the final shape arrived at, the router bit is changed to a sharp bullnose cutter and run around all the edges to produce a pleasing shape.

The center of the hub is best made up with a flanged fitting that can be bolted to a plate on the other side. I usually make a simple pattern

Above left: *The first laminations fitted.* Above right: *The wheel is shaped by running a router around a template.* Below: *The finished steering wheel.*

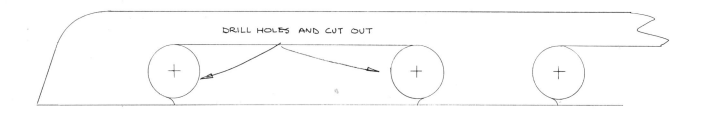

and have it cast in bronze, but it is possible to use an ordinary skin fitting if there is enough metal in the wall section for a keyway to be cut. The skin fitting needs to be well epoxied into the center of the wheel to prevent it from slipping.

As a final touch when the steering system is all set up, the rudder is centered and a 1/2-inch wooden plug is set into the rim of the center spoke, leaving it projecting an eighth inch or so. This can be felt at night time, even through gloves.

GRAB RAILS

It is good practice to provide adequate grab rails along tops of coach roofs and deckhouses where the side decks are narrow. Also from their obvious use, the addition of well-made grab rails does much to enhance the appearance of the deck in general. Grab rails can be positioned to divide differing color schemes or to give emphasis to the line of a house top or coach roof. They are also an excellent means of lashing down the odd piece of equipment, a sail bag, etc.

The most important consideration with any grab rail should be that it be well secured, and the best way to do this is to bolt it down. Even

Above: Figure 41. *Two types of grab rails.*
Below: Figure 42. *Cleats should be shaped in the manner of European style grab rails.*

if this means having a nut and washer on the underside of the deck, it's worth knowing you won't find yourself over the side one day with a grab rail in your hand. The bolts can be reversed, so that just the dome of a coach bolt head is visible on the inside, with the nut and washer recessed in the rail and plugged. Any fastenings through the deck or coach roof should of course be bedded down, and P.R.C. is the material to use for that.

There are two popular shapes for grab rails, with builders usually opting for the easier-to-cut type, which can be sawed on a band saw and shaped with a router. The European types require holes to be drilled first, then they are sawed and shaped.

206

The spacing of the grab-rail bolts should conform to any beams under the deck, but don't make the spans too big. It is better to have an extra fastening between the beams to shorten the spans, even it is a screw.

Grab rails should be about the same size on any boat, since they have to fit the average human hand. They are usually made from one inch to 1-1/4 inch sided material and about 2-1/4 inch molded depth. The cutout should leave a space of about 1-1/4 inches for knuckle clearance.

One of the reasons I prefer the European-type grab rails is that they look like the bases of wooden cleats, which are easily made from scrap pieces of lumber and, like grab rails, should be bolted down. The addition of some glue will make for a firm fastening.

COVE STRIPE

The addition of a cove stripe or line to a hull will usually enhance it considerably, particularly with some of the high-freeboard slab-sided designs that have appeared in recent years. A nicely cut cove stripe will accentuate the sheer and help to diminish the appearance of excessive freeboard, giving the hull a longer and more graceful line.

If you are concerned about painting the stripe or applying gold leaf, there are now excellent, inexpensive adhesive tapes in assorted colors (gold, too) that can be applied easily and will last longer than the real thing. The important requirement is to cut the stripe accurately into the planking. The hull drawings should be consulted to see if the designer has marked such a line on the hull in the sail plan and outboard profile.

Generally, with a normal sheer, the cove stripe is positioned from three to six inches below the deck edge. If the vessel has bulwarks, which are usually higher toward the bow, and the cove stripe is parallel to the deck edge, the distance from the line to the rail cap at the bow will be greater than at the stern. There are no hard and fast rules, however, except that it should be a fair, sweet curve. The cove stripe may be cut before the hull is sheathed, but it is usually done afterward, because the edges need to be cleanly cut if it is to look sharp. Sealing the stripe with epoxy is quite acceptable, though you may prefer to sheathe the stripe groove with a band of Dynel tape.

The usual way of cutting these cove stripes today is to use a router with a rounded cutter, which will cut a uniform groove. A fair batten should be tacked to the hull so that the router can be rested on it. Don't allow chips to lodge on the batten, or the router will ride over them and cause irregularities. The batten can be tacked above the stripe to prevent this, but it requires a strong pair of arms to go the full length of a hull without having the machine bounce away from the batten.

By far the safest method is to cut the stripe with a rounded wooden plane, resting its lower side against a similar batten tacked to the hull. These planes can still be found in some of the special tool shops. There is no "best" tool for this job; it depends on the choice of the worker.

At the ends of the cove stripe there are usually designs—some form of arrowhead or leafy pattern at the bow, and perhaps a feather or a series of dots or trailing leaves or even the vessel's name at the stern. These decorations are usually done with a rounded gouge and mallet, but a router fitted with a base collar and used in conjunction with a plywood template is quick and very efficient if used intelligently.

18

Spar Making

Although most small spars on sailing vessels are built of metal these days, there is still much to be said for well-made wooden spars.

Wooden masts can be made at the job site without the problems and expense of transporting long metal stock extrusions, which may end up not being the best size for a particular boat. Good-quality Sitka spruce is still available, so it is possible to build a wooden spar of comparable strength and weight to a metal one.

Wooden spars are easily tapered, and the thickness of various sections of the spars can be changed to suit certain requirements. The only practical disadvantage of wooden spars over metal ones is the increased maintenance, but modern paints and varnishes have done much to reduce this drawback.

For maximum weight-saving, wooden spars have to be hollow, with waterproof glues bonding the several staves together. By far the most popular section design for light weight and ease of construction is the well-tried box section, which, as the name implies, is constructed with two sides, a front, and a back. Filler blocks are positioned wherever it is necessary to attach solid fittings, such as spreaders, masthead sheaves, and goosenecks, etc., and this core material is inserted during the gluing-up opera-

tion. Other construction methods include laminating the section together into two separate halves with each half being hollowed out before the final gluing operation, and the multiple-stave construction, which was used to build some of the tremendous masts in the old J-class America's Cup yachts. Each type of construction requires different techniques, but they share certain requirements, so it would be best to examine these before progressing much further.

A long, level table or platform, commonly called a spar bench, is needed in building any glued-up spar. A spar bench sounds like a sophisticated arrangement with built-in clamps and heating ducting—and it is true that some spar builders do use this type of bench—but an adequate platform can easily be made to enable a top-quality job to be done with minimum expense.

A spar bench should be at a convenient height, about 30 inches off the ground, where it will be easy to work on the spar during the building, gluing, and final shaping operations. It is best located along a wall so that bearers may be fastened to the wall, perhaps to vertical studs with a bracket or leg to support the other end.

I have done most of the spar-making work on

about five sawhorses, then glued everything together on a series of level blocks along the ground. When dry, the mast was returned to the sawhorses for final shaping and fitting. However, it is often just as quick to set up level bearers with the aid of a string and spirit level at every three or four feet along the length of the spar.

It is often a problem to obtain enough clamps for use during the gluing operation, and a solution to this is to make up clamps of two wooden cross-bearers bolted together on each side of the spar. Banding machines have also been used successfully to hold everything together during the gluing. Some builders screw or nail the staves together, although this practice is somewhat more tedious and requires fastenings to be recessed and covered with plugs. There is no reason, however, why a perfectly good spar cannot be built in this manner.

Good-quality spar-grade spruce is the best mast material; it should be vertical-grain stock and well seasoned. A good alternative to spruce is clear Douglas fir, which is about 10 to 15 percent heavier but also makes fine spars.

Long spars require long lengths of material, so most staves will have at least one scarfed joint in them to produce the needed length. Scarfs should be made to not less than the 1:12 ratio and cut so that the joints will taper outward in a downward direction if the joint is to be visible and the spar varnished. All material must be scarfed up before the shaping is commenced. Any shaping is done on the two sides and front with the trailing edge straight. The spar plan shows the required sections, and the next stage is to mark out the shapes of the staves.

HOLLOW BOX SECTION

A hollow box section mast requires only two different shapes, the two sides and the forward and aft staves. The latter are often of heavier material to allow for the screw fastenings for the mast track. These staves are marked out by stretching a string down the centerline of the full-length material and marking the required

Above: *A simple spar bench. Here the author finishes an edge with a portable power plane.* Below: *Scarfing boards together for a mast.*

widths on each side of the string. A long lofting batten is a good aid in drawing the outline and can be used also as a fence for cutting out the shape with a portable saw. A sharp planer blade will cut very smoothly so the spar will need little, if any, additional planing.

After the forward and aft staves are cut out, I generally prefer to machine a groove in them to receive a tongue cut in the edges of the sides. This has a couple of advantages, particularly if you are short-handed, as it makes for rapid and accurate alignment during the gluing operation. The extra glued surface adds to the strength, and the groove allows plenty of glue to be applied without its running out of the joint. These grooves are cut with a router with a fence; they need to be about 3/16 inch deep and as wide as half the thickness of the sides (*see* illustration). The sides are marked out first by cutting or planing a straight edge, which will be the aft edge, and drawing in the taper from the plan sections with the long batten.

The edges of the sides have to be machined with a router to cut a tongued joint that will match the grooves in the front and back staves. Once this is done, the mast can be assembled in a dry run to make sure everything fits correctly. Next, the core material is fitted to make sure it is not too big, which would prevent the tongue joints from closing completely.

To save time during the gluing operation, it is often best to pre-glue all the core material to the aft stave. This also allows time for completing any wiring that will be secured to the inside of this stave and exit below the level of the deck. On low-voltage systems, wires need to be of ample size: 10 to 12 gauge for 12-volt spreader lights and 12 to 14 gauge for a masthead light on a 50-foot spar is about average. The masthead light wire will probably have to exit through one of the sides below the solid core material so that the wire can bypass the masthead halyard sheaves. This wire can later be placed in a groove just below the surface so it will exit out through the top of the masthead cap fitting. The final assembly of the spar is the most critical time of the entire job, and it should be planned so that

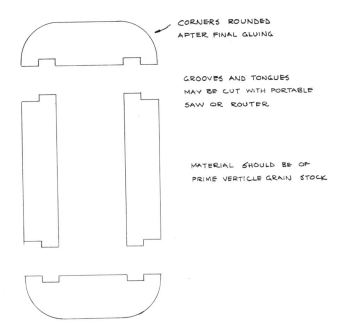

CORNERS ROUNDED AFTER FINAL GLUING

GROOVES AND TONGUES MAY BE CUT WITH PORTABLE SAW OR ROUTER

MATERIAL SHOULD BE OF PRIME VERTICLE GRAIN STOCK

Figure 43. Hollow box spar construction.

the gluing and clamping can be done in the most efficient manner. If you are working in a warm climate, it is best to glue the spar at a favorable time of day—either early in the morning or late in the afternoon—to avoid drying or evaporation of the adhesive.

The choice of adhesive will probably depend on what you are familiar with. I generally use resorcinol glues rather than ureaformaldehyde or epoxy-type resins, although these latter adhesives have certain advantages, such as cost and gap-filling qualities.

All the clamps should be adjusted so that they are set to the correct width. Squares of plywood or cross bearers will prevent the clamps from bruising the spar and also spread the pressure over a wider area. These and the clamps should be spaced out along the spar so that they are ready immediately. If you are well organized, the whole operation can be done without the panic that often attends this kind of job, even in professional yards. It is most important to get the job closed up while the glue is still wet. My wife and I have built several large wooden spars in recent years and glued them up by ourselves. This does not necessarily mean that you should attempt to do the same thing, because over the years, my wife has been part of many projects and knows a good deal more about the procedures than she cares to admit.

Each surface—that is, the tongues and grooves—must be evenly coated with adhesive, and nothing does this better than a small paint roller about one inch to 1-1/2 inches wide. The use of this type of glue spreader allows two or more people to apply the adhesive rapidly so that the side staves may be inserted into the grooves of the back, which should be straight and tacked down to the bench to prevent any possible movement during assembly. Before gluing the remainder of the spar, don't forget to feed the wiring for spreader lights out through the side staves. Another job at this time is to fill up some of the hollow·area inside the mast with crinkled-up aluminum foil, which has the effect of a built-in radar reflector, producing a good echo.

The remaining surfaces to be glued are now coated, and the benefit of the tongued joints is fully realized: the top or front stave can be easily fitted to the sides instead of needing to be aligned and clamped to hold it in position. Clamps are needed, however, to get a tight glue joint and should be spaced at regular intervals, starting from the center and working out toward the ends of the spar. This will squeeze out excess glue from the machined grooves.

The final shaping of the mast should not present much difficulty. The correct corner radius is normally shown on the spar plan and is first marked on the mast as a 45-degree bevel down each edge. The amount of beveled material to be removed will be smaller where the section is smallest for the last third of the length toward the masthead, and this may be marked with a spar gauge or long batten.

The head of the mast will probably need extra material glued to its forward and aft faces to allow any metal tangs to be connected for the forestays and backstays. These tangs are usually incorporated into a complete cap that fits over the masthead and provides for all the running and standing rigging attachments, masthead

light, sheaves for halyards, etc. Wooden spreaders are sometimes supported by transverse metal tangs that lie across the spar under the track. In such cases, you should use a sail track that requires a fillet to be glued between it and the mast. This allows the tangs to lie under the track without creating a bump in the track.

Other types of hollow box spars, such as booms and spinnaker poles, can be made in much the same manner as described above. The assembly of fully tapered spars will probably require the spar bench to be blocked to the required amount as in the case of a tapered spinnaker pole which has its maximum section at mid-length and is tapered at each end on all four sides.

LAMINATED SPARS

Certain sections of masts and booms may require a form of construction different from the box section described above. A shape that is popular with both metal and wooden masts is a slightly squashed section where the forward and aft faces are semicircular and the sides have a slight flatness to them. This type of shape is usually made up by laminating the material together and cutting out any hollow sections before final assembly. The number of laminations required depends on the size of the spar and the material available. The procedure is to make up the mast in two halves split in a fore and aft direction. This often means that the material needs to be somewhat thicker than what is readily available, so it has to be laminated to make up the required size. For example, a maximum section of 7 inch by 9 inch will require two halves of 3-1/2 inches by 9 inches, a difficult stock size to obtain. It is more realistic, then, to use two laminations of 1-3/4 inches by 9 inches to make up each side. The material will be obtained more easily, will probably be better seasoned, and will allow staggering of scarfed joints.

The laminations are first prepared by doing all the scarfing to the required length so they will

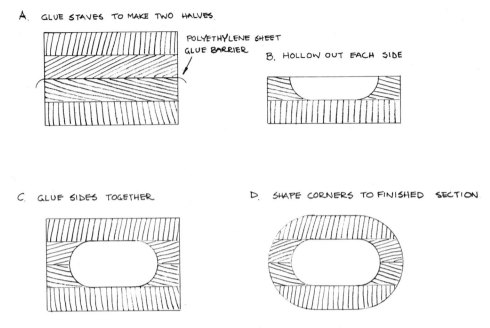

A. GLUE STAVES TO MAKE TWO HALVES.

POLYETHYLENE SHEET
GLUE BARRIER

B. HOLLOW OUT EACH SIDE

C. GLUE SIDES TOGETHER

D. SHAPE CORNERS TO FINISHED SECTION

Figure 44. *Laminated spar construction.*

taper outward and down from the center. It is best to saw each lamination to shape at this stage, because the material will be too thick to cut later. The required shape may be marked out on one lamination, and this can be used as a pattern for the remaining laminations.

Before gluing each side together to make up the half-thickness of the mast, it's best to check the suitability of the lamination surfaces for the glue joint. Machine planing is sometimes poor if the operator has fed more than one plank at a time into the rollers. Any ripples in the surfaces or steps in the ends of the planks caused by their being unsupported during the surfacing should be leveled with a hand plane, or else undesirable voids will result in the glue line. The mast is assembled on one of its sides instead of its afterface, as is done with the box-type construction.

The laminations for each half can now be glued together using a polyethylene sheet to separate the two halves. Edge-nailing is usually required to prevent the surfaces from sliding or skating when pressure is applied with the clamp. A wide paint roller is again the best tool for spreading glue; be sure to use plenty of glue, taking just as much care as described earlier.

When the two sides are ready, the extent of the hollowed-out sections can be marked so that this material may be cut out. There are several ways of doing this other than the laborious way of doing it by hand with a gouge and a round plane. A portable saw is possibly the best tool for the job, but a router can also be used very effectively. The saw should have a sheet of plywood fastened to its bottom so that a fence may be tacked to it, allowing the machine to be guided along parallel to the edge of the material. A series of closely spaced slots will allow the wafer-thin material between them to be broken out to save extra cutting time. By using the plywood base and nailing a fence at an angle to the blade, the saw can be moved along the spar crosswise so that the blade will cut a round radius.

It is necessary to increase the depth of cut gradually when using the saw in this manner, but a ripsaw blade will remove a lot of material quite quickly. Some hand work is necessary at the ends of the hollows, but the main part of the job can be done by machine. Any taper toward the top of the mast will require the depth of cut to be decreased, and the sections on the plan should indicate this amount.

The final gluing together of the two sides should present little difficulty. Once again it pays to check the glue joint with a dry run before any glue is spread.

There may be a considerable amount of material to remove in the final shaping, but generally it is worthwhile to plane off the taper on each side toward the masthead before planing or sawing off the corners.

A well-made laminated spar requires a little more material and time to produce, but the shape is usually more pleasing to the eye.

MULTIPLE-STAVE CONSTRUCTION

Very large hollow wooden masts are seldom built today, for in the larger sizes, the known strength factors of metal are more reliable than individual pieces of wood that have to be assembled by skilled craftsmen. Many of the huge hollow masts on the old J-class yachts were built of wood, which shows what can be done with this remarkable material. Some of those masts were over 175 feet long and were built up piece by piece and stuck together with adhesives that would be considered primitive by today's standards. The sections were frequently large enough to allow a man to be hauled through the spar lying on plank-and-roller skates to inspect the glued joints. It's unlikely we shall ever see such spars again.

Although the magnitude of a job of this size is daunting, the actual construction was not particularly difficult. The spars were made up of several staves that were glued together in a prepared cradle and held with chain clamps. Because of the sheer size of the job and the adhesives available in those days, only one stave could be glued at a time, which meant a lot of man hours wasted in assembling the spar, arranging clamps, then later removing them to allow the next stave to be glued. The chief advantage of multiple-stave spars is that they can be built up from relatively small material without any of the hollowing-out required by the laminated type. Clamping, however, is often difficult without special clamps, but large hose

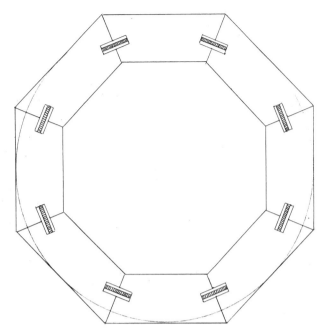

EACH SEGMENT IDENTICAL IN SHAPE AND USING ¼" PLYWOOD SPLINES TO ALIGN STAVES

Figure 45. *Multiple-stave construction.*

clamps or a banding machine will often solve this problem.

To allow accurate alignment of the staves, it is almost essential to cut tongue-and-groove joints in the edges to enable correct positioning. The spar may have to be assembled in two halves so that all the tongues may be glued in evenly.

Solid core material may be installed at this time. This type of construction is certainly more complicated than the box section or laminated methods, but that is mainly because of the greater number of pieces. The technique of fitting all the members together is not unlike strip planking, and accurate preparation of material is the key to success, as it is with all types of spar construction.

As soon as a spar has been finally shaped and sanded, it should be sealed with paint or varnish to prevent checking or splitting. The permanent attachment of fittings is best done after all painting or varnishing is completed. Metal hardware, such as tangs or bands, should be bedded in P.R.C. for absolute waterproofness.

Spreaders should be designed so that water

will not lie where they butt against the mast, a frequent cause of rot in otherwise sound spars. They should be raised at the outboard end so that they bisect the angle of the wire shroud they support. They should be secured firmly so that they can withstand the unfair strains often imposed on them by persons going aloft in a bosun's chair or by the pressure from a full mainsail when running off the wind. The ends of wooden spreaders are usually protected by a metal band shaped to fit a rounded recess for the shroud. Another band placed over this and through-bolted will enable the shroud to be secured firmly. When these bands have been fitted, the edges of the spreader can be rounded to the desired shape.

19

Painting and Varnishing

The quality of painted and varnished surfaces depends very much on the initial preparation of the material that is to be finished. Generally speaking, the average amateur has little difficulty in obtaining satisfactory results with painted surfaces, but there are certain procedures to follow before any paint is applied.

All holes and surface blemishes (such as "half crowns," the bruises left by hammer blows) need to be filled with a suitable filler. Some of the fiberglass fillers used for auto body work are excellent in this respect: they harden quickly, stick well to metal fastenings, and sand easily. These fillers should be mixed in small quantities with a square-ended flexible putty knife, which is the ideal tool for forcing the filler into cavities. Most of these fillers shrink slightly, so it is usually necessary to apply a little extra filler so that subsequent sanding will level it to the surrounding surface.

When sanding flat surfaces, you should use a backing pad or a wooden block to support the paper, or else the only real pressure will be applied with the ends of your fingers. With some of the newer papers—especially wet and dry paper—the skin on fingertips will be cut down rapidly, making them tender and sometimes causing them to bleed. For painted surfaces I like to use 120-grit paper for the final sanding; this provides a smooth finish yet allows a sufficient "key" for the primer-undercoat to penetrate into the wood.

Sheets of sandpaper come in a fairly standard size that measures approximately 9 inches by 11 inches. I was taught very early in my career to fold a sheet in half longitudinally several times and tear it apart so that each piece was 4-1/2 inches by 11 inches. One piece was set aside for later use and the remaining one was folded into three equal divisions with the grit side of the paper exposed. This prevents the grit surfaces from coming into contact with each other and destroying the "bite" of the paper.

A sanding pad of wood or hard rubber that measures about 3 inches by 4-1/2 inches offers ample support for the paper and allows maximum use of the grit surface. The edges can be folded around the sides of the pad for a good grip, and the used surface can be folded away and replaced by a new one when necessary. Stop every so often to remove the paper from the pad and give it a sharp rap to dislodge any buildup of dust in the pores that would otherwise clog up the cutting surface.

After sanding, it is important to dust off the surface with a clean cotton cloth. A good vacuum cleaner is excellent for removing loose dust from the pores of the wood. Naturally the wood surface must be dry and the temperature and humidity within reasonable limits.

PAINTING

All paints, undercoats, and primers in particular need to be well mixed, as the solids will settle in the bottom of a can. A stick is usually necessary to break up these solids, which may be quite thick if the can has been stored for some time. A mixing bit attachment on an electric drill is the fastest way of obtaining a uniform mixture.

The choice of paint largely depends on individual preferences. Epoxy and polyurethane paints offer superior resistance to weathering compared to the older oil-base paints, but they also require careful preparation, as their high gloss shows every defect. Painting a hull or superstructure that has been skinned with fiberglass or Dynel is best done with these synthetic paints, which give a hard, tough surface that will last considerably longer than the oil-base paints.

On bare wood, however, where there is likely to be more movement, the oil-base paints are generally better because they are more flexible. I know several boat owners who use latex house paints on their hulls with apparently excellent results.

The surface of the fiberglass or Dynel on a hull may require extra filling to give a completely smooth surface, and this can be done by filling the paint with powdered talc, which will give it more body. Some paint companies manufacture these fillers, which usually sand down easily with an orbital sander.

A well-prepared surface will usually require about five coats of paint. The initial thinned coat of primer is followed by two coats of undercoat and two of gloss, with several days between the gloss coats. Each coat has to be lightly sanded with about 150- to 180-grit paper and dusted off before the next coat is applied. In a warm climate, wet sanding is a quick and efficient way to do the job: plenty of water keeps the paper from clogging. In colder climates, however, it is generally better to stay with dry sanding so that the surface does not soak up additional moisture.

The chief problem facing amateur painters, and one that has a large bearing on the quality of the paint job, is the type of brush that is used. Professional painters use brushes that often cost $20 to $30 each. Naturally, at these prices they look after them. Like many things in this life, these brushes give better results after they have been used a few times. Choose a brush that is the right size for the job rather than the right price. The topsides of an average-size yacht will require a brush between 3-1/2 inches and 5 inches. Anything smaller will leave a streaked surface with noticeable laps, and will also take too long to apply the paint. One of the methods often used to paint large surfaces is to have one person apply the paint with a roller while another follows up with a brush to level out the paint. On vertical surfaces where the sun will often show shadows from imperfections due to poor brush technique, it is best to apply the paint in horizontal strokes before finally finishing them vertically.

Good brushes, like good tools, should be looked after if they are to last. If they are properly cared for, they will last for years. Use a suitable solvent and a wire brush to remove all traces of paint. Then wash the bristles in warm water and liquid detergent, carefully shaping the bristles so they will dry straight. Brushes should be wrapped in waxed paper and stored so the bristles will not be bent. Paint rollers, on the other hand, are seldom worth saving unless latex paints are used, for the price of the solvent frequently costs more than the roller sleeve itself.

VARNISHING

Good varnished surfaces ("brightwork") on a yacht often do much to enhance the vessel's appearance. The natural look of the varnished wood lends a warm touch to any vessel, particularly when contrasted with some of the rather sterile plastic and metal surfaces that are common today on production hulls. Considerable care is required in making and installing brightwork, for any blemishes or poor joints cannot be covered with fillers, as can be done with painted surfaces. Brightwork has to be planned for from the very onset of the project: joints must be cut neatly and in proper proportion, plugs covering fastenings should be spaced equally, and the wood itself should be chosen to ensure that all pieces are of a similar texture and color. The bare wood must be protected from water, which will cause stains and require sanding or perhaps bleaching to remove them.

Good preparation is the key to successful brightwork. Many builders will not use resorcinol glues for brightwork because the dark glue line shows through the clear varnish. However, if the joints are done well and are symmetrical, the glue line can sometimes be used to advantage, as with laminated hardwood knees, etc. The most common fault with amateur brightwork is that it is not really planned as such. Varnished trim should be shaped so that it can be sanded easily without the paper cutting away corners and exposing bare wood, which will leave light patches visible in the finished job. For this reason, sharp corners are to be avoided. This will also help to avoid "runs" and unequal spreading of the varnished film.

All sanding of the wood must be done with the grain or else the scratches from the paper will be visible through the surface of the varnish. When the scratches are wetted with fresh varnish, they are far more noticeable and will make an otherwise good job look second-rate. Cupboard doors are an example of this problem: the rails have to be sanded as far as the joint where they meet the stiles, with any minor scratches being removed when the stiles are sanded their full length. Sometimes it is impossible to sand with the grain, as with fluted door panels, and the only remedy is to use very fine paper for the final sanding.

Different woods require different paper grits for finish sanding. In general, the harder the wood, the finer the paper should be. Mahogany or teak may be cut down with 100 to 120 grit but will have to be finished with about 180- to 200-grit paper. Nothing makes sanding more boring than poor paper. For a few cents extra, the better-quality papers will sand a lot more material than the bargain variety. The gray-white aluminum oxide papers are excellent, and the black wet-or-dry papers perhaps are even better. On large surfaces, such as door panels, table tops, drawer fronts, etc., a machine sander can often be used to great advantage. Some of the poorer-quality hardwoods, particularly teak, which now comes from all over the Far East, often have beautiful grain effects that make hand finishing a long, tedious task. A machine sander with a soft pad disc can be used by an experienced operator to do a pretty good job of surface preparation in such cases. Although the wood will need to be hand sanded for final finishing to remove any scratches left by the disc, machine sanders still will save a lot of work. High-speed orbital sanders are also good machines, but generally speaking, belt sanders are too clumsy for cabinetwork.

When the wood is prepared for varnishing, you will have to decide whether or not to use a filler or stain on it. Some woods definitely benefit from being treated in this manner, and Philippine mahogany is one of them. Most paint manufacturers have stained fillers available in the various shades to meet all requirements. The paste filler stains should be of a consistency similar to thick cream and may need thinning with turpentine for easy application. Some people prefer to use a brush, and certainly this is often the only practical way of getting the filler stain into the corners and crevices on more open surfaces. However, for a rail cap or a table top, a clean rag is often best. Complete instructions appear on the can, but generally the filler stain is worked into the pores of the wood and vigorously wiped off the surface across the grain, leaving the pores filled. The wood is now a pleasing color that will look even better after varnishing.

It is important that the filler be completely

dry before any varnish is applied. The amount of time required for this will depend on the type of filler used and the climate, but it should be at least 24 hours. Some authorities recommend a light sanding at this stage, but the color can be removed easily by careless work, so it's safer to leave the sanding until after the first coat of varnish has been applied.

To prepare the wood for the first coat of varnish, many boatbuilders are using a technique called "epoxy sealing." This is somewhat similar to the WEST system in concept, as epoxy resins are being used to coat the wood and seal it rather like a varnish primer. Epoxy resin has a color almost exactly the same as varnish when applied to wood, and it forms an excellent filler and barrier film as well as a good base for succeeding coats of varnish.

Due to its consistency, epoxy is difficult to apply in the same manner as varnish. It is generally much thicker, and is hard to brush out with any uniformity. My answer to this problem is to thin the resin slightly with acetone so that it may be brushed on fairly easily and then to carefully wipe the surface with an acetone-dampened rag to remove excess resin. The amount of time required for the surface to dry completely is usually dependent on the surrounding temperature and humidity conditions, but generally 24 hours is enough. After light sanding with about 200-grit paper, you are ready for the first coat of varnish, which you will find goes on much better than on bare wood.

Where epoxy is used to seal large surfaces, such as boat hulls, it is not wise to thin the epoxy, for you want to have a good thick film of resin, particularly if there is no material such as Dynel to hold it. For this type of job, a window cleaner's squeegee is the ideal tool to spread the resin evenly and force it into the pores of the wood and any open joints that have not been filled. Obviously you should experiment with some samples before actually thinning the epoxy. The epoxy I use takes this treatment extremely well, but some brands may not be thinned without it preventing curing.

All your careful preparation work can be wasted if you choose poor materials for the actual varnishing. Just as with paint brushes, buy the best brush you can afford for varnishing. You simply cannot turn out a good job with a poor-quality or dirty brush. Even if a used brush is available, it's worth resisting the temptation, because only after you have started to use a brush will you know if it's really clean. A brush can be washed out in solvent a dozen times and you may think it's clean, yet somehow, after just a few dips in a can of varnish, lumps of old paint and varnish will come out of the bristles in a most disconcerting manner.

The next item is the varnish itself. There are all types and makes to choose from, and much depends on one's personal preference. I generally use one of the older oil-base varnishes for exterior work; it is easy to apply and does not dry too fast. For interior surfaces and cabinetwork, synthetic varnishes give wonderful service and will last for years without refinishing. The big drawback with any varnish is that the sun's ultraviolet rays will break it down much more quickly than pigmented finishes. The synthetic varnishes are considerably harder than the "natural" type, so they are more difficult to remove if the varnish has to be stripped due to weathering. They often dry quickly in open sunlight, which makes application more difficult, but the paint companies' chemists continue to improve the formulas, so it's probably only a matter of time before all paints and varnishes will be made of synthetic materials.

Whichever type you use, do yourself a favor and start with a new can. Old varnish frequently has skin suspended in it, which can do just as much damage as a dirty brush.

Many people prefer to thin the first coat of varnish with about five to 10 percent of thinners for added penetration, but if a new can of varnish is being used, this is seldom necessary. Varnish should not be stirred unless thinner is added, in which case it should be mixed and set aside for a half hour or so. The reason for not stirring is that any solids in the bottom of the can will be mixed and suspended in the liquid. By putting even what you consider to be a clean stirring stick into the varnish, you will, in fact, be contaminating the liquid, and it takes very little dust to ruin a varnished surface.

It cannot be overstressed that cleanliness is of the utmost importance if a decent varnish job is to be accomplished. Every effort should be made to remove dust, not only from the surface you are finishing but also from the surrounding area, particularly if there is any wind or draft that might blow dust onto your wet varnish before it has had enough time to dry. Most paint and hardware stores sell "tack cloths," which are pieces of gauze-like material that have been treated with a sticky varnish-like substance so that when wiped over a prepared surface, all the remaining dust that was not removed by either sweeping or vacuuming will be removed. If you do not have a tack cloth one can be easily made from a clean, lint-free rag (cotton is best) that has been moistened with a little varnish and thinner mixed together. Keep the rag in a clean glass or plastic container with a sealed lid. The tack rag should be the final weapon in your battle against dust and should be used immediately prior to actual varnishing. Be sensible in the clothing you are wearing. It is useless to varnish dressed in dusty garments or even clean ones that give off lint or fluff as you move; in fact, weather permitting, a bathing costume is about the best choice of attire.

Irrespective of your preparations, you will seldom find ideal varnishing conditions, particularly around a boatyard, where there is always dust to be found. I once varnished some brightwork in the middle of an open field thinking I had laid on a perfect coat, only to return a couple of hours later to find that a swarm of tiny midge flies had committed suicide and were stuck over everything. Although we strive for perfection, most of us will have to be satisfied with something a little less, but some consideration given to the preparation as outlined above will materially assist you to produce a professional job and one you can be proud of.

Some people seem to have a born talent for being good varnishers, and my wife is one of them. She has had plenty of experience over the years maintaining our own boat and the various craft I have built. Years ago, I remember trying to explain that the varnish should be "flowed" on instead of brushed on, and when that did not seem to mean very much to her, I simply said, "Brush on a full coat without leaving runs." On a flat, level surface, this could be the wrong thing to say, as the varnish might be loaded on too thickly, but for rounded trim and vertical surfaces, those directions are not too far off the mark. At any rate, the technique is lay the varnish on the surface with the minimum amount of brushing, applying it quickly so that no laps develop.

In hot tropical sunlight, varnishing has to be done with considerable speed to prevent laps. For boat owners in temperate climates, the sun is often the least problem. Moisture from dew or rain is the critical factor; it can ruin hours of work and cause many hours to be spent repairing the damage. So it pays to consider the weather carefully if you are varnishing outside.

New exterior work will require several coats of varnish to build up a thick enough film. The number of coats will depend on the material being covered, the varnish, and the personnel involved, but fewer than five coats is not good enough.

With new work, cleanliness is most important, because it's hard to build up a film thickness if you have to sand out all the lumps for the next coat. With some synthetic two-pot varnishes, one coat may be applied on top of the earlier one without sanding if the surface is still "green" (set, but not cured). In this manner, several coats may be applied in one day, and then they are allowed to harden before sanding for a final coat.

With the oil-base varnishes you cannot do this, as they are cured by exposure to the air rather than by a chemical reaction. Each coat, therefore, must be allowed to dry completely so that it can be sanded lightly with fine paper, about 200 to 280 grit, before the next coat is applied. For the final coat I would suggest investing in a new brush and a fresh can of varnish if you want a good finish, for by now you will have learned how difficult it is to get a brush completely clean.

For really fine surfaces, such as table tops and drawer fronts, the well-hardened finish coat may be rubbed down with "rubbing compound" of the kind generally used on painted auto bodies. This will give a fine-furniture appearance that does not have the shiny, high-gloss look. It must be remembered, however, that these compounds contain wax, and this must be removed from the surface if any further coats of varnish are applied later. Most hardware stores stock liquid wax removers, which should be used before any sanding is done.

20

Repairs and Maintenance

One of the chief misconceptions about modern wooden boat construction is the widespread belief that repair work and maintenance are difficult and require the services of highly skilled personnel. This is simply not so. The very nature of wood allows it to be used in a variety of ways. It can be bent, twisted, glued, shaped, cut, bored, fastened, and made to look beautiful better than most manmade materials. Never before in history has the wooden vessel benefited from so many superior modern products for repair work. Paints and varnishes, sealants and glues, preservatives, fastenings, synthetic materials, fillers, bleaches, and stains—the list is endless. The methods and choices of suitable materials for repairs are limited only by the ingenuity and experience of the worker.

The most widespread concern about a wooden vessel seems to be the fear of some form of fungal decay or rot rather than damage resulting from use of the vessel, which is probably covered by insurance. Rot may be the fault of poor maintenance or unsatisfactory building procedures; it is seldom due to the lumber itself.

In the light of present-day knowledge, it is little wonder that some of the older methods of yacht construction caused rot to develop in inaccessible areas: the practice of installing per-

manent ceiling over frames, decks that were covered with canvas and tucked under moldings, hatch framing, cabin and cockpit coamings that allowed moisture to be drawn into these areas by natural absorption, the oil-base sealants that eventually dried out and allowed fresh water to enter and grow fungus spores. The great wonder is that so many boats built in this manner still survive! However, when a brand-new, expensive product from Detroit can rust out in little more than a couple of years, it's difficult to understand why the owners of those vehicles point such an accusing finger at wood.

A resourceful man can repair just about anything, whether it be built of fiberglass, steel, cement, or what-have-you. Fortunately, wood is one of the easiest materials to work with, and although some of the wooden vessels around may be difficult to rejuvenate, a well-built modern vessel should present no major problem with regard to repairs or maintenance.

I am convinced that the life span and health of a wooden vessel are determined by the initial construction or gestation period rather than by the care the vessel receives later, although naturally the latter is an important aspect.

Most of those problems listed earlier were due to builders bound by traditional construction methods. It is vitally important that a builder realize the shortcomings of every material he uses. Wood rots, steel rusts, fiberglass cracks, as does cement, yet each substance has definite advantages. The wise builder exploits these features so as to complement the others. For example, hull damage due to grounding or collision is probably best resisted by vessels built of steel, which is the reason that material is used so extensively for commercial craft. Not that I am trying to infer that commercial craft are more accident-prone! It is generally accepted, however, that steel will take a lot of punishment, but its big flaw is corrosion resistance. This is what I mean when I suggest balancing the benefits and shortcomings of the modern materials available.

Wood has a remarkable resistance to weathering, and, as mentioned earlier, if it is used intelligently it will last a lifetime. Millions of homes are roofed with untreated cedar shakes, which are subjected to all ranges of temperatures and weather conditions and are generally expected to last at least 20 years, yet many people are still convinced that wood boats will succumb to rot in much less time.

One of the chief objections to cold-molded construction by an uninformed public is that it is difficult to repair. Many people think that hull damage from running aground on a rock or reef will require that successive skins of planking be removed until full-length material can be installed. This was frequently done in the past on double-diagonal construction, where each skin was separated by muslin cloth (another reason for rot), but such removal is seldom required in glued-up cold-molding. Fiberglass construction does not require each successive layer to be peeled back to repair a hole and neither does cold-molded construction. A hole in a sheet of plywood (which, after all, is made up in a similar manner) of bonded laminates is not repaired by stripping back each veneer; it is usually patched by either feathering the edges like a tapered scarf or cutting a rabbet with a router to allow a fitted patch to be glued into position. The same technique applies to cold-molded planking. It is a totally different approach from a repair job on

a conventionally planked carvel hull, since the damage is generally localized rather than spread out over a wide area. A molded boat is a one-piece, homogeneous unit rather than many separate pieces held together with fastenings. Longitudinal stringers are considerably easier to repair than transverse framing, but if thin laminations are glued up into place, even the transverse framing can be repaired by the average handyman.

Repair of cold-molded boats generally employs the same methods and materials as those for the building itself: thin, easily bent lumber glued together with modern waterproof adhesives, synthetic sheathing, and epoxy resins. A patch is usually fitted from the outside and fastened into a series of steps cut back from the edges of a hole in the planking, with additional fastening to stringers or temporary backing to support it. The patch layers should follow the direction of the original lamination.

Few if any yachts are designed to withstand the punishment of being run aground inadvertently, so if you are contemplating doing this with your new vessel, it would be best to select the construction material and design with this kind of treatment in mind. Large steel ships are frequently lost by human navigational errors, yet few people are unreasonable enough to blame the building methods and materials for the accident.

Most of the minor repair work involving boat ownership is due to normal wear and tear: stanchions will be used to fend off a dock, windows will get broken, a line or anchor chain may chafe through the rail cap, or a hatch will be closed over some rope and strain the frame or hinges. Many of these jobs require a patch or what is known as a "graving piece." These patches usually are diamond-shaped and are glued into a similarly shaped recess to cover the damaged area. It is usually best to cut the patch to size first and then place it over the damaged area so that the outline can be marked with a sharp knife. The material may be removed with a chisel or router, and it helps if the patch itself is slightly tapered on its edges so that when it is tapped into place, the joints will be tight. In sheets of plywood, a similar type of patch is set in the outside veneer to cover knot holes during manufacture; these patches are known as "Dutchmen."

That name brings to mind an old friend of mine who was born in Holland and emigrated to Canada. "Why is it," he asked, "that the English language is so hard on the Dutch?" I looked at him somewhat nonplused, so he elaborated, "All the cheap and bad things are referred to as being Dutch: the patches in plywood are Dutchmen, a Dutch treat is when each person pays his own way. It's assumed that a Dutchman's pants have got patches on them. 'Dutch courage' results from a person who is drunk, and being 'in Dutch' means to be in disfavor or disgrace."

I refrained from mentioning that the Phantom of the Seas is known as "The Flying Dutchman," and concluded that my friend did have good cause for complaint.

Minor superficial damage to brightwork can often be repaired invisibly by carefully cleaning and then filling the damaged area with clear epoxy resin, which has a color very similar to varnish. It is necessary to mask off the damaged area with tape and apply enough resin to completely fill the void, taking care that no bubbles are present.

On vertical surfaces, masking tape can be used to hold the wet resin in place. When fully cured, the resin can be sanded down level with the surrounding surface and varnished. Thus treated, a damaged area will be hard to spot.

On small areas scarfing is not critical, but whenever a structural member is being replaced and new material is being scarfed into position, the 1:12 ratio of scarfed joints should be used to give the material ample strength. Perfect joints frequently are difficult to cut, but with some of the gap-filling epoxy glues, this is not a serious shortcoming, although the material must of course be dry.

When working on old boats, it is sometimes necessary to remove long drifts and bolts that have become welded to the surrounding wood. Shipyards often have a special tool for such work that is usually made on the premises. The tool, known as a "dump," has a claw on the end of a steel rod that can be fitted under the head of a bolt or nut, and the other end has a handle. A heavy block of steel can be slid up the rod to strike against the base of the handle with considerable force, which will often dislodge these old fastenings and allow them to be withdrawn. A hydraulic car jack can sometimes be set up to either push or pull the frozen fastenings from the material. A heavy sledgehammer and punch is often the quickest way to do the job, but sometimes space restrictions do not allow this to be done. Application of heat, such as from a blowtorch, is another method used to loosen metal bolts, particularly frozen threads. Use of penetrating oils is another excellent aid in removing frozen threaded fastenings. Small broken bolts and screws can often be removed with tapered bits called "easy-outs." These small tools have a left-handed spiral thread and are inserted into a hole drilled into the center of the broken fastening. A wrench is used to screw the easy-out into the hole so it can grip the fastening, allowing it to be withdrawn. Sometimes the only way to remove a fastening is to drill it out and collapse the wall sufficiently without damaging the thread.

FUNGAL DECAY OR DRY ROT

Given the right conditions or suitable care, wood will last for centuries. There are many examples in Europe, for instance, of wooden buildings and church roofs that are hundreds of years old and have received little or no attention during their life spans. Among the principal enemies of wood are the microscopic, threadlike plants called fungi, which attack wood and use it as food. These fungi are capable of reducing sound lumber to a riddled mass of fragile, crusty flakes that will crumble into powder when probed. The spores of these decay-producing fungi are transmitted through the air by wind currents and can contaminate sound wood if the conditions are suitable. These conditions normally are somewhat critical, but as we shall see, they often exist in the interior of a boat hull. Most of the decay-producing fungi grow rapidly at temperatures that suit normal plant life. Warm, humid climates are ideal, and because of this, boats in tropical climates are more prone to attack than vessels from colder regions. When the temperature drops below 50 degrees, decay becomes relatively slow, and it essentially ceases if the temperature drops close to freezing conditions. The same may be said for the other end of the scale, for temperatures above 100 degrees are unsuitable for fungus growth.

The other vital element for fungus growth is a high moisture content in the wood, which has to be above the fiber saturation point, usually about 30 percent. This is reached when previously dried wood is contacted by water from rain or condensation. The water vapor in humid air by itself will not allow sufficient moisture to support significant decay, although it may permit the growth of mold spores. These minute spores are a type of fungus, and most boat owners will have seen some evidence of mold growth at certain times of the year. It usually is most noticeable on a white surface, such as a deckhead or even sailcloth. In the days of natural fiber sails, when they were made of cotton or flax, it was essential to dry the fabric thoroughly before furling or bagging them. If this was not done, the untreated material could be stained, permanently and in severe cases, completely rotted through. It was a common sight around harbors to see boat owners drying their sails on sunny days. The use of synthetic materials has largely eliminated this practice.

It can be too wet for decay, for the saturation of the wood can allow insufficient air to the interior of the material to support development of decay fungi. There are numerous examples of this. When the elm pilings of the old London Bridge were removed from the mud of the Thames River in the early 1960s, they were found to be in remarkably good condition, having been driven nearly 600 years previously. The giant Kauri pines of New Zealand have been almost logged to extinction, except for the

22,500-acre Waipoura Forest in North Auckland, which is being preserved by the Government. For many years, one of the sources of this excellent lumber has been logs removed from the swamps where they fell, often hundreds of years before.

The chief reason for decay in wooden boats is the very nature of the conditions often present. Warm, unventilated interiors and a supply of freshwater moisture from rain or condensation are ideal for fungal growth, so it is important that the builder and owner be aware of these potential problems and plan a logical method of either preserving an existing boat or adopting an adequate program and choice of materials to prevent fungal decay. As mentioned earlier, the best way to combat the rot problem is good building procedures that include using quality lumber, preservative treatment, and skilled work in preventing the ingress of fresh water into the wood.

BORER DAMAGE

Another hazard to wood construction is attack by some form of borer beetle or ship worm. Boat owners in temperate climates may not be aware of the serious problems that can result from borer attack in tropical areas. By far the most destructive type of borer is the termite, an antlike creature with long wings that appears at certain times of the year in great swarms soon after sunset. They are attracted to light and will frequently be seen flying around street lamps or against lighted windows. They will do this for some time before settling on the ground or some suitable surface, at which point they shed their wings and crawl about looking for a convenient hole or gap in which to start their new home.

Having lived and worked around boats for six years in Honolulu, I became acquainted with these remarkable creatures during repair work on a 40-foot ketch moored near my own *Treasure*. The owner came and asked me if I would do a little job on his boat because one of his crew members had attempted to fend the boat off the dock by pushing against a stanchion and the stanchion had come loose.

The job looked innocent enough; the base of the stanchion was screw-fastened instead of being bolted and a part of the bulwark had been torn out. The ketch was built of strip-planked Douglas fir and was entirely sheathed on the outside with several heavy layers of fiberglass. It was evident as soon as I examined the damaged area that this glass skin had separated from the wood in certain areas and that a large amount of the glass would need to be cut back.

I got my gear together and with power tools was soon able to open up the patient. I found to my surprise that the glass sheathing encased a completely riddled honeycomb structure that extended off into each direction. Extensive areas of the entire boat were in similar condition.

I have heard about doctors who open up a patient and find a disease that they don't have the technology to cure, and my feelings were much the same. I cut out a 10-foot section of the bulwark and laminated new material bread-and-butter style into position. However, it was quite obvious that the termites had completely riddled the entire vessel. It was interesting to note the reaction of the owner when he saw the extent of the damage: he simply refused to believe that it was as bad as it was, which supports my observation that most boating people are optimists.

On another occasion I was awakened during the night on *Treasure* by much shouting and consternation from one of the neighboring boats. I found out the following morning that the old 70-foot schooner *Fiesta,* a veteran of numerous Pacific voyages, had been dismasted by termites. The foremast actually fell over the side when one termite removed the last piece of wood holding it in place.

There were several other craft in the marina there that were classic examples of the very best in dry rot and termite damage, and not for the first time did I encounter the curious humor that attends the misfortunes of concerned owners.

One of the recommended treatments for com-bating these drywood termites was to enclose the vessel completely in a special tent that was pumped full of poison gas and left for 24 hours. This treatment sometimes cured the problem, though some boats seemed to fall apart soon after—almost as though the termites had stopped holding hands.

For two weeks every year in Honolulu, boat dwellers lived aboard in darkness so that the termites would not be attracted in their direction; parents kept children on watch armed with water hoses or fly swatters to dispatch the invading hordes.

Adequate protection of wood from termite damage includes taking the same kind of precautions as for fungal decay. Preservative solutions and painted surfaces are normally quite sufficient, but any trace of borer damage should be recognized as a potential danger, because these creatures stay inside the wood and can do extensive damage before it is apparent.

Of all the marine borers, ship worms are the most destructive. They are mollusks of various species, although in appearance they resemble worms. The best-known types are the several varieties of teredo and bankia, which can cause extensive damage. Present in all the oceans except the Arctic and Antarctic, these wormlike creatures start their lives as tiny, free-swimming organisms. When they find a suitable area of unprotected wood, they quickly develop into a new form and tunnel into the surface. Their principal tools are a couple of shells attached to their heads that quickly grow in size as the creature progresses along the grain of the wood. The tail of the worm remains at the initial entrance hole, and as the shells eat out the wood, it is digested by the tubelike body and excreted out of the tail.

Worms of up to six feet in length have been recovered from the planking of large vessels, and the holes are frequently more than 1/2 inch in diameter. Most wood is susceptible to marine borer attack, so special paints containing copper and other chemicals have been developed to combat these pests. A few mainly tropical woods are very resistant to marine borer attack;

among them are greenheart from South America and totora from New Zealand and several Australian hardwoods, such as turpentine and jarrah. These are often used as wharf pilings or exterior sheathing for boat hulls because of their resistance.

Antifouling bottom paints will prevent marine borer attack on immersed hulls only as long as the paint film is intact. This is where the benefit of a synthetic exterior sheathing material is fully realized.

PRESERVATIVES

Mention has been made that preservatives can be used to prevent rot and termite infestation. There are a variety of preservative treatments that can be used for this purpose. The practice of "pickling" a new vessel with salt was common in the past; it was well known that the rot fungus cannot survive in salt-saturated wood. Vessels that are used regularly and are doused frequently with salt water are far less prone to dry rot attack than idle craft. Although salt is a cheap natural product for combating dry rot spores, it is not practical for the average pleasure yacht, because it will soak up excessive moisture from the atmosphere. There are various rot preservatives on the market today that are far more effective and easier to use.

Once quite popular but now seldom used, creosote, an oily antiseptic liquid obtained by the distillation of wood tar, particularly beach-wood, was regarded as being very effective due to its obnoxious characteristics. It burned any exposed skin it touched, its vapors frequently caused respiratory ailments, and its offensive smell was sufficient reason to cause any self-respecting fungus spore to go elsewhere for more friendly conditions. In spite of all its undesirable features, creosote was not a particularly reliable preservative, and fortunately there are newer products that are much more effective and pleasant to use.

The two most common wood preservatives used today are copper naphthanate and penta-chlorophenol, usually called penta. Both of these solutions have their ingredients suspended in volatile petroleum solvents, which, being very thin, allow excellent penetration of the wood surface.

Copper naphthanate solutions are available in two forms—one is a clear, colorless liquid not unlike kerosene and the other is stained a dark green. Penta also has clear and stained options. The clear varieties generally are the most popular. The stained variety has the ability to leach through several thicknesses of covering paint, so if you intend to paint the wood, the clear variety is undoubtedly the best choice. The green solution does have an advantage in that it is possible to see where you have treated the wood, but if any drops from the brush fall on paint or unfinished brightwork, you will wish you had used the clear type.

There are several new wood preservatives on the market that use Tributal-tin-oxide (T.B.T.O.) as the preserving medium. Some of these solutions also contain wax, which seals in the preserving agents and also prevents water absorption. For bilge areas and out-of-sight, out-of mind locations, these preservative-sealers allow quick treatment, yet since they are clear, the wood can be inspected instantly at a later time. A word or two of caution, however: Because of their wax content, some of these solutions should not be used on wood until all glued construction is complete. Glue simply will not stick to some of these materials, and in fact, I have used certain preservatives on sawhorses, wood clamps, and frames as a release agent. Hardened resorcinol glues, in particular, can be removed easily from surfaces so treated.

One other cautious note regarding these preservatives: being very thin, they splash easily, and if you ever get any in your eyes, you will wish you had not. Always wear protective goggles. The fumes can also be pretty bad, so forced ventilation (perhaps from a reversed vacuum cleaner) is advisable for confined areas. Unless you have a very good face mask, don't try spraying these liquids. Spraying causes minute particles to be suspended in the air, and these can be inhaled into the lungs and cause respiratory problems.

I usually apply all the wood preservative at one time after all the construction is completed. This allows the wood to be saturated, and any surplus preservative can run into the bilge, where it can be collected and re-used.

SEALANTS

Most repair jobs seem to require the use of some type of sealant, and the modern boatbuilder is indeed fortunate to have a full selection of synthetic compounds to choose from. As mentioned earlier, the P.R.C. thiokol sealants come in trigger-operated cartridges that are easy to use for bedding down fittings, glazing windows, paying deck seams, and a host of other applications. This substance sticks well to almost anything, so it can also be used to insulate metal fittings and seal electrical wires where they emerge on deck or out of a spar. Combined with a loose, flexible scrimlike material, it would even be a good adhesive for skinning an old hull, although there are cheaper materials that will do the same task. The material has countless uses, and the modern builder must wonder how boats were ever made watertight without it.

The important thing to remember in repair work is that it is not always necessary to rebuild damaged areas the way they were originally constructed. This does not mean that quality has to be sacrificed, either. It is usually possible to make a neat permanent repair that uses different materials from what was originally chosen. Some of the materials and methods mentioned earlier will certainly be of help, but new products and practices will be developed that may be superior. Take advantage of them if they are better, but remember also that it is necessary to have the experience to judge whether they are reliable.

21

Loose Ends

When a man sees the fruits of his labor, no matter what size it may be, ready at last for the launching with paint and varnish glistening, he is entitled to a certain feeling of inner satisfaction that will be with him always. Some people reading these lines will have built a boat of some kind before and know the special thrill and feeling of satisfaction when the creation from your own hands finally settles into the water. Those who have not experienced it cannot understand the special pride that is the reward of the craftsman who has spent so many long hours patiently constructing his vessel. There were times when he almost wept with frustration when some aspect of the job almost defeated him, plunging his spirits into despair, but he learned to circumvent these setbacks, having the guts to continue, the will to succeed, the dream to pursue.

Launching time is often a difficult period for the builder; it may mean employing expensive equipment and skilled operators to move his vessel from the building site into the water. With large vessels, overland transport is frequently a complex operation, necessitating cooperation and permission from various authorities. Cable television, power, and telephone companies may have to remove low wires along the planned route; transportation departments and local police may have to be approached to supply escorts if the load exceeds a certain width. The latter often requires exact timing so that the trailer will not be on the highway during peak hours and cause traffic jams. Obtaining the necessary clearances from all sources and arranging the details can be a lot of work, and it is best done well before the planned moving date.

The builder is probably working late hours doing all the last-minute jobs; making a suitable cradle for the hull, perhaps moving the vessel out of the building shed, test-running the engine, and final painting. By launch day, he is often emotionally charged up, worried that all these strangers are going to make a hash of the whole operation, damage the boat, and ruin him in the bargain as well. He has heard of the plenty of launch-day disasters: when So-and-So's yacht fell off the cradle, or when a cable broke and the crane jib crashed down onto Joe Soap's boat, almost cutting the hull in half, and when that fellow from over Lyndale way had to remove the deckhouse when he discovered that his boat's only route to the water had a bridge over it with only a 12-foot six-inch clearance. While following the boat along the highway, the builder is almost sick with apprehension every

Buccaneer *enroute to launching. (Sea Spray)*

time the truck negotiates a corner and the camber of the road causes the hull to heel far beyond his expectations. He wonders why all those idiots on deck who are supposed to be watching out for low wires insist on standing together way out at the end of the bow. For many craft, that journey to the sea is the most perilous voyage she will ever make, while for others, it is but the beginning of an adventurous life ahead.

Very few sailing vessels are completed sufficiently at launch time to be ready for even limited sailing, let alone deep-sea work. Spars

usually are stepped after the boat is in the water, with temporary rigging set up to support them so that accurate measurements may be taken for the permanent standing rigging.

After the rigging is completed it will need to be set up correctly and "tuned." Riggers and sailmakers usually prefer their work to be broken in. Wire will stretch slightly and so will sails, particularly along the luffs. Normal standing rigging should be set up firmly, but not bar-tight so that it places excessive strain on the rig. It is normal for the lee rigging to be slack when the sails are set, and on no account should

Opposite: *Launching* Sunrise. Above: Sunrise *sailing in Hawaiian waters.*

you tighten loose wire under these conditions. All adjustments should be made equally so that the tensions are balanced, and this cannot be done if the lee rigging is tensioned.

The alignment of the engine should be checked after launching, and manufacturers' recommendations should be followed in regard to the "running-in period."

There are hundreds of jobs to be done if a vessel is being prepared to go offshore, and this commissioning work is beyond the scope of my book. For the man who has built his own craft, this is usually a most enjoyable time, although the various tasks will take considerably longer than working ashore in the building shed, where the facilities are normally better than alongside a dock.

Finally, never underestimate the power of the sea, for no matter how well you may have built your vessel, it is but a toy when faced with the forces generated by ocean storms. There are limits to which even the best built craft can

succumb, and the man who thinks otherwise is either lucky or a fool.

Few professional occupations in life are as rewarding mentally and spiritually as boatbuilding, considering the amount of time and effort spent during construction. The financial rewards are usually poor when compared with other types of work, but a good craftsman is capable of making a worthwhile living at it without dying of boredom or suffering from ulcers.

Somewhere, years ago, I read a few lines that express my philosophy about boatbuilding. It goes something like this:

> To have lived, a man must have
> Planted a tree,
> Raised a son,
> And built a boat.

I hope that you, too, will feel the same satisfaction from your endeavors.

231

Glossary

BODY PLAN	The hull plan drawing that shows a vessel's sections.
BONDING	The connecting together of submerged metal fittings subject to electrolysis, such as rudder gear, sea cocks, etc.
BOOT TOP	A broad paint stripe immediately above a vessel's waterline.
BRIGHTWORK	Varnished surfaces.
BUSS BARS	Metal strips located between the batteries and switchboard to which electrical wiring is connected.
CANT	A large softwood timber that has been slabbed on each side.
CLAMP	A tool for temporarily holding wooden members together.
CLAMP (SHEER)	A longitudinal structural member to which planking is joined. The clamp is often the same member as the shelf; it is termed a clamp when the molded depth is greater than the sided depth.
CORE	(1) The inside laminates of plywood. (2) A pattern, usually of sand, placed in a mold for molten metal to form around thereby producing a void in the finished casting.
CORE BOX	A female pattern for making cores.
CROSS BANDS	The core material in plywood.
DADO	A shallow groove cut across a wide piece of wood to receive the end of another, similar piece, as in shelving.
DATUM WATERLINE	The designed waterline at which the vessel should float.
DOVETAIL JOINT	The tapered, notched joint used for joining two pieces of wood at 90 degrees to one another.

GLOSSARY

DRAW
The taper on a wooden foundry pattern that allows it to be withdrawn from molding sand.

DRY RUN
A preliminary assembling of materials to check the fit of the various parts of a structure before it is finally glued or fastened together.

DUMP
A tool for removing long drifts and bolts that have become welded to surrounding wood.

DYKE
A North American term for end cutters.

FACE FRAME
In cabinet work, the frame into which doors and drawers are set.

FAIR
A term used to describe a curved line that is without bumps or hollows.

FAIRING UP
(1) In lofting, the process of smoothing out the lines.
(2) Shaping the completed framework of a hull into a smooth line so that the planking will lie fair when it is attached.

FASCIA
Any piece of applied trim or facing.

FIDDLE
A raised piece of wood that forms a lip at the edge of shelving or work tops.

FILLET
A small beading fastened into a corner joint to provide a rounded juncture.

FLITCH
A portion of log sawn on two or more faces.

GANG SAW
A saw commonly used in lumber mills having several vertical blades that rip stock into uniform planks.

GRAVING PIECE
A wood patch, usually diamond shaped, that is let in to repair a damaged section of wood.

GRINDING
Removing unwanted metal from behind the cutting edge of a tool.

HALF CROWNS
Hammer bruises.

JAMBS
The vertical outside framing to which doors are fitted.

KERF
Saw cut.

KING PLANK
The wide, central, longitudinal member of a sprung deck into which the ends of decking are fastened.

KNIGHTHEAD
A member fastened to the outside of the bulwark at both bow and stern to build the bulwark out to the plane of the hull planking.

LIP AND BULLNOSE
A term referring to the rabbeted, rounded edge of a drawer front or door that stands proud of the face frame.

LUGS
Metal pieces welded to fuel tanks that enable tanks to be fastened into position.

MARKING STAFF
A long stick or batten used for obtaining dimensions from the loft floor.

MOCKUP — A temporary construction of materials that gives the builder an idea of what the finished job will be like.

MOLDED MEASUREMENT — The height, or depth, of a member.

MORTISE — The female part of a mortise-and-tenon joint.

MORTISE-AND-TENON JOINT — A much-used joint for joining wood at right angles, the mortise being a slot and the tenon being a male member cut to fit the mortise.

MULLION or **MUNNION** — A vertical member running down the middle of a door.

NIBS — The cut-outs in a king plank or margin piece into which decking is checked.

PANEL — (1) A wide piece of material used for filling an opening, such as in a door.
(2) A piece of plywood.

PATTERN — A form used as a master to produce a duplicate.

PEELER — A log selected for making plywood.

PICKLING — The traditional practice of preserving wood by saturating it with salt.

PIN — The male part of the dovetail joint that fits in between the dovetails.

PLUG — (1) A pattern for making a mold in which a ballast keel is cast.
(2) A male mold or form upon which a cold-molded vessel is sometimes built.
(3) A cylindrically shaped piece of wood used to cover fastenings.

PREACHER — A slotted piece of wood slipped over the edges of plywood structures that is used as a tool for marking the position of framing on the outside of the plywood.

PROFILE — That part of a lines drawing that presents a side view of a vessel.

RABBET — A squared notch cut down the length of a member into which planking is secured.

RAILS — The horizontal framing found in doors and other framework.

RAMMING — In foundry work, the process of packing the molding sand tightly around a pattern.

SHOOTING — Planing the edge of a plank or board to make it straight.

SIDED MEASUREMENT — The width of a structural member in a horizontal plane.

SPILING — The method of developing the shape of curved members such as planking.

TEMPLATE — A temporary shape or form from which is cut a permanent member—e.g., a half template for making a bulkhead.

TENON — The male part of a mortise-and-tenon joint.

Appendix

TABLE 1
CONVERSION TABLES FOR WEIGHT, VOLUME, AND MEASUREMENT

1 Imperial gallon	= 1.2 U.S. gallons		=	4.54 liters
1 U.S. gallon	= .833 Imperial gallons		=	3.78 liters
1 liter	= .22 Imperial gallons		=	.265 U.S. gallons

	Gasoline	*Diesel*	*Freshwater*
1 Imperial gallon weighs	7.42 lbs.	8.55 lbs.	10 lbs.
1 U.S. gallon weighs	6.19 lbs.	7.13 lbs.	8.34 lbs.
1 liter weighs	1.635 lbs.	1.88 lbs.	2.2 lbs.

1 cubic foot	=	6.23 Imperial gallons	
1 cubic foot	=	7.48 U.S. gallons	
1 cubic foot	=	28.317 liters	
1 Imperial gallon	=	277 cubic inches	
1 U.S. gallon	=	231 cubic inches	
1 liter	=	61 cubic inches	
1 cubic meter	=	approximately 35 cubic feet	
1 pound	=	453.59 grams	= 0.4536 kilograms
1 kilogram	=	2.2 pounds	
1 U.S. ton	=	2000 pounds	
1 long ton	=	2240 pounds	
1 metric ton	=	1000 kilograms	= 2204.61 pounds
1 centimeter	=	.39 inch	
1 meter	=	39.37 inches	

TABLE 2

CALCULATING VOLUME FOR TANKS

In calculating tank capacities, it is usually best to reduce all measurements to inches.

To estimate the capacity of a cylinder: multiply the area of one end by the length.

Area $= \pi r^2 = 3.1416 \times$ radius squared in inches

Volume $= 3.1416 \times$ radius squared $\times$ length in inches

To find Imperial gallons: divide sum by 277.

To find U.S. gallons: divide sum by 231.

To find liters: divide sum by 61.

Example:

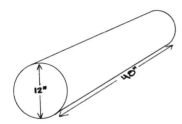

Radius 6^2	=	36
36 × 3.1416	=	113.0976
113.0976 × 48	=	5428.7 cubic inches
5428.7 ÷ 277	=	19.6 Imperial gallons

To find the area of a triangle: multiply the length of the longest side of the height and divide by 2.

Example:

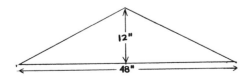

48 × 12 = 576

576 ÷ 2 = 288 square inches

TABLE 3

WORKING OUT ACCURATE ANGLES IN DEGREES

When it is necessary to draw an accurate angle, as when lofting for vee drives and propeller shaft angles, you can mark out a line either 48 inches long or 1 meter long and from one end measure up or down the distance shown in the accompanying tables.

Example:

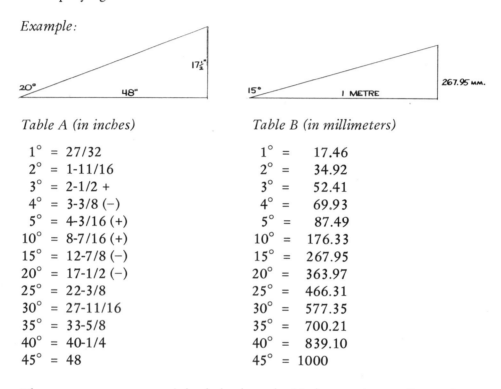

Table A *(in inches)*

1°	=	27/32
2°	=	1-11/16
3°	=	2-1/2 +
4°	=	3-3/8 (−)
5°	=	4-3/16 (+)
10°	=	8-7/16 (+)
15°	=	12-7/8 (−)
20°	=	17-1/2 (−)
25°	=	22-3/8
30°	=	27-11/16
35°	=	33-5/8
40°	=	40-1/4
45°	=	48

Table B *(in millimeters)*

1°	=	17.46
2°	=	34.92
3°	=	52.41
4°	=	69.93
5°	=	87.49
10°	=	176.33
15°	=	267.95
20°	=	363.97
25°	=	466.31
30°	=	577.35
35°	=	700.21
40°	=	839.10
45°	=	1000

These measurements may be halved or doubled to make smaller or larger triangles.

Use the following proportions to make right-angle triangles for marking squares.

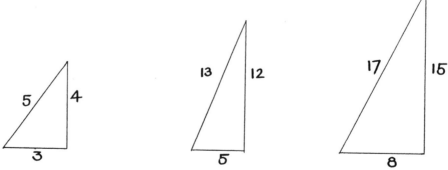

TABLE 4

WEIGHTS OF BOATBUILDING MATERIALS

MATERIAL	*WEIGHT* *(per cubic foot)*
African mahogany	34 pounds
Alaska yellow cedar	30 pounds
Aluminum	168 pounds
Balsa	6-11 pounds
Bronze	481-537 pounds depending on type
Cork	16 pounds
Douglas fir	32 pounds
Ferrocement	185 pounds depending on steel content
Greenheart	66 pounds
Kauri pine	38 pounds
Lead	709 pounds—pure
Lignumvitae	77-83 pounds
Sitka spruce	27 pounds
Steel	490 pounds
Teak	44 pounds
Urethane foam	1.5 pounds
Western red cedar	24 pounds

TABLE 5

QUANTITIES—BOAT NAILS PER POUND

When estimating the quantity of fastenings required for a job it is sometimes necessary to know the approximate number of nails per pound. These figures are for annular ringed bronze nails.

BOAT NAILS

Length (in inches)	Gauge	Approx. number per pound
3/4	12	462
7/8	12	393
1	12	350
1-1/4	12	280
1-1/4	10	155
1-1/2	14	400
1-1/2	12	230
1-1/2	10	135
1-1/2	8	90
1-3/4	10	120
1-3/4	8	83
2	10	105
2	8	75
2-1/4	10	94
2-1/4	8	64
2-1/2	10	84
2-1/2	8	58
2-3/4	8	53
3	8	48

TABLE 6

PHYSICAL PROPERTIES OF THE ELEMENTS

Metal	Symbol	Atomic No.	Weight (lbs./cu.ft.)	Melting Temp.
Aluminum	Al	13	168	660.2°C-1220.4°F
Antimony	Sb	51	412	630.5°C-1166.9°F
Cadmium	Cd	48	540	320.9°C-609.6°F
Chromium	Cr	24	449	1875°C-3407°F
Copper	Cu	29	560	1083°C-1949°F
Gold	Au	79	1206	1063°C-1945°F
Iron	Fe	26	490	1804°C-3279°F
Lead	Pb	82	709	325.6°C-618°F
Magnesium	Mg	12	108	650°C-1202°F
Manganese	Mn	25	466	1245°C-2273°F
Molybdenum	Mo	42	637	2610°C-4730°F
Nickel	Ni	28	556	1453°C-2647°F
Platinum	Pt	78	1339	1769°C-3217°F
Silicon	Si	14	145	1410°C-2570°F
Silver	Ag	47	654	960°C-1760°F
Tin	Sn	50	456	231.9°C-449.4°F
Titanium	Ti	22	281	1668°C-3035°F
Tungsten	W	74	1204	3410°C-6170°F
Uranium	U	92	1190	1132.3°C-2070°F
Zinc	Zn	30	445	420°C-787°F

TABLE 7
PHYSICAL PROPERTIES OF ALLOYS USED
IN MARINE FITTINGS

Alloy	Composition	Melting temperature	
Gunmetal	90 Cu/10 Sn	1000°C	1830°F
Manganese bronze	57.5 Cu/39.25 Zn/1.25 Fe 1.25 Al/0.25 Mn	880°C	1616°F
Monel	67 Ni/30 Cu	1300-1350°C	2370-2460°F
Muntz Metal	60 Cu/40 Zn	905°C	1660°F
Red Brass	85 Cu/15 Zn	1027°C	1880°F
CF-12M alloy (Stainless Steel)	19 Cr/10 Ni/2.5 Mo/012 max. C	1400°C	2550°F
Yellow Brass	65 Cu/35 Zn	930°C	1710°F